George Salmon

Gnosticism and Agnosticism

And Other Sermons

George Salmon

Gnosticism and Agnosticism
And Other Sermons

ISBN/EAN: 9783337160302

Printed in Europe, USA, Canada, Australia, Japan

Cover: Foto ©Lupo / pixelio.de

More available books at **www.hansebooks.com**

GNOSTICISM

AND

AGNOSTICISM

And other Sermons

BY

GEORGE SALMON, D.D.

CHANCELLOR OF ST. PATRICK'S CATHEDRAL, AND REGIUS PROFESSOR OF
DIVINITY IN THE UNIVERSITY OF DUBLIN

London
MACMILLAN AND CO
AND NEW YORK
1887

All rights reserved

CONTENTS

                                                        PAGE

I. GNOSTICISM AND AGNOSTICISM . . . 1

    "We know in part, and we prophesy in part: but when that which is perfect is come, that which is in part shall be done away. When I was a child, I spake as a child, I felt as a child, I thought as a child: now that I am become a man, I have put away childish things."—1 CORINTHIANS xiii. 9-11.

II. UNION WITH CHRIST 24

    "Abide in Me, and I in you. As the branch cannot bear fruit of itself, except it abide in the vine; no more can ye, except ye abide in Me. I am the vine, ye are the branches: he that abideth in Me, and I in him, the same bringeth forth much fruit; for without Me ye can do nothing."—JOHN xv. 4, 5.

III. THE PURE IN HEART SHALL SEE GOD . . 53

    "Blessed are the pure in heart: for they shall see God."—MATTHEW v. 8.

IV. ILL SUCCESS IN SEARCHING AFTER RIGHTEOUSNESS 74

    "The Gentiles, which followed not after righteousness, have attained to righteousness, even the righteousness which is of faith: but Israel, which followed after the law of righteousness, hath not attained to the law of righteousness."—ROMANS ix. 30, 31.

		PAGE
V.	PAIN AND DISEASE	100

"For this cause many are weak and sickly among you, and many sleep."—1 CORINTHIANS xi. 30.

VI.	HUNGER AND THIRST AFTER RIGHTEOUSNESS	124

"Blessed are they which do hunger and thirst after righteousness: for they shall be filled."—MATTHEW v. 6.

VII.	THE KEYNOTE OF THE EPISTLE TO THE HEBREWS	138

"Take heed, brethren, lest haply there shall be in any one of you an evil heart of unbelief, in falling away from the living God: but exhort one another day by day, so long as it is called To-day; lest any one of you be hardened by the deceitfulness of sin: for we are become partakers of Christ, if we hold fast the beginning of our confidence firm unto the end."—HEBREWS iii. 12-14.

VIII.	BOWING IN THE HOUSE OF RIMMON . .	158

"And Naaman said, Shall there not then, I pray thee, be given to thy servant two mules' burden of earth? for thy servant will henceforth offer neither burnt offering nor sacrifice unto other gods, but unto the Lord. In this thing the Lord pardon thy servant, that when my master goeth into the house of Rimmon to worship there, and he leaneth on my hand, and I bow myself in the house of Rimmon: when I bow down myself in the house of Rimmon, the Lord pardon thy servant in this thing. And he said unto him, Go in peace."—2 KINGS v. 17-19.

IX.	SHAME	174

"Let us run with patience the race that is set before us. Looking unto Jesus, the author and finisher of our faith; who, for the joy that was set before Him, endured the cross, despising the shame, and is set down at the right hand of the throne of God."—HEBREWS xii. 2.

	PAGE
X. THE DENIAL OF PETER	188

"When Jesus beheld him, He said, Thou art Simon the son of Jona: thou shalt be called Cephas, which is, by interpretation, a stone."—JOHN i. 42.

XI. CHARITY AND LOVE	205

"And now abideth faith, hope, charity, these three; but the greatest of these is charity."—1 CORINTHIANS xiii. 13.

In the Revised Version it is: "But now abideth faith, hope, love, these three: and the greatest of these is love."

XII. CHARITABLE BELIEF	223

"Charity believeth all things."—1 CORINTHIANS xiii. 7.

XIII. SLAVERY	243

"Whatsoever ye do, do it heartily, as to the Lord, and not unto men; knowing that of the Lord ye shall receive the reward of the inheritance: for ye serve the Lord Christ."—COLOSSIANS iii. 23, 24.

XIV. THE INTERPRETATION OF SCRIPTURE	272

"The Son of man shall come in the glory of His Father, with His angels; and then He shall reward every man according to his works."—MATTHEW xvi. 27.

"For by grace are ye saved through faith; and that not of yourselves: it is the gift of God: not of works, lest any man should boast."—EPHESIANS ii. 8, 9.

XV. REWARD ACCORDING TO WORK	292

"The Son of man shall come in the glory of His Father, with His angels; and then He shall reward every man according to his works."—MATTHEW xvi. 27.

"For by grace are ye saved through faith; and that not of yourselves: it is the gift of God: not of works, lest any man should boast."—Ephesians ii. 8, 9.

XVI. The Two Classes 311

"When the Son of man shall come in His glory, and all the holy angels with Him, then shall He sit upon the throne of His glory: And before Him shall be gathered all nations; and he shall separate them one from another, as a shepherd divideth his sheep from the goats: And He shall set the sheep on His right hand, but the goats on the left."—Matthew xxv. 31-33.

XVII. Working together with God . . . 327

"We, then, as workers together with Him, beseech you also that ye receive not the grace of God in vain." —2 Corinthians vi. 1.

XVIII. The Forgiveness of Sins . . . 349

"And such were some of you: but ye are washed, but ye are sanctified, but ye are justified in the name of the Lord Jesus, and by the Spirit of our God."— 1 Corinthians vi. 11.

I

GNOSTICISM AND AGNOSTICISM

" We know in part, and we prophesy in part : but when that which is perfect is come, that which is in part shall be done away. When I was a child, I spake as a child, I felt as a child, I thought as a child : now that I am become a man, I have put away childish things."—1 CORINTHIANS xiii. 9-11.

THE history of man's search for knowledge in every branch of study has commonly to pass through three stages. First there is the season of toilsome struggle with difficulties, when perplexing problems are grappled with ; a time of labour, no doubt, but of labour rewarded by a sense of constant progress, as difficulty after difficulty is mastered and problem after problem finds its solution. At length we reach a summit from which we can look round with some complacency on our achievements, when we see below us the heights that had been the object of our early ambition, and can delight ourselves with the harmonious landscape which the fields we had traversed present. There for a time our labours cease and many never care to proceed further; but at length, if not the individual, at least the generation, catches sight of new heights that must be scaled. The theories that had explained our early difficulties are seen to leave residual difficulties behind. If these cannot also be made to disappear the theory is convicted of incompleteness if not of error. So further work has to be done: usually what has been already done has carried us some stages on our way; but it may even be that in order to reach what we now perceive to be the real summit, we have to retrace our steps, come down from our boasted eminence, and humbly at the bottom begin the ascent anew.

Thus the most successful theories have had to submit to reconsideration and revision. The Newtonian theory of gravitation, for example, triumphantly established its claims by showing that a number of unconnected laws which had been suggested by observation were all simple consequences of one great principle. Yet the further question had to be faced: Will that principle explain not only all the general features of planetary motion but also all the minor inequalities? And some of these were at times so stubborn that it was seriously investigated whether the law of gravitation would not have to be modified, or at least some hypothesis added as to the time of transmission of its force. The Newtonian theory of light was less fortunate. It too won a first and great success, and Newton's investigations on this subject arrived at some results which cannot be superseded; but though his theory explained some of the more striking phenomena, when tested by more minute details it failed, and so after a temporary reign it has been forced to abdicate.

From the sketch I have given how the finding the answer to one set of questions is sure to suggest other more searching questions, it follows that the difficulty of problems is very differently judged of by a student at different stages of his progress. It is not unnatural to hear that he comes to think of problems as easy which he once esteemed difficult; but it happens too that conversely he comes to think problems difficult which he had once thought easy. Thus, for instance, a schoolboy's idea as to what is an easy book may be very different from that entertained by an accomplished scholar, who may regard that as full of difficulties which the schoolboy pronounces easy. The Gospel according to St. John will be pronounced a delightfully easy book by a schoolboy, glad to find that his painful work with grammar and dictionary is no longer needed, that there is scarcely a word which he does not recognise or a grammatical form with which he does not think himself familiar. Yet there is no New Testament book which more tries the powers of a commentator or presents him with harder problems. How many a crux the scholar will find in the *Æneid* of Virgil or the odes of Horace in places which a schoolboy would skim over in happy ignorance that there was anything at which he need feel embarrassment.

The case is just the same with moral difficulties. To a childish mind what reflections can be more obvious or more satisfactory than those in which it has been stirred up to gratitude towards God?

> "Not more than others I deserve,
>   Yet God has given me more,
> For I have food while others starve
>   And beg from door to door.
>
> "Lord, I ascribe it to Thy grace,
>   And not to chance as others do,
> That I was born of Christian race
>   And not a heathen or a Jew."

It requires a cultured mind to be tormented with the difficulties: "If I deserve no more than others how can it be consistent with the justice of the Father of all that I should be given more? Am I to admire injustice because I profit by it myself? If it is a disadvantage to be born a heathen or a Jew, how can we defend the ways of

Providence which permits so many thousands to suffer the one calamity, so many millions the other?"

The difficulty, however, here presented is one that exists independently of Revelation. It is not more certain that the world is peopled by creatures extremely diverse than it is that among human beings also there are infinite diversities of condition, diversities of capacities and of opportunities for happiness. Dr. Watts has but versified the thanksgiving of the heathen philosopher who blessed his gods because they had made him to be born a man not a woman, a freeman not a slave, an Athenian not a barbarian.

It has seemed to many that Revelation would be a poor thing if the knowledge it supplied, at least when combined with that which could be otherwise obtained, did not suffice to form the basis of a philosophy capable of solving all the problems of life. Accordingly, no sooner had our religion made such progress as to win the adherence of men of culture than they set themselves to frame by its help a philosophy of the universe. They disdained the simplicity of the vulgar, who merely trusted to their faith as a means of salvation. Christianity must do something more for them, and they claimed to be able to add to their faith knowledge. That knowledge professed to include an account of the origin of all things. It explained the process how from one simple, absolute, uncompounded, immaterial essence a multiform and material life had emanated. It traced the different future lots of men to an original radical diversity of nature, and so resembled some modern theories in addressing its message only to an elect seed. To these it professed to teach the true names of the unseen powers and the proper formulæ by which their help could be commanded. And some forms of this philosophy promised to release the initiated from the trammels of the ordinary laws of morality, by communicating to him knowledge which would make it his privilege, nay his duty, to set these laws at defiance. The adepts in this philosophy claimed to be *par excellence* Gnostics. They *knew* where simpler Christians must be content to *believe*. And though this knowledge was for a time guarded as a secret treasure, not to be lightly exhibited to the profane, it was not possible to protect it successfully from the search of curious inquirers, and so, very full details have been preserved to our own day. And what is the opinion of our age as to this vaunted knowledge? Why, that there are no pages of Church History so dreary as those which give the account of these theories, advanced without proof and, according to our judgment, utterly without probability; no pages so irksome to read carefully unless with some special object in view.

Yet it would be an error to suppose that the labour bestowed on the Gnostic speculations was absolutely wasted; for it has left permanent traces in the history of religious thought. If the solutions which this philosophy offered of the problems it attacked must be pronounced entirely unsatisfactory, it at least had the merit of inviting the attention of Christian thinkers to some problems of the highest difficulty and interest. Nor was it without contributing something towards their solution. In no controversy is either party so completely in the right as to have nothing to learn from his opponent in the course of the dispute. Ordinarily, the victor has to make some approximation to the views of his adversary. He finds that he has made some over-statements which must be withdrawn, that defects or weak places in his own system have been pointed out which need to be remedied. And this was true also of the controversy of the Christian Fathers with the Gnostics. Their theories could not be summarily rejected without an attempt to give some other explanation of the problems with which they had grappled, or even without incorporating into Christian philosophy some elements derived from heretical speculation.

For a long time Christian speculators only busied themselves with isolated questions, and it was not for some centuries that an attempt was made to reduce all the results they had arrived at to a complete system. At length the gigantic work was undertaken by the Schoolmen, who, having learned the Aristotelic philosophy and accepted it as the highest product of human science, combined it with principles derived, or supposed to be derived, from Scripture and from the writings of the Fathers, and hoped thereby to obtain a complete philosophy of the universe. There were no questions that could be raised that they had not courage to resolve; they could give any information that might be demanded about the nature of God, about the species and properties of angelic beings, about the Incarnation and its objects, about the whole scheme of Redemption. A few samples of the problems discussed in the "Summa" of Aquinas will suffice:—

Concerning God—

    Utrum in Deo sit idem essentia et esse:
    Utrum Deus intelligat se:
    Utrum Deus comprehendat seipsum.

Concerning angels—

    Utrum angelus sit in loco:

Whether one angel can be in several places at

the same time or several angels in the same place: Whether an angel can change from one place to another without passing through the intervening places: What is the manner of the knowledge and understanding of angels: Whether one can know himself or know another angel: Whether the devil was bad from the first instant of his creation: How long he was in existence before he sinned: Whether a blessed angel is capable of grief: Whether a guardian angel grieves at the sins of his ward: Whether Antichrist will have a guardian angel: What are the different orders of angels and what their respective functions. The problems arising on the supposition that men had never fallen are discussed at length. In what condition would their children have been born: what knowledge and powers would they have possessed at the moment of their birth; would any of them have been of the female sex. Suppose Eve had sinned and Adam not, would the posterity have contracted original sin. Whether, if man had not fallen, the Incarnation would have taken place.

Of the reality and certainty of the knowledge arrived at on such subjects no doubt was entertained, and it was held that by this knowledge all our other knowledge ought to be regulated and controlled; and so Theology was consistently held to be the queen and mistress of all other sciences. To any dictum of hers any conclusion of theirs must give way. It would be premature to pronounce a system to be extinct which is still accepted by so many thousands of our fellow-Christians,—the present Pope not only holding the greatest of the Schoolmen, Thomas Aquinas, in the highest admiration himself, but having not very long since, in a special allocution, directed the members of his communion to this doctor as their most trustworthy guide. Yet though this system is not dead it has received fatal wounds. One deadly blow was dealt it at the Reformation, and still more injury has been done it by the progress of modern philosophy. The progress of literary research has showed that many of the patristical citations on which the Schoolmen relied as authorities were taken from spurious documents; the progress of science has showed that the theology of the Middle Ages, so far from being the mistress of all other sciences, was itself the child of the science of its own time, and contained in it the seeds of decay through having incorporated a philosophy now antiquated. And so even in the communion, where it is most venerated, it has been forced to receive important modifications. By us of other communions, the volumes which contain the best results of mediæval labour are either not opened at all or are only dipped into. We acknowledge the industry, the acuteness of intellect of the writers, but we do not care to sit as disciples at the feet of men whose principles of belief, whose habits of thought, were wholly different from ours ; who, assuming as principles some things which we believe to be true, others which we know to be false, or to have been taken for granted without evidence, occupied their lives in drawing out, by logical process, conclusions from this farrago of truth and falsehood.

At the time of the Reformation, although, as I said, much of the scholastic philosophy was rejected, many of its principles were retained ; but, above all, the hope was retained of giving—though it was thought with better success—satisfactory solutions of the great problems which had perplexed the human mind. Calvin, for instance, might vie with any of the Schoolmen for the boldness and completeness of his system, and for the enthusiastic adherence with which thousands accepted him as having satisfactorily explained all the relations between God and the universe which He had formed. To many minds the boldness and completeness of a system is itself evidence of its truth ; for there are many who would be better pleased to get wrong answers to the questions on which they have had pleasure in speculating than have confession made to them of inability to give any answer at all. I daresay my own experience is not an uncommon one, that on first reading Butler's *Analogy* I felt somewhat scandalised at his timidity in declining to pronounce on such questions as whether God could have saved the world otherwise than by the death of Christ, and by his setting aside other problems, as beyond the reach of human faculties, of which I had thought that I had been in possession of the true answers. But the tendency of modern thought has been to make men dissatisfied with many theories intended to throw light on mysteries of Christian doctrine, and has found that such theories frequently leave behind residual difficulties as formidable as the original difficulties which these theories had been intended to explain. Hence has arisen the growth of what has been called Agnosticism, that is to say, the resolute turning aside from questions which it is supposed the human mind is unable to solve, and the adoption of the maxim of the philosopher of old, What is above us is nothing to us.

This is in truth an extension of the old Stoic philosophy of seeking happiness rather in the suppression of desires than in the gratification of them. That philosophy reached its highest point, and bore its ripest fruits, at the time when the civilised world was tyrannised over by a grinding and meddling despotism, which allowed no man to count on the accomplishment of any of his schemes for the future. His plans might be wisely framed, and have been well adapted for the attainment of that at which they aimed, if it had not been for that irresistible ruling power, which might at any moment interfere for the destruction of the scheme, and possibly of the speculator himself. Thus the constant reminder how much of life there was beyond man's control gave recommendation to a philosophy which proposed to make man independent of external circumstances, and to teach him to make himself happy without what he could have no certainty of attaining. That, however, was after all but a philosophy of despair; and if it had been found possible to take away from human life the stimulus of hope and of desire we should have been deprived of all that has been gained for man's comfort and happiness by manifold inventions, prompted by the spirit which, instead of being content to bear privations and discomforts, struggles to overcome them.

When this philosophy of despair is applied to the subject of knowledge, what sacrifices it demands of its disciples! how much of what for generations has occupied the thoughts and stirred the emotions of men they are condemned to be ignorant of! To name religion is to name one of the main factors in human history—to name what has fixed or formed some of the most intimate combinations of men and stimulated some of their greatest enterprises. And it is a very incomplete account of the matter to say that it was fear which made the gods; an ignoble passion from the tyranny of which philosophy might be regarded as doing no mean service in releasing us. Fear can generate no religion worthy of the name unless it be associated with reverence and awe, and enabled thus to pass into trust and love. Religion has consisted not merely in the recognition of something stronger than man: it has taught him to know something higher and better than himself; to believe in a Being of moral perfection whose justice and goodness are undisturbed by human passions; who gives authority to that voice which man finds in himself, reviewing his own conduct, and visiting it with censure when he has gone astray. From the belief that the Ruler of the universe is wise and just and good, religion draws the consequence that He is One in whom we can put our trust, One to whose disposal we may resign ourselves, and acquiesce in His decisions in perfect confidence that He doeth all things well. And the Jewish religion did more than teach such resignation as the Stoics inculcated, to the sovereign will of the irresistible Supreme Ruler: it taught that that Ruler loves us—loves us individually; that He is one whom we may love, to whom we may pour out our whole soul, and be assured of His willingness to hear us. These lessons of Judaism were intensified in Christian teaching, which gave new assurance of the love of Him who spared not His own Son, but freely gave Him up for us all. And so the humblest Christian has felt himself entitled to a privilege which it seems marvellous that we creatures of the dust can venture to claim— the privilege of communion with God. This short phrase sums up in three words a vast territory of thoughts and feelings, to all which the Agnostic abandons the right to enter. So I repeat it, what a sacrifice it is! We can think of a world without music, a world without art, a world without poetry. None of these is a world so colourless, so dreary, as a world without God, a world without hope of immortality. We justly feel ourselves higher in the scale of creation than the beasts of the field, who are condemned with downward eye ever to contemplate the world beneath, and know nothing of the glories of the heavens and of the distant worlds they reveal. Is it not also a descent in the scale of being when man, to whom a capacity for something higher had been opened, casts down his dazzled eyes and resigns himself thenceforward to know of none but material earthly interests, and in them to find all his employment and his happiness—such happiness, at least, as the instability of all things here will allow him?

No doubt it is not without a sigh that the Agnostic resigns himself to do without that in which so many thousands of his fellow-creatures have found their highest happiness. But he consoles himself perhaps with the flattering sense of his superiority in philosophic modesty: if he has not the knowledge which they value so highly it is because he alone is wise enough to know that he knows nothing. But let it be clearly understood that whatever other merits Agnosticism may claim, modesty is the last that can be ascribed to it. It may seem paradoxical to say it, but when it is reflected on it will be found to be an obvious truth, that Agnosticism is the very highest point of Gnosticism. For who can venture to say what cannot be known but one who thoroughly knows all that can be known? Who can have the presumption to bar the way of explorers by setting finger-posts at different openings—Enter not here, for this way there is no thoroughfare—unless one who had thoroughly explored the way and had ascertained that there was no outlet? To arrive at the stage of being able to pronounce problems insoluble is the very highest achievement of science. Many an aspiring geometer has vexed his soul in fruitless efforts to trisect an angle or to square the circle ; and one of his equals who could only tell him that hitherto none had succeeded in solving these problems might do more to fire his ambition than to cool his ardour. It would require the authority of one who stood on a higher mathematical level than himself to convince him that in attacking these problems he was spending his labour in vain. The same thing may be said of the algebraic solution of the higher equations : the thing has not been done, and all the more eagerly was the problem attempted by one aspirant after another, each hoping that he might succeed where his predecessors had failed; but the investigation whether at all the problem is soluble belongs to a far higher department of mathematical science, and is indeed one of such difficulty that you might count on your fingers the living men who had qualified themselves to pronounce an independent opinion on the validity of the argument. Thus you see that while I myself pointed out at the beginning how much of human labour has been misdirected to the acquisition of pretentious knowledge, falsely so called, and while I therefore freely acknowledge that a service is rendered men by drawing them away from making ropes of sand and from employing their energies in work which can have no fruitful result, still I hold that to be in a position to render such a service a man must be on a commanding eminence whence he can survey the whole field of labour. It would be a service, I daresay, to weed a library of useless books; but clearly none but a man of first-rate knowledge could be trusted to perform that service. Otherwise we should have good reason to fear lest some of the chief treasures of the library might be cast out by one incompetent to appreciate their value. In sum, then, while I acknowledge that in the difficulty of finding time and opportunity to learn all that we should wish to know, no mean service is rendered us by one who can tell us with authority what things it is best not to try to know, I say also that it is clear that such a service can only be rendered us by one himself possessed of the highest knowledge.

It follows, then, as I have said, that Agnosticism is the most arrogant form of Gnosticism. The subject of religion is one which so vitally concerns man's highest interests that ignorance of it, from indifference or from mental indolence, would argue total incapacity to enter into some of the most elevating and ennobling thoughts that have filled the human mind. Agnosticism, then, would be too contemptible to deserve argument if it did not profess to rest on a philosophic conviction founded on a survey of the human powers that knowledge on such subjects is unattainable. Others may profess that they know God, but the Agnostic knows that there is none: that is to say for practical purposes none, since a God is for all practical purposes a nonentity if it can do us no good to concern our thoughts about Him or to seek His favour, and if we are in every respect to act just as we should act if we were assured He did not exist. Thus you see that while the Agnostic in words makes a modest confession of ignorance, in reality he lays claim to the possession of certain knowledge on a subject to which mankind have for generations applied their best thoughts, and yet, if this modern school is to be believed, gone hopelessly astray.

Is it the case that all who now call themselves Agnostics are entitled to claim the superiority to other men which their theory implies? I think not. I believe the true type of these Agnostics to be the sailors of Columbus, who begged and implored him to turn his ship round, confident as they were that he was on a path on which nothing could be found. But this confidence arose from no philosophic knowledge that investigation must be fruitless. It was nothing but indolent impatience of the toil of search, inability to recognise the tokens of success which had already presented themselves, incapacity to share the scientific faith in things unseen which assured their master that if they would but persevere in the way by which he led them they should certainly reach the land of promise which lay beyond.

We have had reason to see that there was arrogant presumption in the Gnosticism of those Christian speculators who ventured to say "We know": little less presumption in the assertion "We know not, and cannot know." What, then, is the truth? Is it not as the Apostle has said, "We know in part." We know, as children know the occupations and anxieties of mature life.

An intelligent child may easily form a general idea of the character of what is likely to be his future occupation, but his conceptions of the details will be confused and inaccurate; and as to the plans and interests which it will involve, he can know absolutely nothing. Of the future which is to follow this earthly life we can know far less than any child does of the affairs of manhood; nor is it in the least necessary that we should. It is enough for us that we can say with the Apostle, "We know not what hereafter we shall be: but we know that, when He shall appear, we shall be like Him."

The sense of the necessary dimness and incompleteness of our knowledge of the future life ought to teach us the wisdom of modesty and caution in our criticisms and predictions concerning it. Many things, for instance, have been said on the subject of the continuance of evil in the world beyond the grave, in the conclusiveness of which no one can feel much confidence who has realised the extreme fallibility of our moral judgment in cases where our knowledge of the facts is imperfect. "Shall not the Judge of all the earth do right?" is a question to which only one answer can be given. Yet if we proceed to argue, such and such things are in our judgment not right, therefore it is incredible that the Judge of all the earth can do them, we may easily find ourselves refuted by facts. Thus when Abraham, whose words I have quoted, refused to believe that in the destruction of a doomed city the innocent might share the fate of the guilty, he refused to believe what we in our wider experience know to have happened times without number. Are we then to say that we have no capacity for measuring the morality of the divine actions, and that goodness and justice in the case of the Supreme are names denoting ideas quite different from those which in human intercourse are attached to these words? It might as well be said that a child is incapable of understanding what a grown person means by truth and justice, purity and goodness.

But though on these subjects a child can easily learn enough to guide his own conduct, his moral judgments may be widely astray when he criticises the conduct of his elders. For childish morality ordinarily reduces itself to the observance of certain fixed rules as to the reasons for which no inquiry is made ; and to which no exceptions are recognised, and to the breach of them no indulgence given.

Many of you will know the clever rhetorical use made of this characteristic of childish morality by Southey in his verses on the Battle of Blenheim. He contemplates the battle from a child's point of view, as just the killing or maiming for life of so many thousands of human beings, and has no difficulty in arriving at the conclusion that a glorious victory is a very wicked thing. Yet whatever opinion we form as to the lawfulness of war, it is quite plain that the question is a complicated one, and that it is a mere rhetorical artifice to try to dispose of it summarily by the consideration that there is a commandment Thou shalt not kill. If, with regard to the sixth commandment, a child is liable to form erroneous judgment, it is needless to say that with regard to the seventh he can hardly form any opinion at all. And going through the other commandments it would be easy to give other illustrations how wide of the mark the criticisms of a child might be.

But fortunately it costs a child no effort to refrain from criticising. Though his understanding is not developed, and his mind ill stored with facts, he is quite capable of trusting and loving. He can know that his father loves him, he can believe that he is wise and good; and if there are things in his conduct which seem strange to him, they only cause him passing wonder and do not dwell in his mind as sources of serious perplexity. And so with us; faith can well supply the defects of knowledge. We can be sure that the Judge *will* do right, even though we cannot be safe in concluding that He will do this or that because this or that seems to us to be right. And the clouds that obscure the region of speculation do not descend upon the region of practice. Whatever else we may be ignorant of we have no difficulty in knowing what course of conduct is pleasing to God and approved of men. In the text the Apostle contrasts our imperfect and provisional knowledge with charity which never faileth. The time will come, he teaches, when our best earthly speculations shall be set aside in the light of fuller knowledge, as a boy's notions about the business of life are replaced by better knowledge. But a character trained up by faith and hope and love will endure and be a source of blessing throughout eternity.

II

UNION WITH CHRIST

"Abide in Me, and I in you. As the branch cannot bear fruit of itself, except it abide in the vine; no more can ye, except ye abide in Me. I am the vine, ye are the branches: he that abideth in Me, and I in him, the same bringeth forth much fruit; for without Me ye can do nothing."—JOHN xv. 4, 5.

THE course of modern controversies has forced us to take notice of the diversity of the authors whose agency has been employed in the composition of the Holy Scriptures. It was easy for interpreters of former days, in the fulness of their conviction that all was God's Book, to lose sight of the human element in Scripture. Thus they might establish their doctrines by arbitrarily combining sayings of writers who lived hundreds of years apart, and were, to all appearance, speaking of different subjects: they might be blind to all differences between the various writers except when their attention was roused by some striking apparent discrepancy which demanded explanation. Our tendencies to error lie in the opposite direction. In our days some of the most laborious students of the Bible have been men who absolutely refuse to recognise any Divine element in it. They have busied themselves in noting the characteristics of the various writers, their peculiarities in form of expression or turn of thought. It has been no shock to them to discover, or think they discovered, discordances in statement of fact or in modes of presenting religious truth. Nay, so super-subtle have they been in finding such differences, that they have persuaded themselves they saw them in what a more sober criticism has no hesitation in recognising as works of the same author, and have been led to cut homogeneous books into fragments, supposed to be inconsistent in their character. But when all exaggeration and fanciful speculation have been stripped away, there remain, as results of modern criticism, a number of facts which no honest student of God's Word can refuse to include in his system; nor is any theory of inspiration now likely to be advocated which does not fully recognise the character imprinted on the Bible by the diversity of agents through whom the Holy Spirit worked.

And when we consider the matter we see that, whatever we might beforehand have thought likely, this arrangement, in which our sacred volume is not a book, but a library, not a single document written in a uniform style, but coloured with the personality of several individual writers, is intimately connected with the fact that ours is a historical religion. It rests on our belief of certain great facts attested by chosen witnesses who live for us in their writings. We know each by his style, his favourite expressions, his turn of thought. There are few living persons of whose character we have as vivid a conception as that of St. Paul. His character impresses itself on believers and unbelievers alike. All admit that he was incapable of deceit, and so whatever theory of our Lord's resurrection is framed must reconcile itself with the fact that one who was on the most familiar terms with the first asserters of the miracle, both most fully believed their story and claimed to have had himself personal confirmation of its truth. Again, the fact that the witnesses are not one, but many, gives a cumulative force to their testimony. It is well known to you what use Paley made of the argument from coincidences, in establishing the historical credibility of our documents. But also in ascertaining the doctrines of the Christian revelation, attention may rightly be called to the force added to the proof when we have the agreement of different witnesses. Divines of a former generation might have been content to point out that such and such a doctrine was proved by so many Scripture texts. It is no disadvantage to us that the course of modern controversies forces us to take notice that these texts are in many cases taken from different writings. We are thus enabled to see how the Church from the first performed her office of witnessing to the truth, when we can call up members of the Apostolic Church and find them in complete agreement, not only with regard to such external facts as our Lord's death and resurrection, but also with respect to what may be called revealed facts, such as our Lord's pre-existence, His share in the work of creation, the rule which He now exercises sitting at the right hand of God, His future return to judgment.

It is my purpose in this sermon to exemplify this accordance of teaching with regard to the doctrine contained in the text, the Union of Christ with His Church; to show that this idea, which is certainly not an obvious one, or one likely to have occurred independently to different disciples (for I do not know that the followers of any philosopher, or of any other religious teacher, imagined any such relation to exist between them and their master), was common to the different New Testament writers, and was made the basis of their system of doctrines. I will first speak of the surface agreement, I mean the direct statement of the doctrine in various passages, and then of the deeper, underlying agreement disclosed in doctrines which all the Christian teachers included in their system, and which have their root and their justification in this principle of the intimate union between Christ's people and their Head.

The Synoptic Gospels professedly deal with the history of our Lord in His life of humiliation, and therefore cannot be expected to give much evidence as to the relations between the risen Saviour and the Church, which at the time of which these Gospels treat, can hardly be said to have been in existence. But we may take notice of the closing promise which St. Matthew records as made by our Lord ere He parted with His disciples, " Lo, I am with you always, even unto the end of the world." In these words we have the difference on which I just remarked between the conception which the Christians entertained of the relation between them and their Founder, and that which prevailed in other philosophic or religious sects. Others were zealous to venerate the memory of the great man to whose instruction they had been indebted for their knowledge, or by whose laws they were glad to be governed, but his activity was in their idea a thing of the past. Christians thought of their Master as ever with them, and trusted for safety in all their trials to the abiding presence of Him who possessed all power in heaven and earth.

In an earlier chapter of St. Matthew the doctrine of Christ's identification of Himself with His people is put in a striking way. You remember the description of Christ's coming in His glory, and all the holy angels with Him; and how He rewards those placed on His right hand, because when He had been an hungered they had given Him meat; thirsty, they had given Him drink; a stranger, and they had taken Him in; naked, and they had clothed Him; sick and in prison, and they had visited Him. And when they disclaim having rendered Him any such service He tells them, " Inasmuch as ye did it unto the least of these My brethren, ye did it unto Me." This saying of our Lord is not recorded by St. Luke, yet in his second work the third Evangelist has given different expression to the same idea. When Saul of Tarsus made havoc of the Church and wasted it, Jesus is introduced as acknowledging His Church's trials as His own, and as stopping the career of the persecutor with the words, " Saul, Saul, why persecutest thou Me?"

But one thing more in the Synoptic Gospels must not be passed over, that story which all three are careful to tell, how our Lord, the same night that He was betrayed, commanded His disciples thenceforward to show forth His death by eating His body and drinking His blood. It would lead us away from our subject if I were to enter into any minute discussion what sense is to be given to these words; but this lies on the surface of them, that our Lord instructed His disciples that they were in some way to enter into communion of the most intimate kind with His own personality. And this is confirmed by the fourth Evangelist. He does not repeat what his predecessors had told of the institution of that sacred feast, but he records another discourse in which Jesus describes Himself as the living bread which came down from heaven, speaks of His flesh and His blood, given for the life of the world, as the true meat and drink, makes the participation of them the essential condition of obtaining eternal life, and states as the result of this participation that he that eateth that flesh and drinketh that blood dwelleth in Christ, and Christ in him. One whose attention had not been called to it would scarcely conceive how completely St. John's mind was pervaded by the idea of this mutual indwelling of Christ and His people. It runs through his first epistle from one end to the other. And as St. John also held the doctrine of a complete union between the Son and the Father, he interchanges with the assertion of an indwelling of Christ, a similar assertion of an indwelling of the Father. And among the many proofs of common authorship of St. John's Gospel and his Epistles, the identity of language on the subject we are considering deserves to hold a high place. In our Lord's prayer for His disciples, recorded in John xvii., He asks for them "that they all may be one; as Thou, Father, art in Me, and I in Thee, that they also may be one in us . . . : that they may be one, even as we are one: I in them, and Thou in Me, that they may be made perfect in one." The Epistle opens with the assertion, "Our fellowship is with the Father, and with His Son Jesus Christ." It closes with, "We are in Him that is true, even in His Son Jesus Christ." To be "in Him" was the privilege to which every professing member of the Church aspired, and of the validity of their claim to which they were bound to assure themselves. "Hereby know we that we are in Him. He that saith he abideth in Him, ought himself also so to walk, even as He walked." "Whosoever abideth in Him sinneth not: whosoever sinneth hath not seen Him, neither known Him." "He that keepeth His commandment dwelleth in Him, and He in him: Hereby we know that He abideth in us, by the Spirit which He hath given us." "Whosoever shall confess that Jesus is the Son of God, God dwelleth in him, and he in God." Thus all through St. John's Epistle we meet constant echoes of the doctrine formally expressed in the discourse from which the text is taken, that union between Christ and His people is as intimate as that between the vine and his branches; this union being the source of all the branches' fertility, as, on the other hand, their failing to produce fruit is the mark of separation from Him.

Of the New Testament writers there are no two more unlike and independent of each other than St. John and St. Paul, and therefore their complete agreement in a doctrine is strong proof that that doctrine must have been part of the common possession of the Church. Now in this doctrine of the necessity of Christ dwelling in them, St. Paul's language is an echo of St. John's. "Know ye not," he says to the Corinthians, "how that Jesus Christ is in you except ye be reprobates?" To the Romans he says, "If any man have not the Spirit of Christ he is none of His. And if Christ be in you, the body is dead because of sin; but the Spirit is life because of righteousness. But if the Spirit of Him that raised up Jesus from the dead dwell in you, He that raised up Christ from the dead shall also quicken your mortal bodies by His Spirit that dwelleth in you." One of St. Paul's favourite images, occurring in several distinct letters, is the comparison of Christians to a temple built for the dwelling of the Holy Ghost, of which the several Christians are living stones, Jesus Christ Himself being the chief corner-stone,—language, I may add, with regard to which there is strong coincidence between the Epistle to the Ephesians and St. Peter's First Epistle. But St. Paul uses another comparison still more closely akin to St. John's figure of the vine: Christians are a body of which Christ is the Head. Each member has its several functions, but from Him the nourishment is derived by which the whole body makes its increase. "No man ever yet hated his own flesh; but nourisheth and cherisheth it, even as the Lord the Church; for we are members of His body, of His flesh, and of His bones."

It is unnecessary for me to multiply proofs how completely the belief pervaded the Christian Church, that in some mystical but very real manner a union existed between them and their ascended Lord, which was the source of the spiritual life of every member. I go on then to speak of the less direct evidence, that the belief of which I am speaking was an essential part of Christian teaching, afforded by the other doctrines which have their explanation and justification in this central truth. And first with regard to the doctrine of the Atonement. We have heard many discussions in our day as to the ethics of vicarious suffering, on the questions whether it is just and right that one person should suffer for another, and whether such suffering can make satisfaction for that other's sins, questions scarcely touched on by the sacred writers. And, perhaps, the reason is that they did not look so exclusively as some modern writers do, on that aspect of that Atonement in which it may be illustrated by the payment of a debt, a transaction in which it is of course immaterial whether the satisfaction be made by the person who owes it, or by another for him. But an essential part of the New Testament doctrine of the Atonement is that the satisfaction is performed by no stranger, but by One bound by the closest ties to those for whom it is made,—by the Head of the family who are to be thereby reconciled. And in this point of view the Atonement is illustrated by a class of analogies quite different from those which are used when it is regarded as the payment of a ransom or debt.

To suffer for others, to make atonement for

others, is one of the most constantly recurring experiences of life. Human life owes almost all its security, and the greater part of its happiness, to the fact that, whether by nature or by choice, by the ties of common family, common country, or voluntary association, different individuals are bound together into one body. And the law of such bodies is not only that if one member be honoured the others rejoice with it, but that if one member suffer the others must suffer with it. For as in the natural body the nerves, along which in health thrill so many sensations of pleasure, at times rack the frame with cruel achings, so those ties of union which in various ways bind us in one body with our fellowmen do at times bring us pain instead of happiness, pain which we are content to accept on account of the vastly greater happiness which has come through the same channels. We owe so much, for instance, to our country and its laws, which give us security for property, and life, and family comfort, that it is justly accounted the grossest ingratitude if we do not love our fatherland, or if we hesitate to give our substance or our life for it should its needs require. Yet this tie of union with the other men who inhabit with us the same land may bring on us calamities which no sins of our own had deserved. The misconduct of those who have been chosen to govern, their unjust ambition, their rashness, their want of foresight leading to measures which we have condemned and against which we have protested, may involve the country in sufferings of which we must take our share ; we must, by our exertions and our sacrifices, contribute to the atonement necessary to undo the evil which has been done. Nor will those without, to whom compensation may be due, distinguish between the innocent and the guilty, bound together in a common solidarity. Not to draw any illustration from current events, how many Frenchmen were there in 1870 who had entirely disapproved the policy which had plunged their country into war, yet had to make bitter atonement for their ruler's mistakes; and that not wrested from them reluctantly, but given of their own choice, because they deemed that no matter by whose fault their country had been brought into distress, it had a right to claim from them in its hour of trial, their substance, their lives, and their children. Family life, source though it be of our purest enjoyments, will at times bring its pains. The heart of the parent may be wrung by the misconduct of a child, and he may think it the least of his sufferings that he has to make atonement to others for the injury which the prodigal has caused them. On the other hand, often has the Jewish proverb been verified, "The fathers have eaten sour grapes, and the children's teeth are set on edge." Often has the son had to pay in health or fortune the penalty of his father's recklessness; and it has not rarely happened that the son has undertaken the voluntary burden of making satisfaction for his parent's wrongs by the discharge of his neglected obligations. The innocent wife of a guilty husband must share the penalty of his wrong-doing, having as little the power as the will to separate her lot from his. In theory these may be instances of vicarious suffering, but they are not felt so. Could you dissuade a woman from following her husband into exile on the ground that it was not just that she should suffer for another? Would she not reply that he for whom she was suffering was not another, but in such sense one with herself that their joys and sorrows must of necessity be common?

Thus we see that we give an imperfect representation of the doctrine of the Atonement if we discuss the possibility or the justice of the penalty of our sins being borne by another. For an essential part of the doctrine is that He who bore our sins and carried our sorrows was no stranger, but One in the closest union with those whom He saved; the Head of their family; related to them in the same way as Adam to the human race, or, as the relation is elsewhere figured, bound to them in mystical union closer than that of human marriage. When this is borne in mind it seems less to call for explanation that the sorrows of those whom He loves should be His, that His victory over sin and death should be theirs. Thus it would appear that the doctrine of the Atonement is involved in the very fact of the Incarnation. When once it is revealed that Christ took upon Him the nature of men, is not ashamed to call them brethren, made Himself partaker, like them, of flesh and blood, it seems to follow that He must bear the griefs and carry the sorrows of those with whom He entered into so intimate a partnership, and surely also that those sufferings borne by Him who was Himself sinless should avail to make reconciliation for the sins of the people whom He had made His own. Whether there be a logical necessity or not, there is, at all events, complete harmony between the doctrine that Christ took on Him man's nature—that he filled the place of the second Adam, that is to say, Head of the redeemed family—and the doctrine that He made satisfaction for those with whom He entered into so close a relation, and that He has made them to share in His privileges and benefit by His triumphs. It is on the last point that I have next to speak, the privileges of Christ's people, my object being to show that the New Testament language on this subject is all pervaded by the same conception of the union between them and their Head.

And in the first place I would direct your attention to the promises made to prayer in the name of Christ. Twice St. John introduces our Lord solemnly promising, " Verily, verily, I say unto you, whatsoever ye shall ask the Father in My name, He will give it you." Elsewhere it runs, " If ye shall ask anything in My name I will do it." Consequently that prayer should be offered in the name of Christ has become an elementary and fundamental principle of Christian worship. This rule of worship has existed as far back as we can trace the history of the Christian Church. Within the last few years the earliest extant document of the sub-Apostolic Church, the Epistle of Clement of Rome, has been completed by the recovery of the contents of the missing leaf of the only MS. until lately known to contain it. Great part of this is occupied with a prayer, which probably reproduces for us the liturgical use of the Church of Rome before the end of the first century. And how does this prayer end? " Through the High Priest and Guardian of our souls, Jesus Christ, through whom be glory and majesty unto Thee, both now and for all generations, and for ever and ever." It has been disputed whether the Gospel of St. John was written before the end of the first century. This prayer of Clement's shows us one of two things: either that that Gospel was in A.D. 97 already known and honoured, and that the Church had derived from it the rule of offering its praises and confessions through Christ, or else that that rule expresses the practice of the Church from a time before that Gospel had been committed to writing. But if so, we cannot doubt that that Gospel truly explains the origin of the practice; namely, special promises of acceptance to prayer so offered, made by our Lord Himself during His earthly sojourn.

And this rule of prayer has, we all know, continued from the first century to the nineteenth. It is the more striking in our own form of prayer, because, like the other Western Churches, we use not one long continuous prayer, but break up our prayer into a number of collects, each closing with the same formula. Our ears are so familiar with the sounds "through Jesus Christ our Lord," or "for Jesus Christ's sake," that, perpetually as they occur in the course of our service, they scarcely attract our notice, or induce us to ask ourselves what we mean when we utter them. Yet surely if we once allow our minds to dwell on the words, we see that they are alive with doctrine. In the first place, what a conception does the use of this form imply of the dignity of Christ: that when addressing our Father and our Maker, who, we may believe, loves the creatures whom His hand has formed, and whose willingness to hear their petitions was recognised by Old Testament saints, we still put forward no other claim for acceptance of our request than that we are privileged to address our prayers through Christ, for whose worthiness we hope to be granted that which in our own name we had not dared to ask! And in the second place what a conception it gives us of our union with Christ that we should feel ourselves warranted to make this use of His name! In our intercourse with each other, there is no privilege we are more chary of bestowing than the right to use our name. The circumstances must be very special when we would give to one about to ask a favour from a third party authority to say that the benefit bestowed on him might be regarded as an obligation conferred on ourselves. Yet surely nothing less than this is implied when we ask a petition for Jesus Christ's sake. We do really plead in prayer that saying of our Lord to which I have already referred, " Inasmuch as ye did it unto one of the least of these my brethren, ye did it unto Me." In these words He taught us that He regarded the meanest of His people as so one with Him that He would own mercy shown to them for His sake as if He were Himself the destitute suppliant who demanded aid. It is wonderful love and condescension that He has thus knit together the members of His mystical body by their common relation to Him, and enabled each to claim the love and good offices of the others, as they love and value their Lord, from whom flows the spiritual life of all. Yet far more wonderful it is that He gives us authority to use the same plea in our addresses to the Supreme, and reveals to us that the love which the eternal Father bears to His only begotten Son must embrace all who are one with Him. Nay, if we examine more closely the phrase, " prayer through Christ," we find reason to think that it has a deeper meaning still. Those words I quoted from Clement, " Through our High Priest Christ," I think allow us to see what the ancient Church understood by them. As in the old dispensation the high priest offered for the sins of the people and presented their incense before the mercy-seat of God, so Christ having once for all made satisfaction for the sins of men, remaining a High Priest for ever, presents the incense of His people's prayers and thanksgivings before the mercy-seat on high. Thus the privilege of making prayer through Christ is represented not by the analogy of one who is entitled to use the name of an absent third person, but by that of one who has that person as a present advocate and intercessor, who will make the request of the petitioner his own.

I think that when we allow our minds to dwell on all that is meant by praying in the name of Christ, and praying through Christ, we cannot appreciate the greatness of the privilege without being forced to ask ourselves, Can I, without any feeling of unreality, come to God and claim blessings from Him, on the ground of my being so united to Christ that I am entitled to plead His promise that He counts what is done to His people as done to Himself? And again, Are the objects of my desire, the things that I wish to pray for, such that I can without any sense of unfitness entrust my requests to Christ, and ask Him to make my petitions His? We are sometimes tempted to think of prayer as a kind of magic charm, which will give us the power of getting the benefits we wish for, and turning away the calamities we are afraid of, and overlook that we are only entitled to claim the New Testament promises to prayer on the terms of being united to Christ by living faith, and of being, in virtue of that union, assimilated to His character. Christ's promise is, " If ye abide in Me, and My words abide in you, ye shall ask what ye will, and it shall be done unto you." Elsewhere the Apostle says, " This is the confidence that we have in Him, that if we ask anything according to His will He heareth us."

It might seem as if the Apostle's words, " If we ask anything according to His will," put on the success of prayer a limitation not contained in our Lord's promise. Yet the difference between these two phrases, " whatsoever ye will," " whatsoever is according to His will," is found to disappear when it is stated that the suppliant must be in union with Christ, that is to say, in union with One the principle of whose whole life was the doing His Father's will, who made it the daily prayer of His disciples, "Thy will be done in earth as it is in heaven," whose own prayer in His last agony was, " Father, not My will, but Thine be done." In another verse of this fifteenth chapter of John it is implied that the promises of answer to prayer, however absolute in form, are really conditioned, it being required that they who ask should be living and fruitful members of the true Vine—verse 16: " I have chosen you and ordained you, that ye should go and bring forth fruit, and that your fruit should remain ; that whatsoever ye shall ask of the Father in My name, He may give it you." In these words it is clearly implied that this union with Christ exhibited by the fruits of holiness is a condition necessary in order to enable any to claim the promise that the Father will give what is asked in the name of His Son.

And this brings me to speak of the Christian doctrine of sanctification, in which we find surprising unity between the doctrine of the New Testament teachers. It is quite intelligible that they who lived in the company of Jesus of Nazareth, and who had been witnesses of the spotless purity of His life, His meekness, His unselfishness, His implicit trust in His Father, His zeal for His glory, His love for men's souls and bodies, should feel strongly themselves, and should impress on their disciples the duty of imitating so perfect a model. I do not know, therefore, that much stress from an evidential point of view can be laid on the undoubted fact that all the New Testament writers agree in dwelling on Christ as our Example, except that if the case were otherwise, we might have cause to suspect that His life had not been such as we now know it to have been. St. Matthew represents our Lord as saying, "Take My yoke upon you, and learn of Me; for I am meek and lowly in heart." St. John in his Gospel, " I have given you an example, that ye should do as I have done to you." St. Paul, "Let this mind be in you, which was also in Christ Jesus." St. Peter, "Christ also suffered for us, leaving us an example, that ye should follow His steps: who did no sin, neither was guile found in His mouth: who when He was reviled, reviled not again; when He suffered, He threatened not; but committed Himself to Him that judgeth righteously." And St. John in his Epistle gives as the test of union with Christ, "He that saith he abideth in Him, ought himself also so to walk, even as He walked."

But the New Testament doctrine goes beyond this inculcation of likeness to Christ as a duty incumbent on all who claim to be united with Him. It asserts that union with Christ bestows a power to attain this likeness to Christ, and is a necessary condition to the attainment of such power. This doctrine, which is fully expressed in the parable from St. John which I have taken as my text, so pervades Paul's Epistles that it is difficult to select quotations to establish it. He describes the believer as buried with Christ in baptism; and, the old man thereby being crucified and slain, as rising again with Him to newness of life. "I am crucified with Christ: nevertheless I live; yet not I, but Christ liveth in me: and the life which I now live in the flesh I live by the faith of the Son of God, who loved me and gave Himself for me." So he writes to the Galatians. To the Colossians he says, "If ye then be risen with Christ, seek those things which are above, where Christ sitteth on the right hand of God. Set your affection on things above, not on things of the earth. For ye are dead, and your life is hid with Christ in God." This language might sound mystical if it stood alone, but light is thrown on it by the comparisons elsewhere used by the Apostle, in particular where he compares Christ to the Head of the body, "from which all the body by joints and bands having nourishment ministered and knit together, increaseth with the increase of God." In other words, the doctrine is that the spiritual life of every Christian depends on his being united with Christ, and in virtue of that union drawing from Him continued supplies of grace and strength, by which alone he can make growth and exhibit fruit.

Once more the same principle, which is made the root of the Christian's present holiness, is also made that of his future blessedness. It has often been remarked how vague the New Testament is in its description of the happiness of the future state. This much seems to have been regarded as sufficient for us to know, that if we have been united to Christ here, we cannot be separated from Him hereafter, and that whatever we shall be, we shall be like Him. "If we be dead with Christ we believe that we shall also live with Him." "When Christ, who is our life, shall appear, then shall we also appear with Him in glory." "It doth not yet appear what we shall be: but we know that, when He shall appear, we shall be like Him; for we shall see Him as He is." The thought perpetually recurs that Christ shares with His people His own glory. In St. Luke our Lord is related to have said to His disciples, "I appoint unto you a kingdom as My Father hath appointed unto Me." We have the same thought in different words in the Book of the Revelation: "To him that overcometh will I grant to sit with Me in My throne, even as I also overcame, and am set down with My Father in His throne." And the whole idea is expanded in our Lord's prayer, recorded in John xvii.: "The glory which Thou gavest Me I have given them; that they may be one, even as We are one: I in them, and Thou in Me, that they may be made perfect in one; and that the world may know that Thou hast sent Me, and hast loved them, as Thou hast loved Me. Father, I will that they also whom Thou hast given Me be with Me where I am; that they may behold My glory, which Thou hast given Me: for Thou lovedst Me before the foundation of the world." Thus you will see that the idea of future blessedness presented in all the New Testament books where it is spoken of is something based on union with Christ, participation through Christ's goodness of the glory which the Father had bestowed on Him, being with Christ where He is, being in every sense like Christ.

The examination we have made enables us to understand why it is that Socinianism proper is now an extinct heresy, a deserted half-way house which no one now stops at. There are many now who believe Jesus of Nazareth to have been mere man, a Jewish sage it may be, of exceptional wisdom and goodness, but still in no essential respect different in nature from other men. But those who so believe do not attempt to establish their creed by Scripture, nor have they any solicitude to reconcile themselves with the teaching of the early Church. If they think but humbly of our Lord, they have still less reverence for His immediate followers, and would not scruple to claim to be on a multitude of points wiser than they. So they have got long past the stage of those who equally taught the bare humanity of our Lord, but who conceived themselves bound to maintain that such a doctrine was primitive Christianity. As I have said, the passages of the New Testament which have come under our study are enough to exhibit the hopelessness of reconciling

Socinian views of our Lord's nature with the belief of His followers as recorded in the New Testament. I have not brought before you to-day any of the texts which are commonly quoted to prove our Lord's divinity ; and I have thrown into the background those which speak of the unity between our Lord and His people as but a feeble counterpart of the unity between our Lord and His Father which existed before the world was. But we have seen evidence that the first disciples looked on their Master as holding a position corresponding to that of Adam as federal Head of a new creation ; that they believed that all who find God's favour do so because so united to Christ that their sins brought suffering on Him, that His righteousness brought salvation to them ; that they believed that that righteousness, the righteousness of Christ, must be worked out in the lives of His people ; that they held themselves entitled in coming to God in prayer to plead Christ's merits as giving them a claim to His favour ; and looked forward to no happiness hereafter but what they should gain as joined to their risen and ascended Lord. These are not the views of any single authority, but the evidence is harmonious of every writer from whom we learn anything as to what primitive Christianity was ; and the agreement extends to every detail of the doctrine.

It is simply impossible to suppose that they who believed thus of our Lord looked on Him as a man like others ; and, therefore, we feel under no temptation to look for strained methods of interpretation when we read that they worshipped Him as their Lord and their God, that they owned Him as the Word of God by whom all things were made, which was in the beginning with God, and which was God.

It needs to say but few words in conclusion as to the practical bearing of the doctrines we have been considering. It is not merely in an evidential point of view that it is important to notice the perfect harmony of the Christian doctrines, some, which at first sight might be supposed to be independent and distinct, turning out on closer examination to be only different aspects of the same truth. But it is quite as important practically to bear in mind the essential unity of the different parts of the Christian scheme. There have been ungodly men who have turned the grace of our God to lasciviousness, who have caught eagerly at the doctrine that the penalty of our sins has been borne by another, and who have inferred that we ourselves being now secure from paying what has been discharged already, need neither trouble ourselves with sorrow for sin past, nor be solicitous about precautions against sin future.

To all of us it is delightful to think that the eyes of the Lord are upon us, and His ears open to our prayers, joyful to believe that our inheritance shall be with Christ in glory. But we have seen that the privileges and the duties of the Christian life are inseparably connected. Antinomianism is a thing impossible if we once clearly understand that all our hopes, all our claims on God's favour rest on our being one with Christ, a union which implies sympathy with the mind of Christ, zeal for the things for which He was solicitous, hatred of what He hated, perfect likeness to His character. Brethren, may God grant to each of you that Christ may dwell in your heart by faith, that you may be strengthened by His Spirit in the inner man; gaining from Him power to overcome your spiritual enemies; continually changed from glory to glory till you attain complete likeness to His image.

III

THE PURE IN HEART SHALL SEE GOD [1]

"Blessed are the pure in heart: for they shall see God."—
MATTHEW v. 8.

ONE of the most authentic and most interesting accounts of Christian martyrdoms is to be found in the history of the persecution of which Lyons was the centre in the year 177. Beginning in popular clamour and continually urged on by the violence of excited mobs, it was not only taken up by the authority of the local magistrates, but on account of the Roman citizenship of some of the victims it became necessary to consult the Emperor; and the final deeds of blood were committed under direct imperial sanction. And the notable thing is that the Emperor, who thus became responsible for crimes committed under the name of law, which we cannot read without shuddering to learn what a wild beast man can be to man, was no other than he, the self-denial

[1] Preached at Great St. Mary's, Cambridge, June 1, 1884.

(may we not say the holiness?) of whose life approached nearest to Christianity,—Marcus Aurelius. The world has seldom seen an example of power so unlimited, wielded so conscientiously by a perfectly irresponsible ruler, whose one object was not to gain enjoyment for himself, but to fulfil what he believed to be his duty. Indeed we feel it now to be the weakest point in his philosophy, that it was so joyless, and could do so little for the happiness of its professors. In this respect the Emperor contrasts unexpectedly with those whom he committed to the sword as criminals. Which might we expect to be the happier, the ruler of the civilised world, who had only to form a wish and his commands were executed, or those outcasts of society whom their fellow-citizens regarded with such horror and loathing that the physical pain they had to endure was a less trial than their knowledge that every fresh cruelty ordered by the magistrates was considered by the clamouring spectators to be punishment too mild for their guilt? Yet in the history of the martyrdoms the prominent feature is the enthusiastic joy of the sufferers. Those, indeed, whose constancy failed in the trial, hung their heads downcast for shame, but the steadfast were seen with countenances radiant with joy, so rapt in ecstatic contemplation that they had scarce consciousness of the tortures applied to them. And meanwhile the Emperor himself, at whose word these things were done, rather tolerated than enjoyed life. That he refrained from suicide was due rather to a sense of duty than to any pleasure this life gave him. Whether Stoicism or Christianity be the truer system of philosophy may be a subject for discussion, but if the question were put which was more capable of bringing to its professors happiness and joy, the most ardent Stoic might yield the point without a struggle.

The two systems of philosophy, however, agreed in teaching the lesson, "Love not the world, nor the things which are in the world;" and what has led me to speak of Marcus Aurelius now is in order that we may consider the argument by which he disciplined himself, and justified himself in his disregard of the things in which other men find happiness and pleasure. Consider, he says, any of the things in which other men place their delight, and analyse it, and you will find it undeserving of the esteem they set on it. Do they take pleasure in music? Well, take one note, sound it, and listen to it, and is there any beauty in it? sound the next note, listen to that too, is it any better? and so on for every note. The whole thing when pulled to pieces is found to have nothing in it. So in like manner if they take pleasure in looking at dancing : consider any one attitude of the dancers, fix it and regard it, and where is the beauty of it ? So likewise for the pancration and everything else in which men imagine they find pleasure ; analyse them and you will find that not one can stand the test ; not one when pulled to pieces will be found to have anything in it. We need not doubt that this argument was used seriously by the Emperor in his reasonings with himself, and that it was part of the process by which he disciplined his mind to that detachment from the world at which he aimed ; but I am sure we must feel, too, that if he hoped by means of it to influence the feelings or the conduct of other people, there are few indeed to whom it would carry any persuasion.

But it seems to me that the argument is neither more nor less sophistical than that analysis, claiming to be scientific, by which in the same manner that Marcus Aurelius tried to show that there was nothing real in our conceptions of beauty, others have tried to show that there was nothing real in our notions of God. In fact, the weapons that have been used to demolish old religious beliefs are much more powerful than those who wielded them were aware of. Bishop Butler showed long ago that the chief arguments which had been directed against the special system of Christianity could not in consistency be employed by the Deists who used them, since if the principles involved in their objections were rigorously carried out, it would not be possible to believe that the world we live in was controlled by an intelligent and benevolent Ruler. In the modern state of the infidel controversy this way of repelling assaults on Christianity has lost its effectiveness because a great mass of the most troublesome assailants now are willing to carry out their principles to the full, and to give up not only their Christianity but their old-fashioned Theism; hoping, however, by some new religion of science or art to give some other satisfaction to the wants in man's nature which religion aimed at supplying. They little know, however, how potent are the instruments they have used in their assaults on traditional beliefs, and how little resistance anything they are minded to retain is able to make to similar attacks.

They cannot help acknowledging what an important part religion has played in the history of mankind. They know that to the great majority of their fellow-citizens the beliefs which they reject still continue to be the source of their strongest, purest, and noblest emotions, their consolation in time of trial, their strength in time of temptation. When affliction befalls where else can such a foundation for patient submission be found as in the belief that it has been sent by a wise and loving Father? when the allurements of temptation are most attractive, what thought has such force to repel them as "How can I do this wickedness and sin against God?" But I need not enlarge on what is not likely to be denied, namely, that the belief that they have a Father in heaven is one held by a great many, and that it is a belief which makes them happier and makes them better. But the question of questions is whether the belief is true. This conception of a divine Friend, whose love it is delightful to contemplate, whose purity is our noblest model, has it any objective reality, or is it all but the creation of the minds of those whose thoughts have dwelt upon it? To those who have habitually walked by faith in the unseen it will seem as unpractical to ask such a question as it is to propound doubts concerning the existence of the external world. Metaphysicians have employed themselves with the question how we can ever get beyond our own sensations and know with any certainty that there are external objects which excite them. When we dream we are for the time convinced of the reality of all we think we see or hear, and yet we wake and find it to have been delusion. Can we be sure that there is anything more substantial in our waking perceptions, and that they are anything more than a longer-continued, more consistent dream? It is of little consequence whether the answers that have been given to these questions are logically sufficient to bear a searching criticism, for no speculative difficulties that can be raised about the matter disturb for a moment the practical convictions of the most ingenious sceptic. There are many who feel in precisely the same way with respect to doubts raised as to the existence of Him, communion with whom has been their highest happiness, the desire to please whom their habitual rule of life. They care not for speculative difficulties because they have a practical conviction founded on experience and knowledge.

But, it will be said, such persons are a minority. It is quite true that it is idle to think that any possible amount of speculative difficulties could shake the practical conviction which every one feels as to the objective existence of an external world; but then that is precisely because it is a conviction felt by everybody. If there was anything like so universal a consensus to belief in the existence of God we should own doubt to be unreasonable.

Well, then, let the religious emotions be compared with those which are excited by the perception of beauty in sights or sounds, and let us see whether we can either scorn the latter as unreal or fantastical, or else deny that the former are quite as essential a part of our nature. It need hardly be said how far indeed from being universal is any agreement as to the objects capable of affording the pleasure of which I speak. We can barely show that a capacity for such pleasure is natural to our race by appealing to the delight which the most untutored savages show in decking themselves with ornament. But how vast is the interval between the æsthetic conceptions of such a savage and those of an art student of the present day! It is notorious how slowly men's education in matters of taste has proceeded. It is little more than a century since it was discovered that the snow peaks and glaciers of a Swiss mountain were capable of inspiring other emotions than those of terror; about as long a time since a Gothic cathedral was regarded as but a frightful monstrosity exhibiting the rude taste of a barbarous age. How widely differences of culture at the present day produce corresponding differences of taste is too notorious to need to be dwelt on. Does it follow, then, that the emotions which the supposed perception of beauty excites are to be despised as unreal, and that we are to hold that the more a man purges his mind from them the more he deserves the character of a wise man, resolved to see things as they really are, and freed from the fantastical additions which different men's imaginations have made to them? I have already told you the process by which Marcus Aurelius imagined he could convince himself that he had demonstrated the nothingness of the vain pleasures by which the unlearned allowed themselves to be beguiled. It was an attempted demonstration in the success of which the world would have had no cause for rejoicing. What reason for triumph would there have been if the imperial philosopher had succeeded in robbing life of a large portion of its happiness, and rendering the existence of all others as joyless as his own? In point of fact, he never had a chance of succeeding; for he could not get a hearing for speculations which seemed as visionary as attempts to demonstrate the non-existence of the external world. If we have a right to ascribe objective reality to the unknown cause of the sensations which we know other men experience like ourselves, have we not as good a right to ascribe reality to the source of the emotions which we know that others as well as we experience? When men knew as a matter of fact that certain sights or sounds gave them exquisite pleasure, what availed a demonstration that the pleasure was imaginary, or that it was irrational, when their experience assured them that it was real? And they felt assured also that to lose a capacity for such pleasure would not be an advance in the direction of simplicity and truth, but a retrograde step in the history of the culture of the human race.

But if they had condescended to argument it would have been easy to show that one who should resolve to see things exactly as they are, and to part with all that the human mind has added to the bare facts of nature, must in consistency carry out very far the disintegration of ordinary conceptions. Marcus Aurelius refused to own that it was legitimate to derive any pleasure from hearing a succession of sounds unless when you attend to each sound by itself you can find the pleasure in that. But even the single musical note has not the unity which he was willing to acknowledge in it. What is it but a succession of pulsations differing only in rapidity from what we should count as distinct noises? But we may go further. What is now known as to the convertibility of forces leads us to regard heat, light, electricity, as all but different modes of motion differing from each other only according to the magnitude or rapidity of the moving particles. That these should present to us now distinct ideas may be pronounced to be altogether the work of the human mind. But further still, the grouping of the different atoms into substances regarded as separate units is also the work of the mind. It is a grouping altogether relative to our organs of perception, and we have reason to know that if we could see things exactly as they are, that which now appears to us a single quiescent solid mass would be perceived to be a congeries of molecules each in rapid motion, seeming to be at rest only because the range of their vibrations is too small for our existing organs to take cognisance of, and seeming to form one body only because the intervals of separation are also too small for us to discern, but really only one in the sense that the planetary system may be said to be one. Thus, then, if we could see things precisely as they are, and stript of the illusions with which the constitution of our minds has surrounded them, all that we should see in this universe of ours would be a multitude of independent particles in incessant aimless motion, approaching each other, colliding, repelled again, some making oscillations of small, others of larger, amplitude, some groups continuing for a time in the close neighbourhood of each other, until, as in their mad dance they come into collision with other groups, the temporary combination is dispersed. Man is truly, in a sense Bacon did not contemplate, the interpreter of nature. It is man who discovers the plan that rules the mighty maze, and recognises in some of these groups of vibrating molecules sentient reasoning beings like himself.

If we thoroughly understood the function that mind plays in revealing to us the universe which we perceive, we should acknowledge that it is unreasonable to impose on the revelations of our souls the limitations of physical philosophy. All that physical philosophy can do is to tell us the laws of motion. When first that philosophy became a science it made known the laws which regulate the motion of the larger masses. The more recent sciences of chemistry and electricity throw light on the motions of the smaller particles of which our senses cannot take direct cognisance; but in the last analysis it is still of nothing but of motion that they tell. The great modern law of the persistence and conservation of force is no more than a statement that the quantity of motion in the world remains constant. In any other sense it is not true. Ask the mourners by the grave of a great man whether it is true that the world has lost nothing by his death, seeing that the amount of force in the world cannot be diminished. True, accumulated stores of rare learning have been dissipated ; ripe experience from which wise counsel had never been sought in vain has now become no longer accessible; love proved by years and sacrifices has been taken away; but there is a due equivalent for what is gone in the chemical reactions of the decaying animal matter left behind. The simple fact is that for everything in the living man which admitted of being translated into modes of motion there remains an equivalent in some other form of motion, but grief proves that life and thought are felt to be things of a different kind, which when lost are not replaced. If the word "progress" is the watchword of our civilisation, that word is evidence that we are in a region governed by different laws from those which rule the conservation of motion. The quantity of motion in the world remains constant; we cannot produce new motion except by the destruction and conversion of some previously existing form, but the nature of life is to propagate itself and increase; a single seed of life introduced into our globe had within it the potentiality of indefinite multiplication. And so likewise of thought. To employ the phrase "germs of thought," is scarcely to use a metaphor, so notoriously do ideas communicated to another fructify and expand to results of which the originator never dreamed. And the benefit thus given to another causes no loss of power to him who gives it. By lighting a neighbour's torch our own taper shines no less brilliantly.

When it is understood in how completely different a sphere lie the ideas with which religion is concerned from those which are dealt with by the sciences which undertake to analyse the laws which regulate the transformation of the different modes of motion, it will be felt how idle is the apprehension that the culture of the physical sciences can be injurious to religion. It might as well be feared that the culture of science can be injurious to art by leading to some discovery which would show that the works of the great masters were not fit objects of admiration. On the domain of art true science is able to cast a useful light, but there is no danger that a Helmholtz can either overthrow or replace a Beethoven.

Just as little need we fear that religion can be unfavourably affected by any progress of research into the laws which govern the material world. We need not fear that that science which reveals the relation of the soul to God can be overthrown even though an anatomist may have dissected hundreds of bodies and never been able to see a soul, or though an astronomer may have explored the whole of the planetary system without having been able to see anything of that huge brain without which some would tell us that there could be no intelligence presiding over nature. Religion like art deals with facts and experiences of its own, and these experiences such that he who has known them understands that they belong to the higher part of his nature, and that not to have felt them would indicate that some part of his constitution was either defective or had not been properly cultivated. A philosophy which ignores such facts or treats them as illusions condemns itself as ignorant; and it is only in proportion as it recognises and sympathises with them that it deserves to be listened to. For it is not to be denied that there may be a true philosophy of religion. The savage bowing before his rude image may testify that the instinct of worship is natural to man, but his religious conceptions will no more content a civilised man than the ornaments with which he decks himself will satisfy the demands of civilised art. There is no part of our nature which is not improved by culture and education, and it need not be supposed that what we may call the religious faculty is any exception to this rule, or that our advances in thought and knowledge, if rightly used, will do nothing in elevating our conception of God.

How, then, are we to educate and improve in ourselves that faculty which discerns the divine? Different answers to this question have been given.

There have been many who have thought that since the object was to penetrate into the unseen world and to discover something more than sense could reveal, the more communication with the material world was closed the clearer must be the spiritual discernment; and so they have striven by fasting and other mortifications to dull the organs of sense in the idea that the things of earth being shut out they might then hope to see God. There are others, again, who think of God as that everpresent force which rules and sustains the material universe, and have thought that in the study of its laws they could best see God, and so they have found a God without justice, without love, without pity, indifferent alike to human suffering or human crime. Very different from either is the way suggested in our blessed Lord's utterance, " The pure in heart shall see God." Where in fact do we find the clearest revelation of God? Not so much in the spectacle of the order of the universe and the manifold contrivances which seem so clearly to indicate a wise and benevolent Designer. Far more in the voice of conscience within, which claims for its dictates an authority superior to ourselves, which warns, rebukes, punishes as if it were something different from and above ourselves. If we disregard her remonstrances, then drifting unruled ourselves on the waves of impulse and passion, it costs us less to believe that the world is without a ruler, nor do we much care to discover One whose friend we know we do not deserve to be. But on the contrary, what can more purge the spiritual vision than what is meant by that specially Christian word, purity? a word meaning so much more than virtue; not the mere giving other men their due, and so gaining their approval, but the striving under the eye of an invisible Master to become cleansed from all defilement, and so be made a vessel unto honour, sanctified and meet for the Master's use, and prepared for every good work. What way so sure of seeing Him whose will it is our constant aim to do, whose ineffable purity is the pattern we strive to imitate?

Far be it from me to suggest that unbelief must necessarily have its root in moral impurity. There were indeed unbelievers in former days, and the race is not quite extinct, who showed utter want of sympathy with those high and noble aspirations which our religion is certainly an attempt to satisfy; and who, while by their ribald attacks on things sacred they made many a victim among the vicious and profane, yet repelled and disgusted those whose tone of moral feeling was more lofty. But it is only justice to own that there are among the unbelievers of the present day many with the high tone of whose morality we can find no fault, though we may doubt whether it could have been conceived except by minds trained up in Christianity and from early years imbued with its spirit, and may doubt whether it could retain a permanent hold on the generality of men, if Christianity, the root from which it has sprung, were destroyed. But while we do not judge others, it is right that we should examine ourselves. That time of life at which the growth of our intellectual powers gives us confidence in our capacity to form an independent judgment, and to put to the test the traditional beliefs of early years, is also the time of life when the temptations to fleshly lusts are the strongest. He then whose vision of God has been clouded over has reason to examine himself whether the cause may not be that he has permitted his own organs of spiritual perception to become impaired. There is no such parent of doubt as the trifling with known obligations. Let no one complain that he cannot find the evidences of our religion perfectly convincing, if his own conduct be such as will sufficiently account for the perplexity which he feels : if he have fallen into the habit of neglecting known duties, such as the use of the means of grace—private prayer, study of God's Word, public worship ; if he deliberately reject the call which each returning Lord's Day makes on him to lift his thoughts for a time above the petty concerns of this life; if he suffer himself to be always engrossed with this world's pleasures and its cares; if he go on to be guilty of that against which his conscience still more loudly protests; if he habitually allow his imagination to be polluted by impure thoughts; or if he gives himself up in act to licentious pleasures; then it is only natural that, his heart being hardened by the deceitfulness of sin, the eyes of his understanding also should be darkened; that he should lose his power of spiritual perception, and have no share in the promise reserved for the pure in heart,—that "they shall see God." For the habitual sense of the presence of God, the conviction that there is something higher and nobler than the objects of sense, deserving of our love and affections, is a conviction that can only be preserved by acting in conformity with it, and honestly following where it leads us. It is only by habitual affectionate obedience to God that we can preserve the power of realising things not seen.

In what I have said to-day I have brought before you no specially Christian doctrine; for the course of modern assaults on revelation makes it necessary for us from time to time to labour in the defence of principles which are common to us with every one who believes in a God. I will not conclude, however, without citing another passage of Scripture which may be regarded as complementary to that which I have taken as my text. "No man hath seen God at any time: the only begotten Son, which is in the bosom of the Father, He hath declared Him." Our blessed Lord has not only taught His disciples that in moral purity must be laid the foundation of any religion worthy of the name, He showed in His own person how the divine life in this world was practicable. And so in the New Testament we find exhortations not less noble but less vague than the Old Testament precept, "Be ye holy, even as I am holy." The hope of Christ's disciples is that when He shall appear they shall be like Him, and they are taught that every one that hath this hope in Him purifieth himself even as He is pure. The exhortations to them run :—" Let this mind be in you which was also in Christ Jesus." "Christ left us an example that we should follow in His steps: who did no sin, neither was guile found in His mouth." "Who His own self bare our sins in His own body on the tree, that we, being dead to sins, should live unto righteousness : by whose stripes ye are healed."

Nor did Christ merely leave His people an example. He provided them also with means of attaining conformity to it—the chief being that gift of the

Holy Spirit whose coming we commemorate to-day. His office is to take of the things of Christ and show them to you; by revealing to you what Jesus was, at once to inspire you with the wish and give you the power to be like Him. In the Apostle's words, I then exhort you, "Walk not you as those walk who have the understanding darkened, being alienated from the life of God through the ignorance that is in them, because of the hardness of their heart: who, being past feeling, have given themselves over unto lasciviousness, to work all uncleanness with greediness."

"Ye have not so learned Christ; if so be that ye have heard Him, and have been taught by Him, as the truth is in Jesus: that ye put off, concerning the former conversation, the old man, which is corrupt according to the deceitful lusts; and be renewed in the spirit of your mind; and that ye put on the new man, which after God is created in righteousness and true holiness."

"Grieve not the Holy Spirit of God, whereby ye are sealed unto the day of redemption."

IV

ILL SUCCESS IN SEARCHING AFTER RIGHTEOUSNESS[1]

"The Gentiles, which followed not after righteousness, have attained to righteousness, even the righteousness which is of faith: but Israel, which followed after the law of righteousness, hath not attained to the law of righteousness."—ROMANS ix. 30, 31.

AMONG the moral essays published about the beginning of this century, one of the most striking was that by Mrs. Barbauld on the inconsistency of human expectations. It was mainly taken up with insisting on the truth that what a man soweth, that, and not something else, is what he will reap; and it explained the majority of men's disappointments as arising from the fact that they sow one thing and expect to reap another: they expect to gain the end when they have neglected or disdained to use the means necessary to obtain it. You complain, for instance, that the good things of this world are ill distributed, that riches and honours fall to the lot of men un-

[1] Preached at Great St. Mary's, Cambridge, June 8, 1884.

worthy of them. Examine into the matter and perhaps you find that the man whose riches you envy has given up his whole mind to the pursuit of them. He has been so absorbed in his ventures and his investments that he has had no thought to give, not to say to science, or literature, or art, but scarcely to the enjoyment of the society of his own family. You feel that such a sacrifice is more than you would be willing to make, and perhaps you are right in your decision; but then do not complain that he who has been willing to pay the price should get what he gave it for. Another has made the pursuit of worldly advancement his great object in life: he has canvassed, puffed himself, intrigued; you disdain to employ the arts he has used, yet inconsistently you grudge him what these arts have gained for him. Once more, you complain that dull men get all the honours and prizes of this world, the fact being that you think the plodding industry to which they stoop too degrading to your genius. You would not be guilty of their stupidity in giving up the pleasures of society, or the enjoyments of lighter literature or other recreations. Well, you have your reward in whatever pleasures these can yield: do not grudge them theirs.

In short, the doctrine of this essay is: make up your mind what objects you consider desirable, and then give yourself up to the pursuit of them. The world is so constituted that diligent exertion will, in all likelihood, meet with success. If you think riches the greatest good, then give yourself up to the pursuit of wealth. Your mind will probably not be very expanded, nor your sentiments very liberal: but it is likely you will be rich. If you think learning the greatest good, give your days and nights to study. Your body may not be very healthy, but it is likely you will be learned. Whatever you think worth working for you are very likely to get; but do not complain if you do not also get other things when you have not thought proper to use the means necessary for attaining them.

There is much good sense and truth in the doctrine of the essay to which I have referred; but there is hardly any truth without a counter-truth. The general rule undoubtedly is that men get what they work for; but there are quite enough of exceptions to it to account for men's calculating that their experience will be otherwise. On the one hand, men sometimes get that on which they have bestowed no labour. A man completely neglects his own interests in his zeal to do some great work for the bodies or souls of other men, and it happens that the gratitude felt for the good he has done makes him more a gainer than if he had laboured for himself. Or he has had to cast away the good opinion of his fellow-men. In obedience to his conscience he has had to brave their disapprobation, to submit to misrepresentation and calumny, and in time his consistent steadiness vindicates itself; the mists of prejudice clear away, and he stands far higher in their respect and favour than if he had shaped his conduct with a view to win them. Our Lord Himself encouraged His disciples to expect in some such way to receive that which they were forbidden to seek. He bids them to take no thought what they should eat or drink or wherewith they should be clothed: but He adds, "Seek ye first the kingdom of God, and His righteousness; and these things shall be added unto you." He bids them take for themselves the lowest place, but He allows them to hope that the Master will afterwards say to them, "Friend, come up higher." And so the Apostle describes godliness as having the promise of the life that now is as well as of that which is to come. And it has become a popular saying that it is possible to make the best of both worlds,—to get all the good things of this, without losing claim to the blessedness of the future. The result is that we are not disposed to acquiesce in the view that men will reap what they sow; that it is natural that men should have riches and honours who have worked hard to get them, and that those should be without them who have taken no trouble for them. We think there ought to be more poetical justice in this life; that its good things should belong, not to those who work for them, but to those who deserve to have them; nay, to them so much the more, the less they have grasped them for themselves. And as I have said, the case of rewards being given to those who have not sought them occurs quite often enough to raise the expectation that it may take place in general.

But if it were only this, that some get more than they have worked for, it would be less surprising; the really strange thing is that others who do work are disappointed, so that it seems as if they would have had better success if they had not striven for it at all. I do not now speak of such cases as when a man allows his conduct to be guided by the search for popularity, and when his object is plainly seen, the popularity he desires cannot be had; or as when a man so exclusively pursues his own interests that his selfishness provokes the hostility of others, and he finds in the end that he would have advanced his interests more had he thought about them less. In these cases, if the law, "Seek and ye shall find," does not strictly hold, we might account for it by the fact that there was something reprehensible in the seeking. But what are we to say to cases where to seek is not only not wrong but is our bounden duty. To seek to obtain the favour of Almighty God is surely the duty of all His creatures, and yet many who have sought it earnestly have not sought it successfully. I have chosen as my text the passage in which the Apostle Paul observes the paradox that the Jews who had devoted themselves to seeking to obtain righteousness before God by the works of the law which He had given them, had failed in their pursuit, while the Gentiles without effort had been successful, so that the words spoken by Isaiah long before were verified, " I was found of them that sought Me not: I was made manifest unto them that asked not after Me."

It is exactly the same paradox that is presented in the story of the Pharisee and the Publican. To gain the favour of God was the great object of the Pharisee's life. To this end he fasted, and made long prayers and paid tithes of mint, anise, and cummin; he thought it not enough to observe the precepts of the law, but added for further security a multitude of traditional commands. That he should avoid the grosser vices was a matter of course. He was not an extortioner, unjust, an adulterer ; yet we are told that the publican, whose life was disfigured by stains which seemed to the Pharisee shocking and disgraceful, went down to his house justified rather than he. And the same story has constantly repeated itself in the history of our own religion. Men have given up all the ordinary business and all the pleasures of life, and made it their one object to seek to save their souls. They have retired to deserts, they have macerated themselves with fasting, they have disciplined themselves with scourging; in their anxiety to escape hell they have made a hell of this earth ; so that it seems cruel to ask the question, Have all their pains and sacrifices brought them nearer to the end they were aiming at?

One daughter disdains the happiness of this life, and resolves by her sanctity to merit for herself something higher. She enters a nunnery, and distinguishes herself among the sisters by her peculiar austerities. As far as nature will permit, she denies herself food ; when constrained to take it, lest she should take pleasure in the act, she mixes what she eats with ashes and bitter herbs ; that she may not indulge in sleep she fills her bed with tiles and broken stones ; she disciplines her tender skin with scourging till the walls and floor of her cell are spattered with her blood ; she wears a hair shirt, and presses on her brow a metal crown of thorns. As her bodily strength decays her spiritual insight increases; she sees visions, she becomes an *Ecstatica*, and when she has brought herself to an early grave, the admiring gratitude of her community obtains her enrolment in the calendar of saints. I am drawing no imaginary picture. I have taken my model from the life of a saint,[1] recorded for the admiration of her co-religionists; for repeatedly has it happened that by the application of moral force alone tortures which would be thought too severe for an atrocious criminal have been inflicted on an unoffending girl with no other fault than that of a weak and superstitious mind.

Meanwhile her sister, who has never aspired to tread any heroic paths of sanctity, discharges with unpretending simplicity the ordinary duties of life. She becomes a happy wife and mother, the ruler of an attached family. She has no title to any higher praise than that she corresponds to the description in the Book of Proverbs: "She looketh well to the ways of her household, and eateth not the bread of idleness. She stretcheth out her hand to the poor; yea, she reacheth forth her hands to the needy. She openeth her mouth with wisdom; and in her tongue is the law of

[1] St. Rose of Lima.

kindness. The heart of her husband doth safely trust in her, for she will do him good, and not evil, all the days of her life. Her children arise up, and call her blessed; her husband also, and he praiseth her. Many daughters have done virtuously, but thou excellest them all." She has had all this world's happiness, which her sister whose thoughts were bent upon the future has not dared to touch; yet I suppose there is scarcely any one here who thinks that the great inequality in their conditions in this life is likely to be compensated by an inverse distribution of happiness in the next, or who believes that the voluntary sufferings of the one will be more likely to gain God's favour than the other's homely fulfilment of duty.

But let us not be misled by the clearness with which we can see the mistakes committed by persons of different religion and different habits of thought from ourselves. The way to profit by such mistakes is to ask ourselves, May not we also deceive ourselves when we think ourselves religious, or admire others as religious or as advancing the interests of religion, and may it not be that a higher place in God's favour may be obtained by others who seem to us to have neglected to seek it?

Perhaps, however, it may be thought that the

ill-success of many in seeking to earn for themselves a claim to future happiness is to be accounted for by there being something wrong in the spirit which prompted their search. It may be said that the spirit which urges some men to grasp at happiness in another life may be nothing more than the same selfish spirit which urges them to advance their interests in this, and that it ought not to surprise or offend us more in one case than in the other, if their calculations are disappointed. But this explanation will not suffice to account for the difficulty we are considering. For the same phenomenon of some men obtaining with little effort what others labour for in vain presents itself when the object aimed at is not selfish at all, but is directly to do good to other men. The fact of the complete failure of many exertions made for charitable objects has more than once been brought under public notice. I do not now speak of such cases as charitable endowments dishonestly misappropriated to purposes different from what the founder intended, or of charitable organisations mainly worked for the benefit of the officials employed in promoting them. I refer to cases where the failure arose, not from any misadventure in the working of the scheme, but was inherent in the scheme itself. Endowments have been given for the poor of a particular parish, and instead of the founder's hope being fulfilled that the parish in which he took an interest would be exceptionally free from pauperism, his benefaction has only had the effect of attracting thither a number of the idle and worthless from other places, so that the more that was done to relieve misery the greater seemed the misery that needed to be relieved.

And those who have not waited to make their benefactions till they were dead have often not been more successful in their endeavours to diminish the misery of the world. A wealthy and kind-hearted person has flung his money broadcast round the district in which he resided, only with the effect of making his neighbours more helpless and more idle, little better off while they received his bounty than they had been before it was granted, and ready to sink into deeper destitution if it should be withdrawn. He simply verifies in his experience what Archbishop Whately was in the habit of saying: that men will do what they are paid for doing. If you pay men for working you can collect about you an army of workmen. If you pay men for begging you will collect about you an army of beggars. Perhaps such a man is succeeded by another who is little susceptible of benevolent aspirations. Not with any view of doing good to his neighbours, but merely in order to make a profit for himself, he establishes a new industry; and the wretchedness which when combated directly seemed inexhaustible now completely disappears. The warmhearted man who tried to help his neighbours fails; and the cold-hearted man succeeds who has been able to put it in their power to help themselves.

So again it has happened that a despot whose actions have been solely directed to the gratification of his own ambition, and who has squandered men's lives without scruple when the sacrifice would advance his ends, has yet by his able rule conferred permanent benefits on the people he governed, which they would not have enjoyed under the government of a more amiable and more conscientious sovereign. I suppose, after all deductions have been made, it was better for France to have been ruled by the first Napoleon than by Louis XVI. However this may be, cases are numerous enough in which most good has been done by persons who thought least about it, so that we are reminded of instances in which a wooer by his nervous and awkward solicitude to please has repelled the coy beauty whom he sought to win, and has had to yield the conquest to another, whose chief merit was that he had less set his heart on gaining it.

What, then, is the practical conclusion to be drawn from the instances I have brought before you? Are we to sum up the result of our experience in the formula, "Seek and you shall not find; if you want to do good to your fellow-creatures, don't try." Nay, the doctrine arrived at would not stop with teaching us to abandon all charitable exertions; it would lead us on to the secularist conclusion that, inasmuch as so many who have ruled their lives with the object of gaining God's favour, have clearly failed, the best way to please God, if there be a God, is to think as little as possible about Him; that our best rule of conduct is to do all we can to advance our own interests; that in so doing we are taking as likely a course as any other to benefit other people, and that if we do all we can to make ourselves happy in this world, we are also making the best provision for our being happy in another life, if there should be one.

I know it will not need much discussion to persuade you that there must be some fallacy in the arguments which lead to such a conclusion; and you will be quite right in not allowing any paradoxical enumeration of contrary instances to make you doubt the truth of the rule that what a man soweth he will reap. The simple truth is that it *is* what he sows that he reaps, and not always what he thinks he sows or what he would like to reap. A man may be very diligent in sowing; but if it be not the right kind of seed the harvest may be very different from what he wishes to get. God governs the world by laws which will not make allowance for good intentions, and so it happens that a vast amount of mischief is done by perfectly well-meaning people. We are sometimes tempted to be shocked at the hardness, we might almost say the cruelty of our ancestors, and at the indifference with which they witnessed different forms of human suffering. Yet experience is teaching us that for the effectual relief of that suffering a wise head is quite as necessary as a tender heart; for it has happened more than once that the shrieks of philanthropists have been a real hindrance to the diminution of the misery that is in the world, because in their impatience of some particular form of suffering which has come under their notice, they have never stopped to consider whether in their attempt to suppress it they might not be the cause of much greater misery.

The popular conception even still is that any-one can do good to his fellow-creatures if he has only got money enough. It requires experience to teach men that to do good instead of being one of the easiest things in the world is one of the hardest. Many a man in former days has given all his goods to feed the poor with no other result than that there was one pauper more in the world than there had been before. In modern times we have less of zeal to make such sacrifices, but often not more knowledge. The total amount given for charitable objects is probably greater than ever it was; for if there are fewer who give all they have, there are more who give of their superfluity; and with the national progress in wealth, the portion available for charitable purposes shares in the general increase. But with the majority, giving is so indolent an act that it scarcely deserves the name of charity. Money is given that is not missed; sometimes as a matter of routine; sometimes because to refuse it when asked for it is more troublesome than to grant it; sometimes because the giving relieves the pain with which amiable people hear or read of stories of distress. But in comparatively few cases do those who give their money give their thoughts, their care, or their personal exertions; and so it happens that of what is given a large portion is simply wasted, and some is actually injurious. The story is told by those who have worked in the East of London, that in seasons of exceptional distress appeals made by letters in the *Times* have been instantly responded to by enormous benefactions from the wealthy; and that the result has been that notwithstanding all the money that has been poured in, the distress was not only not lightened, but actually became worse the more that was done to relieve it. For industry was discouraged when easier ways of getting money were discovered, new claimants flocked to the place where they heard that distributions were made, and prices rose as unworthy recipients were prodigal of their lightly-acquired gain.

Yet surely when it has been proved that unconsidered reckless giving is useless or mischievous, it does not follow that we are wrong in being solicitous for the good of others and in making sacrifices for that end. If to offer unto God that which costs us nothing does not gain a blessing from Him, it does not follow that we do wrong in dedicating to Him our service. Nay He who has said that even a cup of cold water given in His name shall not lose its reward, has deigned to recompense acts of kindness the moral value of which we must own to be very small. To yield to the instincts of compassion roused by the hearing a tale of distress, to give hastily something from our superfluity that we do not miss, and give ourselves little further trouble what becomes of our benefaction, is, as I have said, an act of such slight moral worth that we have no right to complain if such giving effects little good. Yet we have little doubt which to prefer when we balance this against the alternative of not yielding to the instincts of compassion. To begin with, if it be a doubtful matter whether what has been given has always benefited those on whom it was bestowed, it is quite certain that to stifle the tender voice of pity would injure those who withheld their bounty; its suppression would be a brutalisation of their souls. Take the charitable institutions of England as a whole, and let it be granted that a strong case can be made out that there is much mismanagement, much waste, much collision and overlapping of effort, yet what would our land be if there were no such institutions, if there were no signs of sympathy of the rich with the poor, if every one who failed to fight successfully the battle of life were without pity hustled down and trampled on by his more successful neighbour? And it is exactly because God's call on us to do His work in the world has been, however feebly and inadequately, obeyed, that He whose rule is that to him that hath shall more be given, is teaching us how that work can be done more effectually. If those ruder methods of charity had not been tried, we should never have set ourselves to find a still more excellent way.

And as I have spoken of the abuses of charity,

let me say that I do not know any form of charity which is less liable to those abuses than that in which you are asked to assist to-day,[1]—the hospital relief of the sick poor. I do not deny that even in such institutions there is liability to abuse, and need of caution and good sense on the part of those who manage them; but at least this has not, like some forms of bounty, a natural tendency to increase the misery it attempts to relieve. The existence of such institutions makes no one more reckless in incurring sickness; and if we provided the ablest surgeons in the world, no one would break his leg or his arm in order to have the advantage of their skill. Again, if we are convinced that we do far less good by helping other people than by enabling them to help themselves, it is surely a wise and economical form of assistance if when a man, who hitherto has been able and willing to help himself, is reduced by God's providence to temporary necessity, we take means to provide that his disablement shall be as short as possible; when we take care that an accident happening to the breadwinner of a dependent family shall not reduce the whole to pauperism, but that by timely skilful assistance he may be again placed in a condition to work for them.

What I have said as to the difficulties which

[1] A collection was made for Addenbrooke's Hospital.

have been raised about charitable giving will sufficiently explain how I would deal with corresponding difficulties on the question how men can find acceptance with God. We have seen that though many men who have tried to do good to others have nearly quite failed, or have even done mischief, it does not follow that the impulse to benevolence ought to be checked. What does follow is that the impulse has need to be guided by the most enlightened knowledge. And in like manner, though many mistakes have been made by men who desire to win God's favour, and even sins committed under the idea of doing Him service, we are not driven to the secularist conclusion that we are to remove the wish to please Him from among our conscious motives to action. What does follow is the duty of obtaining an enlightened knowledge of His will by every means through which He has been pleased to reveal it, whether through the laws of nature or in His Word, in order that we may be saved from the mistake of hoping to win His favour by actually opposing His will. For if we transgress His laws, neither our ignorance nor our good intentions will save us from having to pay the penalty which the violation entails. Indeed, it has often surprised me to mark how in the ordinary course of God's providential government of the world, the same man for the same actions will receive his reward for that which is good in them, and yet have to pay the penalty for that which is evil in them.

Some of the most absurd actions done to gain God's favour have not been without their reward at least in this life. I suppose if one were to try to imagine a method of forfeiting all chance of influencing or benefiting one's fellow-men without gaining any compensating divine approbation for himself, he could think of nothing better than the method adopted by the pillar saints of old. To retire as far as possible from the society of his fellow-men, and lest even in the desert his solitude should be invaded, to mount a pillar some forty cubits high, there to spend his time in bowing his body up and down, is, I suppose, a prescription for as unprofitable an existence as the wit of man can devise. Yet it is certain that Simeon the Stylite exercised a very powerful influence on his contemporaries; the more he seemed to wish to withdraw himself from their society the more they flocked to him : his counsel was taken in political decisions of great moment, the Emperor revoking decrees on his remonstrance, and what seems more surprising, we are told that thousands of heathen were converted to Christ by the spectacle of his aerial martyrdom. Can a bramble bring forth grapes? we may ask. It certainly cannot. And if such a life as this effected any good, it must have been that notwithstanding the folly and superstition of the man there was sincerity and unworldliness which forced for itself recognition from men, and gained its due reward. So again, the lives of the self-torturing saints were probably not as miserable as the recital of them sounds. It is not so hard to bear suffering when we do so of our own choice, and in recompense they must have been conscious that they were the objects of very profound admiration from those who surrounded them. And shall I say that in this world only they had their reward ? If they built on the true foundation: however much of wood, hay, and stubble they built on it, however much their disappointment to see the structure they gave their life to raise swept away, the Apostle teaches us that whatever loss they suffered, they themselves might be saved though so as by fire. I do not think the man a worse Protestant who expressed the charitable belief that many a tonsured head might now be resting in Abraham's bosom; many a body worn by fasting and disfigured by voluntary suffering, yet have been a temple of the Holy Ghost.[1]

Still after all charitable care has been taken not to exaggerate the amount of injury which some have suffered from imperfect knowledge of

[1] Maitland, *Strictures on Milner's Church History*, p. 9.

Christ's way of salvation, there remains beyond dispute a sad history of wasted lives: of "money given for that which is not bread, and labour bestowed on that which satisfieth not," which proves of how little worth religious zeal is if it be not guided by knowledge. On this principle rests the vindication of the importance of dogmatic religion. On this day[1] the Church directs our attention to mysteries of our faith, concerning which the light of nature could have told us nothing, and these, no doubt, will have furnished the subject of thousands of discourses to-day. There are many who think time wasted in such discussions, and who hold that the preacher's time could be better occupied in enforcing some practical points of duty. But the question whether a knowledge of the doctrines of our religion is important is settled if it be granted that our religion is a divine revelation. Experience has proved to us that ignorance of the laws of nature does not excuse a man from having to pay the penalty which attends the violation of them. And so, if God has revealed any truths which it concerns us to know, it cannot be harmless if we neglect to make ourselves acquainted with them, and to apprehend their meaning.

If, then, you desire to please God, you must

[1] Trinity Sunday.

begin by striving to know His will by every means by which He has revealed it: striving in a spirit of humility, not supposing your knowledge to be already perfect, or refusing to be taught on any points on which you may now be ignorant or mistaken. But you cannot expect to gain this further light unless you faithfully act on such light as God has already given you. It is by striving, however feebly and imperfectly, to fulfil the duty which He has enabled you to see that even by your errors and failures He will teach you His way more perfectly.

May He, then, from whom every good gift cometh grant you rightly to perceive and know what things you ought to do, and also give you grace and power faithfully to fulfil the same.

I do not think it necessary to add much in the way of advocacy of the institution to which you are invited to contribute to-day. If I had desired to find an illustration of the remark I already made, how God often causes good seed sown at His command to bear fruit, on which they who sow have never calculated, I could find none better than the case of the exertions that have been made for the relief of the sick poor. Those who first founded such institutions as that for which your help is asked, certainly had no other thought than by relieving the distress which they witnessed to show themselves true disciples of Him who has declared that He accepts acts of kindness shown to his brethren as if they had been done to Himself, and owns them with the acknowledgment, "*I was sick and ye visited me.*" Yet experience has now taught us that if the rich merely followed the dictates of enlightened selfishness, they could, in their own interests, have done nothing more prudent than take steps for the extirpation of disease from among the surrounding poor. For disease once generated is no respecter of boundaries, and infection passes lightly from the poor man's cottage to the rich man's mansion. But still more in another way has the rich man found the work of benevolence bring a benefit to himself. When sickness invades his own family he calls in the services of a skilled physician; but where has that physician acquired his skill? How has he obtained that intimate familiarity with various forms of disease which prevents him from being easily taken by surprise, or being often perplexed at the sight of symptoms such as he had never witnessed before? I need not tell you how it is that a student of two or three years' standing can now acquire an experience such as without the help of hospitals he could only have gained at the end of a long life of practice, and how, instead of having to buy his experience by trials and failures

H

of his own, he has been able in the very beginning of his career to witness the treatment approved by the best medical science of his day. It is notorious that a young man who had not "walked the hospitals" would be regarded as unfit to enter the medical profession; so that if you could even be insensible to human suffering we could establish the claims of these institutions as indispensable means of medical education.

And this consideration gives appropriateness to an appeal on their behalf from the University pulpit. This University is justly proud of its Medical School. Great as is the vigour with which other branches of learning are pursued in Cambridge, I do not think that any school in the University has shown more activity or made greater advances in public estimation than its Medical School, which in quite recent years has risen from a position of comparative insignificance to take rank with those foremost in reputation for scientific knowledge. But a medical school without means of efficient hospital training is maimed in a vital part.

I have not thought it necessary to make myself specially acquainted with the working of the particular institution for which I now ask your help, except that I have learned that it deserves particular praise for the excellence of its nursing arrangements.

There are many here who must possess more knowledge of it than any which I as a stranger would be likely to acquire. It is enough for me that I can take for granted that, if you own the duty which lies on those to whom God has given the means to help their poorer brethren in those times of suffering which all the resources of wealth cannot wholly deprive of their terrors, the form in which you in this place can best show your sense of that duty is that which is now presented to you.

V

PAIN AND DISEASE[1]

"For this cause many are weak and sickly among you, and many sleep."—1 CORINTHIANS xi. 30.

IF the collection to be made to-day did not suggest the topic, the subject of sickness is one which it would not have occurred to me to bring before a congregation such as the present, the majority of whom, being in healthy vigorous youth, have had little experience of illness. As a speculative question, however, the problem of disease must have presented difficulties to students of natural theology. Some of the strongest arguments for the wisdom and goodness of the Creator are drawn from the study of the anatomy of the human frame. Man's body is found to be a machine constructed with consummate art, full of what we can describe by no other word than contrivances, mechanical and chemical laws being dexterously taken advantage of, so as in every

[1] Preached on Hospital Sunday, 1886.

way to provide for the wellbeing of their subject. That any one of these arrangements could be the result of undesigning chance is intensely improbable; but to suppose that chance could account for such a combination of successful arrangements compressed into a small compass is an outrageous absurdity. Nor can we regard the modern explanation as adequate which regards existing forms as presenting an appearance of perfection only because they are the survivals of failures which have disappeared. It is indeed an interesting and valuable observation that of what may be called the chance variations that take place in species, only those which give the individual an advantage in the struggle for existence are likely to be perpetuated. We can see how in this way provision has been made for the modification of species so as better to adapt themselves to any change in their surroundings. But no predecessor of existing forms of which we have any knowledge can properly be described as a failure. Each, when regarded in connection with the circumstances in which it was destined to live, presents marks of design as apparent as in any existing forms, and might equally be used to give evidence of the wisdom and goodness of its Creator. We must likewise bear in mind the harmony and balance of the organs of existing creatures. We can conceive a chance variation causing in an individual a beneficial modification of one organ, but if we look to mere chance the chances are enormous that favourable modifications of other organs would not take place in the same individual. The individual in which the organ of sight had developed itself would not be likely to be capable of rapid motion or gifted with exceptional power to seize its prey. No hypothesis of the origin of living creatures which excludes the notion of plan and design can possibly be modified so as not to be equally at variance with all we know of the history and with antecedent probability.

But then we come face to face with the difficulty, How is it that a machine constructed with so much skill should be so liable to get out of order? The very delicacy and art of its construction multiplies the unfavourable chances to which it is exposed. How easy it would be for an arraigner of Providence to draw a picture of the sorrows and sufferings of human life; to tell of the privations endured by families whose main support has been prostrated by disease; to speak of tortures endured by the sufferer himself, which if inflicted by human hands would stamp their author as a monster of cruelty. In the book of Job, for instance, we have description of pains overtasking the sufferer's powers of endurance. "Wearisome nights are appointed to me. When I lie down, I say, When shall I arise, and the night be gone? and I am full of tossings to and fro unto the dawning of the day. . . . My soul chooseth strangling, and death rather than my life. I loathe it; I would not live alway: let me alone; for my days are vanity." And not to take extreme cases, the amount of pain and discomfort inflicted by diseases which do not threaten life and which are therefore felt to make scarcely any demand on the sympathy of others, such as toothache, dyspepsia, neuralgia, is such as to suggest many perplexing questions. All this pain and disease does not disprove the *goodness* of the Creator; for, as Paley has well remarked, pain seems never to be the object of the Creator's design. There are numberless arrangements in the human body to which I have given the name of contrivances, suggesting as they do irresistibly that they were combined with design and purpose. That purpose is always a beneficent one. Not a single one of these arrangements can be named of which it can be said that the object was to cause pain or inconvenience to the subject of them. But if the goodness of the Creator remains unimpeached, what shall we say of His power? Does it not seem as if notwithstanding all His skill His work had but an imperfect success, the materials on which He had to work being so refractory that He was unable completely to master them.

It is evident, however, that the problem of the existence of pain and disease in the world is only part of the larger question of the existence of evil in the world. The passage I have taken for my text speaks of disease as the punishment, or at least the consequence, of sin—a subject on which I shall have more to say presently. Now we can neither wonder nor complain that wherever sin is possible suffering should be possible. Our difficulty on this point is not as to the severity but as to the mercy of the Creator of the universe. We own it to be a proof of His goodness that He has constituted the world so that suffering follows sin ; if we complain, it is that He has not made it follow sin so speedily and so inevitably that no one should be tempted to commit it.

But you will easily understand that I am not now going to discuss with you the problem of the origin of evil, and that I am not so confident as to expect to dispose in half an hour of difficulties which have occupied the minds of thinking men for so many generations. The subject, indeed, is one which seems to be beyond human faculties. I daresay the solution lies in the direction indicated by Leibnitz, unmercifully ridiculed though his theory was, that ours is the best, not of all imaginable, but of all possible worlds ; and it is certainly easy to show of any suggested improvement in the existing constitution of the world that it would introduce a state of things less desirable than that which we experience. But what faculties have we to judge of the possibilities of worlds? It is likely that for want of knowledge and want of impartiality our speculations as to the uses of pain have no more value than the results arrived at by a company of young schoolboys who should debate whether or not their master ought to have the power of punishment.

It is well, however, to point out that those difficulties which we cannot solve lie altogether in the region of speculation, and do not at all affect practice. We are not practically concerned to know why the constitution of things is not other than it is ; what we are practically concerned to know is what that constitution actually is, and how we are to order ourselves in respect of it. What God is in Himself is a purely speculative question, with regard to which both reason and revelation are almost quite silent ; what we need to know are His attributes, which affect us and of which in our conduct we are bound to take account. Now I have already pointed out that the difficulties which have come before us throw no doubt on the moral attributes of God, but only raise the question whether we can say that there are limits to His omnipotence. We have no cause to doubt that we are right in ascribing to the Author of nature benevolence and moral goodness. These attributes are stamped on all the laws of nature: they are the qualities which He rewards in us, and on the measure of our possessing which our happiness depends. But we can raise the questions, Are the things that are impossible to us impossible to God? Could He make two contradictory propositions both true? Can He give creatures a power of choice and at the same time make it impossible for them to choose wrong? Can He act contrary to His own nature? Can He make vice happy? Is it that He cannot or that He will not? If He cannot, then the impossibilities in the nature of things which we allege are something antecedent to and stronger than God. Now, however, these questions are to be answered, it is plain that they lie altogether in the region of abstract metaphysics. It is practically important to us to know whether two objects of our choice are incompatible; but whence that incompatibility arises—whether from the arbitrary appointment of God, or from the inherent nature of God, or from something in the nature of things antecedent to God,—is as purely speculative a question as can be imagined.

Supposing that we are satisfied to accept as a fact the existence of those incompatibilities which our experience tells us of, it is easy to see that many of the things we complain of as evils could not be removed except on the terms of having a world so utterly different from ours that we have no power of judging whether or not it would be a better one. Pain and disease, for example, we could not wish removed except on the terms that there should be no such thing as death,—that we should have no bodies capable of dissolution. We cannot say that it would be better if death invariably took place at a fixed age, or that it occurred suddenly and without any preparation of natural decay. If our bodily frame is to be susceptible of dissolution it is well that we should have immediate notice of any derangement of its functions; and, as has been often remarked, that is one of the beneficent uses fulfilled by pain. Pain warns us at once when anything goes wrong, provides, by the immediate penalty it exacts, against imprudent use of the diseased part, and directs us where it is needful that a remedy should be applied. We are not left by slow experience to learn that it is imprudent to walk with a sprained limb or work with an inflamed eye.

The pain such conduct at once produces is the best security against our wishing to do it. Pain is constantly the physician's guide in localising the seat of a disease ; and often when the patient feels no pain the physician will try by pressure to produce it in order to assist his diagnosis. Without this wholesome warning we should in ordinary life be constantly exposed to the danger to which we are told travellers benumbed by Arctic cold are liable—of losing part of our bodies without being aware of it. As things are, the ordinary rule, subject no doubt to some exceptions, is that every derangement of an organ signals its presence by pain. And one at least of the exceptions to that rule may perhaps be taken as indicating the benevolent purpose of the ordinary law, namely, that when mortification has proceeded so far that remedy is no longer possible, pain ceases.

What I have said describes the use of pain in causing a remedy to be applied and a stop put to mischief which has already begun to work ; but there is something more important, namely, its educational use in warning him who has suffered once, or known others suffer, to avoid that which would cause like suffering again. And this brings me to the larger subject,—the educational use of pain, disease, suffering of all kinds as penalties for the breach of God's laws; serving alike to diffuse the knowledge of these laws and to deter men from violating them. If I were asked to describe the object of our being placed in this world, the chief end that our Creator appears to have had in view, I should answer, our education. The Author of nature undoubtedly shows that He desires the happiness of His creatures; but He does not make that the end to which all else is subordinate. He will not grant them happiness unconditionally, but only on the terms of obeying His laws. In the discipline of life rewards as well as punishments are freely used to train and draw forth man's powers. The race as well as the individual makes daily progress in knowledge and in ability to command the forces of nature. The knowledge of those arts of life which we now regard as indispensable to our comfort was no original possession of our race, but was gained in successive generations as enquirer after enquirer found his diligence and ingenuity rewarded by success. It certainly seems as if our Creator cared less that we should possess knowledge than that we should be induced and trained to search for it.

And man himself likes it better so. It were no happy world if what poets have fabled concerning the golden age were realised,—if the leaves dropped honey, and if you might everywhere see streams running wine, and if the earth spontaneous yielded her fruits without any demand of man. To the cares that have sharpened mortal wits we owe much of our happiness. How wretched would it be if in our childhood we were endowed with all the knowledge we were ever to gain, and thus were never permitted to know the pleasure of research and discovery! If all the physical wants of man were supplied without any effort of his, and if that "magister artis ingenique largitor" gave no lessons, the life of contented animal existence we should be apt to lead would, according to our present feelings, not be worth living. Why, at the present day those who are endowed with such riches that all their wants are supplied without any exertion of theirs, find life too monotonous unless they can find something to call forth their powers. If no more worthy pursuit presents itself, they are glad to return, at least in mimic presentation, to the time when man had to live by the produce of the chase. Nor even then can they find pleasure if their task is too easy. Who would think it sport to be invited to join in a slaughter of barn-door fowl? Uncertainty, liability to disappointment, toil, even danger; these are the things which give to sport its zest. The Alpine climber who courts the pain of fatigue and makes light of the perils of his task could not easily be persuaded of the truth of the Eastern saying, that standing is better than walking, and sitting better than standing, and lying better than sitting; at least he would feel that if this were true it were also true that sleeping is better than waking, death better than life. When we thus see that men will not only disregard pain in order to gain some worthy end, but will even find in the pleasure of an uncalled-for exercising of their powers a sufficient inducement for courting pain and danger, we cannot wonder if the Creator has shown Himself more solicitous to educate man's powers than to spare him risk of pain or disappointment.

But the drawing out of man's physical powers is a small thing compared with his moral education, and in this pain is a most potent instrument. It is not easy to see how we should be able to feel any hatred of sin or any dread of falling into it if the practice of it were perfectly consistent with happiness. Suppose that pain of all kinds were abolished, pain of body and pain of mind; if sin were followed by no bodily inconvenience, by no pain of disapprobation of others, no pain of disapprobation from our own conscience, if we could feel as completely happy after sin as before, how could we persuade ourselves that God was really displeased with our conduct? At present even a delay in retribution tends to lead men to reconcile themselves with the ways of evil; for as the wise man said of old, "Because sentence against an evil work is not executed speedily, therefore the heart of the sons of men is fully set in them to do evil." It is through the discipline of pain that our moral judgments have been built up. Just as the child learns by his own experience or by the experience of others that he must not put his finger in the candle-flame, so other less obvious laws of nature become known through the penalties incurred by breaking them. Society follows the same method. By a resolute infliction of penalties it can mould public opinion. It can, for instance, cause bribery at elections, which was once practised without scruple by men of the highest character, to be regarded as a disgraceful offence, whereas on the other hand robbery and murder will be treated as venial transgressions in a community which sees them constantly meet with impunity. Mr. Darwin has, as you know, pointed out that the processes by which man moulds species to his advantage have been anticipated in the ordinary working of nature; and so likewise it is true that the processes by which human laws and their penalties mould the moral judgments of society have been anticipated in the ordinary working of nature, which by the infliction of penalties teaches man what to avoid and what to condemn.

Among these penalties disease is one. Death is the wages of sin, and disease is part-payment of that wages. Are we to suppose that every sick man is specially a sinner? I am old enough to remember the first invasion of Asiatic cholera into these kingdoms, and I remember how many well-meaning people undertook to point out the national sins which had brought this national judgment on us. When our Lord was told of the men whose blood Pilate had mingled with their sacrifices, and when He asked, Suppose you that these men were sinners above all that dwelt in Jerusalem? He did not say that these men were not sinners, He did not say that their fate was entirely undeserved; but He stirred the consciences of His hearers to think of sins of their own just as likely to draw down judgment—"Except ye repent, ye shall all likewise perish." As the world is constituted there are some calamities which we describe as accidental; that is to say, we do not understand the laws of their occurrence, and human prudence is unable to avoid them: others which we recognise as preventible; and therefore those who suffer by them must be described as suffering the penalty of a breach of nature's laws. Human life thus becomes a game of mingled chance and skill: unskilful play may through favourable chances for a time escape its penalty; but that element in the game which is independent of chance is so powerful, and acts so perpetually, that it cannot fail to decide the ultimate result. Now if we divide diseases into those which are preventible and those which we must still describe as accidental, we find that as human knowledge increases, the list of the latter is constantly being diminished through a transference of its members to the former class. In some cases, and those more than many persons are aware of, disease is the penalty of what we must call sin,—that is to say the breach of laws which we recognise as moral, laws of temperance and chastity,—the penalty frequently not falling exclusively on the wrongdoer himself but being extended to his posterity, for we are so interlaced one with another that it is scarcely possible for one man to suffer alone, and when, for example, a profligate squanders his resources, innocent wife and children have to share his poverty. Other diseases result from a breach of laws of which it is only in modern times that we have begun to take notice,—the law of cleanliness, for example, and the law of exercise, which is necessary to the healthy condition of every organ.

But it may be asked Why inflict penalties for breaches of a law which the transgressor has not been informed of? Ought not ignorance of a law to be a sufficient excuse for having broken it? Certainly in the course of nature it is not so regarded. Our Creator, as I said before, subordinates our comfort to our education, and scruples not by the infliction of pain to stir us up to exercise our faculties. There are few ways in which the human faculties have been more nobly exercised than in the study of diseases, their causes and their remedies, or in which skilful study has obtained more splendid rewards, in the relief of pain, in the averting sorrow from households threatened with the loss of a beloved member, in the general increase of both the comfort and the duration of human life.

If we are tempted to think pain and sorrow such dreadful things that the Author of nature ought not to have used them even for our discipline, we must reflect whether we ourselves think pain or danger so very dreadful. The line that separates pain and pleasure is often very shadowy. There are some pains, such as the pain of fatigue, which, as I already said, we court in very sport merely to break the monotony of life. Still more when pain and toil have won some worthy prize, we look back on the pain with more pleasure than regret, and feel that it endears to us that which we have gained. "A woman when she is in travail hath sorrow, because her hour is come: but as soon as she is delivered of the child, she remembereth no more the anguish, for joy that a man is born into the world." But the woman's sorrows do not come to an end with the birth of the child. What weary hours she still must pass in nursing its helplessness: how many nights are robbed of sleep as she has to quiet its querulous fretfulness; every pain the infant suffers strikes a pain into the mother's breast. It would be easy to make a picture of the pains which the care of unreasoning infancy involves. But ask the mother herself Are these things pains? She will tell you they are pleasures. And here we come to a larger subject—the passing of pain into pleasure.

I know few things in modern literature more striking, and to a certain extent more true, than the image under which Mr. Huxley has represented human life. He takes as the basis of his metaphor the famous picture in which Retzsch depicted Satan as playing at chess with man for his soul. But for the mocking fiend Huxley substitutes a calm strong angel who is playing for love, as we say, and would rather lose than win. The chess-board, he says, is the world, the pieces are the phenomena of the universe, the rules of the game are what we call the laws of nature. The player on the other side is hidden from us. We know that his play is always fair, just, and patient; but also we know to our cost that he never overlooks a mistake or makes the smallest allowance for ignorance. To the man who plays well the highest stakes are paid with that sort of overflowing generosity with which the strong man shows delight in strength; and one who plays ill is checkmated without haste but without remorse.[1]

The illustration is admirable for enforcing the lesson which it was intended to teach, namely, the duty of learning the rules of the game on the correct playing of which our happiness depends. I often think of it when I see young men through want of thought or want of knowledge make wrong moves, the mischievous consequences of which will be felt through their whole subsequent life. But the illustration does not fairly represent the character of our antagonist. He is not a calm strong angel, paying his winnings or exacting his penalties with equal unconcern. He is always ready to provide consolation for the loser; and will freely grant him his revenge, not as sharpers will do, with the wish to win more from him, but with the sincere desire that the human

[1] Huxley's *Lay Sermons*, "On a Liberal Education."

player shall win far more than if he had not been worsted in the first encounter.

He who in the path of life has taken a wrong turning, and has exchanged smooth and easy walking for a rough and thorny road, need not imagine that his journey has been brought to a disastrous end. That rugged path made toilsome by his own errors will still, if he pursue it courageously, lead him to the desired goal. On that road he can still find a Father's guidance if he but seek it in faith and repentance; and struggling on in cloud and storm he may receive a blessing which he would never have known in the full sunshine of prosperity. Many can echo the Psalmist's experience, "It is good for me that I have been afflicted." Nay, I know not whether he who has never known sorrow is more than half a man. That joyous prosperous man with whom things have always gone well is apt to have the best part of his nature undeveloped, and he who has been trained in sorrow's school might wisely say that he would not change with him. What stronger proof have we that He who deals with us does not afflict willingly than when we find that His very punishments are blessings? For our transgressions a heavy burden is put on our shoulders; we shrink from it; we doubt our strength to bear it, but we are forced to submit;

and when we have gone away with our burden we find we have carried off a load of treasure.

Nothing impresses me more with a sense of the goodness of the Creator than to observe how the very pains and sorrows of life seem unable to resist the universal tendency to turn themselves into sources of happiness. What could seem more destructive of happiness than sickness? A strong man delighting in the vigorous exercise of his faculties is suddenly reduced to helplessness; he is not only rendered incapable of carrying on his ordinary work, but he becomes dependent on others for common services, and has the distress of feeling that he is not only useless but is a cause of trouble and anxiety to those about him: pain is added—it may be life imperilled, and yet any of you who have known it can tell whether that has been a time of unmixed misery. Far from it, I have no doubt you will say. The causes of pain bring into operation reacting causes of happiness, and these far more powerful. What bodily pain can be set against the happiness of loving and being loved? and seldom is that happiness felt so keenly as when on the one hand love is called on to show how it delights in sacrifice, and on the other hand that love is appreciated and returned as it never might have been but for those tender ministrations which soothe the hours of nature's weakness.

Perhaps I ought not to omit to add that but for sickness we should not know the joys of convalescence; when we learn to set a new value on the common blessings of freedom from pain, and nights of refreshing sleep. At a German watering-place may be read lines which declare that though it is commonly said that the greatest happiness on earth is the possession of health: this is not true. A greater is the recovery of health.[1] But there are English lines with which you are more likely to be familiar; so familiar indeed that some apology is needed for making so hackneyed a quotation—

> "See the wretch that long has tost
> On the thorny bed of pain,
> At length regain his vigour lost
> And breathe and walk again.
> The meanest floweret of the vale,
> The simplest note that swells the gale—
> The common sun, the air, the skies,
> To him are opening paradise."

On the whole we may pronounce those to be under a delusion who imagine that the music of life would be made richer if every discord were

---

[1] The reference is to an inscription on a pillar erected on the Promenade by the river at Ischl:—

> "Man nennt als grösstes Gluck auf Erden
> Gesund zu sein:
> Ich sage, nein!
> Ein grösseres ist, gesund zu werden."

struck out. Life is a conflict not without its dangers of wounds and defeat, but also one which elevates by its tension of our powers, and which promises a noble victory as its reward. Should we do well to exchange it for an inglorious and enervating peace? What would become of heroism and fortitude were there no ills to bear, no dangers to despise, no difficulties to overcome? Without pain this earth would be no nursery of human virtue, and something tells us that virtue is a higher thing than happiness.

Among those virtues for which pain and sickness give occasion are those which I have just glanced at—sympathy with the sorrows of others, compassion, tenderness, love.

You will perceive that I have come very near the subject of our appeal to-day. I have remarked how in family life the sufferings of one member draw out the sympathy and affectionate solicitude of others,—that love and sympathy being constantly felt to more than compensate for the sufferings which drew them forth. The inequalities of worldly condition too often tempt us to forget that our Master Christ intended that His people should form one great family, and that we should be all members one of another. Happily we are so constituted as not to be able to see with indifference the pain and suffering even of those whom we have allowed ourselves to regard as strangers. And when we come to their relief we learn to recognise our kindred, and the mutually estranged members of the family are again drawn together. In many ways the rich have benefited by these institutions primarily intended for the relief of the poor; benefited by the suppression of infectious disease and by the increase of medical knowledge, but in no way have they profited more than in their moral education. By their exertions for their brethren's sake they are roused out of that state of heartless God-forgetting material prosperity which those who would wish pain banished from the world seem to think of as the ideal perfection of human society, but which a truer view pronounces to be its lowest degradation.

It is well that this congregation, though from the circumstances of its members naturally not able to contribute so largely as others, should be allowed to join in the effort which is being made to-day. Perhaps the appeal ought to affect you more strongly than others. Those who give elsewhere do not contemplate the possibility that they should ever be inmates of these institutions themselves. But I have known more cases than one where students attacked by sickness, from which no age is exempt, have found in these institutions watchful care and nursing which they could not have had in their lonely college chambers. But I should be sorry to rest the case on any such selfish grounds. It is in another way that I believe you will do yourselves good by opening your hearts to this appeal. In your younger days you experienced all the tender kindnesses of family life. Later you will probably know family life again: happier then because giving more than receiving. But in early manhood the temptation to selfishness is strongest. Then a man stands most alone, and is apt to think it his sole duty to push himself on in the world. Thankfully then accept the opportunity of counteracting this tendency by showing sympathy with the needy and the suffering; so that however small your means of helping them may be, you may still be entitled one day to receive from our Lord the acknowledgment, " I was sick and ye visited me."

VI

HUNGER AND THIRST AFTER RIGHTEOUSNESS.

"Blessed are they which do hunger and thirst after righteousness: for they shall be filled."—MATTHEW v. 6.

WHAT is meant by hunger and thirst for food and drink? Does it mean this, that your understandings have been convinced that if you neglect to take nourishment you will lose your strength; that you will be unable to perform the duties of your daily life; and that if your neglect continue long you will die? Does it mean, in short, that you choose to take nourishment because of the good consequences that you are persuaded will follow from your doing so? or rather does it not mean that you feel a craving for the food itself without any thought of future consequences, and that it is immediate pain to you to be deprived of it?

Imagine that it were possible for you to travel to some other planet, and that you there heard a preacher delivering an eloquent sermon on the duty of taking food and drink; that he showed by solid arguments how the tissues of the body are wasted in all the processes of life, and how it is absolutely necessary that this waste should be repaired by nourishment in order that the work of life should be carried on. If you heard such an argument, the more elaborate and conclusive and thoroughly satisfying it was, the more would the conclusion force itself on you, the people for whom all this reasoning is necessary can have no idea what hunger and thirst are.

It is a striking characteristic of our Lord's teaching that He puts forward righteousness not so much as a thing, the absence of which will entail certain dangerous consequences, as rather a thing necessary to satisfy the cravings of the soul. He makes a capacity to feel such cravings the essential evidence of the soul's life and health. It is sufficient to compare the beatitudes of the Sermon on the Mount with the beatitudes of the Pentateuch. The reward promised to obedience in the Book of Deuteronomy is "Blessed shalt thou be in the city, and blessed shalt thou be in the field. Blessed shall be the fruit of thy body, and the fruit of thy ground, and the fruit of thy cattle, the increase of thy kine, and the flocks of thy sheep. Blessed shall be thy basket and thy store. Blessed shalt thou

be when thou comest in, and blessed shalt thou be when thou goest out. . . . The Lord shall command the blessing upon thee in thy store-houses, and in all that thou settest thine hand unto; and He shall bless thee in the land which the Lord thy God giveth thee." And in fuller detail are enumerated the penalties which would follow on disobedience. All through, righteousness is commended as a thing desirable, not so much for its own sake as in order to gain the external prosperity and escape the plagues which God has instituted as the sanctions for His commands. And in modern preaching this Old Testament method is very commonly adopted. It is true that under our dispensation we are not able, as Moses was, to promise that temporal prosperity and adversity shall correspond to men's deserts; but we have a clearer view than Moses of the rewards and punishments of another life. And so the Christian preacher has been able to draw more glorious pictures of the happiness that will crown obedience than that given in Deuteronomy xxvii., and more terrible pictures of the misery of God's enemies than that given in the xxviii. And consequently if one of us had to express in his own words the idea of the text in the form in which he has received it, it would be apt to run—
" Blessed are ye who hunger and thirst for salvation, for ye shall obtain it."

It is quite a different key which is struck in our Lord's beatitudes—"Blessed are they which do hunger and thirst after righteousness: for they shall be filled. Blessed are the merciful: for they shall obtain mercy. Blessed are the pure in heart: for they shall see God. Blessed are the peacemakers: for they shall be called the children of God." Thus, then, though it is perfectly true that the righteousness spoken of in the text is, according to the rule of God's government of the world, rewarded, and its absence punished, yet the prudential seeking after righteousness in order to gain these rewards or escape those punishments is no more hunger and thirst for righteousness than a sick man's taking food for which he does not care, but which is prescribed as necessary to keep him alive, can be called hunger. The blessedness spoken of in the text is that of those who feel in their souls a real craving for righteousness. The reward offered is nothing external, it is simply that that craving shall be satisfied.

The illustration I have just glanced at shows clearly enough that a capacity to feel such cravings is in itself blessedness. It occurs to us from time to time to see realised Job's description of the sick man chastened with pain upon his bed, so that his life abhorreth bread, and his soul dainty meat. In vain his attendants strive with delicacies to tempt his appetite; their well-meant efforts are loathed, and it is only as a matter of prudence and duty that he can force himself to accept what they bring. When, as the violence of the disease abates, the natural appetite returns, and he himself begins to desire the food which he had repelled, then he begins to know the blessedness of returning health.

The test suggested by the illustration that has been employed induces us readily to acknowledge the truth of the doctrine of Scripture that man's present state is not that perfect state in which he was created, but one which must be described as a state of disease. Can we say that those objects after which men's desires now ordinarily crave constitute the true food of the soul? Their own consciences bear witness to the contrary. They must own that too true an image of their conduct is presented by the prodigal who filled his belly with the husks which the swine did eat,—the food of beasts, ignoble and unworthy of man, insufficient to satisfy his real wants or give his soul the nourishment it requires. Nay, the objects of their perverted desires may be actually poisonous, destructive of the soul's true life. And when their reason has taught them their need of the righteousness which is the true food of the soul, and the danger of being without it, still this food is tasteless and insipid to them; they find they have no appetite for it; like sick persons they turn from it with disgust, or force themselves to take it without relish. This is surely very unlike the experience described by the Psalmist: " Like as the hart desireth the water brooks, so longeth my soul after Thee, O God. My soul is athirst for God, yea, even for the living God." " Thou art my God, early will I seek Thee; my soul thirsteth for Thee in a barren and dry land where no water is." " My soul breaketh out for the very fervent desire that it hath alway unto Thy judgments. Teach me, O Lord, the way of Thy statutes, and I shall keep it unto the end. O Lord what love have I unto Thy law: all the day long is my study in it. I have longed for Thy salvation, O Lord, and Thy law is my delight." And doubtless these descriptions of the Psalmist were true of him who wrote them in a far lower sense than they were of Him to whom David and the other prophets bore witness, and who could say, " My meat is to do the will of Him that sent me, and to finish His work."

Taught by His example, our Lord's disciples learned to know what righteousness was, and how much they came short of it. They learned from Him the extent of the commandment to love the Lord their God with all their heart and soul and strength, and their neighbour as themselves. He taught them how defective was that which passed for righteousness in their day; how merely external it was; how partial the fulfilment of duties on which men prided themselves. And He insisted that their righteousness must exceed the righteousness of the scribes and Pharisees—in other words, must exceed the righteousness of those who passed for the most righteous men in the nation. He taught them the worthlessness of religion itself, if it bore no fruit in the life. The Pharisees might for a show make long prayers, and their condemnation would be all the greater. Devotion to Himself He would not accept, except on the terms of obedience to His commands. "Why call ye Me, Lord, Lord, and do not the things which I say?" All hypocrisy and self-flattery He condemned; all saying and not doing; and when they had done all they could He taught them to know that they were unprofitable servants. Tried by such a standard as this, they felt how much they were below it, and having learned to love the righteousness of which they saw embodied the most perfect pattern, they longed to realise it in their own persons, and so felt the stirrings of that hunger and thirst after righteousness which are the signs of the new life that Christ gives to those that believe on Him; the signs that the old malady of their nature has begun to be overcome.

Blessed are they who feel such hunger and thirst, not only because these are the signs of health and life, but also because they have the promise that they shall be filled. In this world every desire and appetite God has implanted in His creatures corresponds with a provision He has made for satisfying it. And so it is in this case. That Holy Spirit whose office and work it is to excite the craving for spiritual food leads us to Christ in whom it can be satisfied. He is the bread of life. That our Lord should have used such words about Himself is enough to show that He claimed to be something more than a human teacher, showing by His example the blessedness of those who make it their meat and drink to do God's will. He insists on union with Himself as the means by which that heavenly hunger can be appeased. And Christ has not merely done a work for men which makes their heavenly life possible. That alone would not be enough, as it is not enough that food should be prepared if it be not received, digested, and incorporated. So Christ does not give life to our souls merely by dying for us, or by being exhibited to us in the Gospel, but as He is received by faith, so that dwelling in our hearts He becomes one with us and we with Him. Thus He is able to promise the fullest contentment for those desires which by

His Spirit He creates. "If any man thirst," He cried, "let him come to Me, and drink." "Whosoever drinketh of earthly water shall thirst again: but whosoever drinketh of the water that I shall give him shall never thirst; but the water that I shall give him shall be in him a well of water springing up into everlasting life."

You will have observed that in my exposition of the text I do not interpret the righteousness spoken of as justifying righteousness, the outward righteousness of pardon, but I treat the hunger and thirst described as the eager, earnest, inward desire for personal real goodness and holiness, the constant persevering effort to win higher and higher attainments of righteousness in Christ under the sanctifying Spirit.

It is perfectly true that Christ's righteousness is the only real and trustworthy righteousness in which the sinner can abide the severity of God's judgment, and that really to feel the need of pardon, and to long for that righteousness, is the first step towards being filled with it. Still the whole context is opposed to the deduction of this doctrine from this part of the Sermon on the Mount. Our Lord is all through engaged in showing how His disciples must by their lives adorn the Christian profession. They must be merciful, meek, pure in heart. They are to be the light of the world. They are to let their light so shine that men may see their good works and glorify their heavenly Father. Our Lord is not come to destroy the law but to fulfil. Whosoever shall break one of its least commandments and teach men so, shall be the least in the kingdom of heaven. Whosoever shall do and teach them shall be called great in the kingdom of heaven. Then He tells them that their righteousness must exceed the righteousness of the scribes and Pharisees, and goes on to show how much more searching are His precepts than theirs. The whole context then binds us to interpret the righteousness spoken of as that which was to be exhibited in the lives of those who hungered and thirsted after it.

It need not be feared that by thus interpreting we should teach men to put confidence in their works of righteousness as means of salvation, for the very notion of hunger after righteousness is opposed to the notion of confidence that we have attained righteousness. It implies a confession of want, an acknowledgment that we have it not in ourselves, and that we must look outside ourselves for the means of obtaining it. On the other hand, as I pointed out at the beginning, it puts far too low a meaning on the text to treat it as if hunger after righteousness meant no more than a desire to be saved from the wrath to come. There are many who profess to feel a longing for pardon who are merely alarmed as to possible danger in a future state, but who have no real conviction of sin, no craving after righteousness. And this is plain from the vagueness of their language. They complain of the sense of sin, and mourn that they are in the abstract miserable sinners, but their conscience tells them nothing of any particular sins, and they would be angry if some were pointed out to them which are most patent to the eyes of others. And when they believe that they have found pardon they consider that it would be an insult to the freedom of God's grace if they were thenceforward to harass their minds by anxiety about moral conduct, it being assumed that this will be sure to come right of itself in the case of those who have accepted Christ's Gospel. Such was not the method of Paul, to whose strenuous proclamation of the doctrine of justification by faith without the deeds of the law, we owe the prominence which that doctrine holds in the teaching of every reformed church. He does not content himself with using general terms about sin and righteousness, but in almost every epistle gives detailed moral precepts, and describes in language familiar to every reader of his epistles what he means by the works of the flesh and the fruits of the Spirit.

Mistakes indeed of opposite kinds have been made.

To return to the illustration which I employed in the beginning, though it is hard even by way of illustration to conceive beings incapable of feeling hunger and thirst; yet, if we can imagine such beings convinced by argument of the necessity of taking food, but without any appetite to guide them as to the quality or amount of what they were to take, it would be more likely than not that they would make mistakes, that they would spend their money for that which is not bread, and their labour for that which satisfieth not. Of such a kind are the mistakes made by men who being without any real craving for righteousness, but convinced that something of the kind is necessary for their safety, attempt to gain their salvation by works of their own devising. The history of religions true and false is a record of strange devices used by men to gain the favour of their divinities; and though foremost among these methods is the performance of supposed works of righteousness, yet the works recommended commonly have not tended to the advancement in true holiness of him who performs them. And while men were taught that things were essential which God had not required, while in following false ways of salvation His true way was neglected, the double result was produced which the prophet has described as characterising the work of the false teachers of his time. "With lies you have made the hearts of the righteous sad, whom I have not made sad, and strengthened the hands of the wicked, that he should not return from his wicked way by promising him life."

Again the craving after pardon without any craving after righteousness is as it were a desire to have life on the terms of never having need of food. This, according to any form of life within our experience, is a thing impossible; for the very essence of life, as we know it, is work, waste, and reparation. And equally impossible is it to have heavenly life without that constant feeding on Christ by faith, the effect of which is assimilation with Him. It does not appear to be the intention of our Maker to give us happiness without righteousness. In His government of the world our happiness is always subordinated to our growth in holiness. He allows us to taste the bitter fruits of misdoing, and by personal experience to learn how evil and bitter a thing it is to forsake the Lord our God. He chastens us with suffering; He ripens graces in us by the discipline of affliction. Nay, Christ's end in our redemption is stated to be our sanctification. "He gave Himself for us, that He might redeem us from all iniquity, and purify unto Himself a peculiar people, zealous of good works." Those then invert Christ's order who treat good works as a means of gaining redemption; and those mistake His plan altogether who teach that the one great thing is to accept Christ's offer of redemption, and who if they do not in so many words say that subsequent holy living is unnecessary, practically produce this impression by their complete silence on this subject. Good works, as our Article asserts, are not the means of gaining life in Christ; they are the consequences and evidences of that life. But righteousness and true holiness is the very essence of that life.

Remember, then, that working for a religious object is *not* religion : talking about religion is not religion. All the doctrines, all the facts of our religion, are means to the great end of making us such as Christ was. Let nothing else obscure in your minds the importance of the question, Are you proving the reality of your life in Him by daily growing more and more like Him in meekness, patience, self-denial, love ? For if these graces be wanting, however much a man may seem to be religious, he deceiveth his own heart, his religion is vain.

VII

THE KEYNOTE OF THE EPISTLE TO THE HEBREWS

"Take heed, brethren, lest haply there shall be in any one of you an evil heart of unbelief, in falling away from the living God: but exhort one another day by day, so long as it is called To-day; lest any one of you be hardened by the deceitfulness of sin: for we are become partakers of Christ, if we hold fast the beginning of our confidence firm unto the end."—HEBREWS iii. 12-14.

THAT Paul was the author of this Epistle to the Hebrews, was from very early times the received belief of the Eastern Church. Even scholars who had difficulties in subscribing to it unreservedly assumed its truth in their popular addresses. In the West the Pauline authorship was for a couple of centuries ignored or denied; and it was not till the beginning of the fifth century that, mainly through the influence of Jerome and Augustine, the Eastern belief established itself firmly in the West. At the Reformation, with the revival of learning there revived also the difficulties which the early critics had felt as to acknowledging Paul as the author; such as the absence of his name from any opening salutation, contrary to the practice of all his acknowledged letters, the difference in style, and still more the unlikeness of this writer's acknowledgment that he had but a secondhand knowledge of the things spoken by the Lord (" which at the first were spoken by the Lord and were confirmed unto us by them that heard him ") to Paul's claim to have himself seen our Lord, and to have derived his doctrines not from men but from the immediate instruction of his Divine Master. It was this last argument especially which weighed with Luther and Calvin, both of whom thought it likely that not Paul, but some member of his circle, such as Apollos, was the author. Since their time not only has popular opinion generally ascribed the authorship to Paul, but that opinion has had its countenance, if not its origin, in the official language of the Church. Twice in our Prayer-Book Paul is spoken of as the author of the Epistle to the Hebrews, and the title the book bears in the Authorised Version is " The Epistle of Paul the Apostle to the Hebrews." Even in the recently revised version this title is continued, the revisers explaining in their preface that they had not been expressly directed to extend their revision to the titles. It may reasonably be doubted whether this limitation of their commission would have been discovered by any one if they had thought proper to disregard it; but it is very intelligible that a Board of Revisers, including men who represented not only various schools of thought within our own Church, but even different denominations of Christians, might be able to arrive at tolerably unanimous conclusions on questions of grammar or even of textual criticism, but would find themselves embarked in long debates if called on to pronounce an authoritative judgment on the authorship of every one of the New Testament books; and therefore it may have been quite wisely that the entering on such questions was declined. Suffice it then to say that, notwithstanding that our Church appeared to have taken a side on this question, some of her most orthodox members have felt themselves free to separate the question of the authority of this Epistle from that of its authorship, and, on the latter question, to arrive at a conclusion adverse to the Pauline authorship. Such, I am inclined to believe, would have been the conclusion of a majority of the Board of Revisers if they had thought proper to pronounce on the question. At all events the question is a completely open one in our Church. For you will observe that this is not the case of a writer who assumes the name of Paul, and who must be pronounced guilty of forgery if that name does not really belong to him ; the claim of Pauline authorship is not made by the writer himself, and so it is no disparagement to him to inquire whether it has been rightly made for him by others.

It is not my intention, however, to enter into that inquiry now, further than may be necessary to bring out the full meaning of the passage I have taken for my text. No unprejudiced critic, I think, can read the Epistle without feeling that the Paulinism of its doctrine is unmistakable. The writer is either Paul himself, or else one who has sat at the feet of Paul ; who not only agrees with him in teaching those truths which every preacher of Christianity must have published, but also who has imbibed from him all that we regard as characteristic in the Pauline method of presenting Gospel truths. Nor is it only in the substance of its doctrine that this Epistle is Pauline ; the language also is so in a high degree. There are many coincidences of expression with Paul's acknowledged letters which either prove common authorship or, if they do not, at least show that the writer of the Epistle to the Hebrews was well acquainted with some of Paul's epistles, in particular that to the Romans. On the other hand, one cannot but be impressed by the fact of which Origen took notice, that the Greek of the Epistle to the Hebrews is of a rhetorical character, unlike that of Paul's writings; so that even if we believe that the Apostle commissioned the writing of the Epistle, and adopted it when written, still it would be reasonable to think that he had employed in the composition the hand of some other person.

But it seems to me that even this suggestion of the Alexandrian critics fails to take account of what I regard as indications of a date a little later than that of the circle of Pauline writings. The question of the final perseverance of the saints,—in other words, the question whether it is possible that one who is really a child of God can totally and finally fall away,—is one that has been warmly debated among Protestant theologians. Those who on this subject speak in the language of most confident assurance have always found passages in Paul's writings most apposite for quotation, such as "Being confident of this very thing that He who hath begun a good work in you will perform it until the day of Jesus Christ." But I do not know whether it has been sufficiently remarked that if one had to derive a system of doctrine from the Epistle to the Hebrews alone, controversy on the subject of which I speak could scarcely arise, for it would be determined in quite the opposite way. The danger of his disciples falling away seems to be weighing heavily on the writer's mind. He recurs to the subject again and again, multiplying his exhortations and his warnings. The Epistle opens by contrasting the former dispensations in which God spoke to the fathers by the prophets, with the new dispensation of which His Blessed Son was the Mediator; and the practical conclusion is immediately drawn that the dignity of the Messenger throws a greater responsibility on those to whom the message has been sent; makes the duty of adherence to it the greater, and the danger of falling from it the more terrible. It is with a practical, not a dogmatic, object that the superangelic character of the Son of God is insisted on in the first chapter. The conclusion is at once drawn how much more dangerous the rejection of the word spoken by the Son than of that dispensation which was given by the instrumentality of angels. "Therefore we ought to give the more earnest heed to the things which we have heard, lest at any time we should let them slip;" or, as the Revised Version has it, "lest haply we drift away from them. For if the word spoken through angels proved stedfast, and every transgression and disobedience received a just recompense of reward, how shall we escape if we neglect so great salvation?" Then the writer compares Christ with Moses, and goes on, "Moses indeed was faithful in all his house as a servant, but Christ as a son, over His house; whose house are we, if we hold fast our boldness and the glorying of our hope firm unto the end." Then he warns his disciples by the example of the Jews to whom Moses spake, and who, as we read in the 95th Psalm, provoked God to swear in His wrath that they should not enter into His rest. Then he proceeds, as you heard in the text: " Take heed, brethren, lest haply there shall be in any one of you an evil heart of unbelief, in falling away from the living God: but exhort one another day by day, so long as it is called To-day; lest any one of you be hardened by the deceitfulness of sin: for we are become partakers of Christ, if we hold fast the beginning of our confidence firm unto the end." Then, reminding them of the fate of those who were unbelieving and disobedient, and whose carcases fell in the wilderness, he exhorts again: " Let us fear therefore, lest haply, a promise being left of entering into His rest, any one of you should seem to have come short of it. For indeed we have had good tidings preached unto us, even as also they: but the word of hearing did not profit them." " Having then a great high priest, who hath passed through the heavens, Jesus the Son of God, let us hold fast our confession." And having spoken somewhat on the high priesthood

of Christ, he comes back to his warnings, in words
the sternness of which has made them hard to be
received. "As touching those who were once enlightened and tasted of the heavenly gift, and
were made partakers of the Holy Ghost, and tasted
the good word of God, and the powers of the age
to come, and then fell away, it is impossible to
renew them again unto repentance; seeing they
crucify to themselves the Son of God afresh, and
put Him to an open shame." "But, beloved, we
are persuaded better things of you, and we desire
that each one of you may show diligence unto the
fulness of hope even to the end, that ye be not
sluggish, but imitators of them who through faith
and patience inherit the promises." The writer
then sets forth at length the superiority of Christ's
atonement over the Mosaic sacrifices, and then
returns to his constant topic of exhortation: "Let
us hold fast the confession of our hope that it
waver not; for He is faithful that promised: and
let us consider one another to provoke unto love
and good works; not forsaking the assembling of
ourselves together, as the custom of some is, but
exhorting one another; and so much the more, as
ye see the day drawing nigh. For if we sin wilfully after that we have received the knowledge of
the truth, there remaineth no more a sacrifice for
sins, but a certain fearful expectation of judgment,

and a fierceness of fire which shall devour the adversaries. A man that hath set at nought Moses' law dieth without compassion on the word of two or three witnesses: of how much sorer punishment, think ye, shall he be judged worthy, who hath trodden under foot the Son of God, and hath counted the blood of the covenant wherewith he was sanctified an unholy thing, and hath done despite unto the Spirit of grace? For we know Him that said, Vengeance belongeth unto Me, I will recompense. And again, The Lord shall judge His people. It is a fearful thing to fall into the hands of the living God." The writer then reminds his disciples of the proofs of the sincerity of their faith, which they had already given, and exhorts: "Cast not away therefore your boldness, which hath great recompense of reward. For ye have need of patience, that, having done the will of God, ye may receive the promise. For yet a very little while, He that cometh shall come, and shall not tarry. But my righteous one shall live by faith, and if he shrink back my soul hath no pleasure in him. But we are not of them that shrink back unto perdition; but of them that have faith unto the saving of the soul." In the passage just cited occurs perhaps the only, or nearly the only, instance in which a charge of bias can with any appearance of justice be brought against the translators of the Authorised Version. For without any authority from the original, they interpolate the words "any man." "The just shall live by faith: but if any man draw back, My soul shall have no pleasure in him," an interpolation apparently dictated by dislike to the doctrinal inference suggested by the literal translation : "The just shall live by faith : but if he draw back, My soul shall have no pleasure in him." After this the writer, having in his noble eleventh chapter sung the praises of faith, returns to exhort his disciples to patience under the temporal sufferings they were undergoing. He reminds them of the example of Christ in enduring the contradiction of sinners, that they wax not weary, fainting in their souls. He tells them of the purposes for which their Father saw it good that they should receive chastening ; and he proceeds, " Follow after peace with all men, and the sanctification without which no man shall see the Lord : looking carefully lest there be any man that falleth short of the grace of God ;" or, as it is in the margin of the Revised Version, " that falleth back from the grace of God ;" " lest any root of bitterness springing up trouble you, and thereby the many be defiled ; lest there be any fornicator, or profane person, as Esau, who for one mess of meat sold his own birthright. For ye know that even when he afterward desired to inherit the blessing, he was rejected, for he found no place of repentance, though he sought it diligently with tears."

I have made quotations from the Epistle at great, I only hope not wearisome, length. I have felt this fulness of quotation to be necessary on account of the manner of reading the Bible which is habitual to all of us. In church or in family use we read one chapter at a time; and in this piecemeal method of study we are altogether unable to perceive the general drift of a long epistle taken as a whole. It is often even worse in our private study of Scripture. Too many then look out not a chapter, but a text, seeking to find, it may be, in some incidental words a proof by which to establish a doctrine, and scarcely troubling themselves to inquire how their interpretation fits in with what goes before and after. In the present case it would have been impossible without very full quotation to exhibit how the whole letter is pervaded by the thought that the faith of its readers was being subjected to severe trials, tempting them sorely to apostasy, that they had need of patience and endurance to hold fast the good confession they had made, and must be reminded of the rewards of perseverance, as well as admonished by Old Testament examples of the irretrievable ruin which would follow falling away.

Now I hope you will not imagine that I wish to make out that there is a difference of doctrine between the writer of the Epistle to the Hebrews and St. Paul; that I am arguing that the Epistle to the Hebrews cannot have been written by St. Paul because, to state the matter coarsely, St. Paul was a Calvinist, and the writer of that epistle an Arminian. Such an idea could only be suggested to any one by our unhistorical method of reading the New Testament, our habit of searching it only in order to find out a text which may furnish a ruling on some disputed point of modern controversy, regardless what were the circumstances of the sacred writer, what the thoughts of which his mind was full, and whether it was of that controversy it was his object to speak. I have no desire to disparage the interests of the subjects on which in modern days controversy has arisen : what are the beginnings of the spiritual life, what the signs by which it manifests itself, whether the subject of it can recognise those signs by infallible indications, and what confidence he can build on them for the future. But it may easily be that if we read with these questions in view we may fail to throw ourselves into the circumstances of the sacred writer, and to perceive what were the thoughts and feelings of which his mind was full. In the present case the writer of the Epistle to the Hebrews has not in his thoughts the case of the secret decadence of the spiritual life in the soul of one whose heart had at one time burned with zeal for the Gospel cause, but whose love had grown cold, and concerning whose restoration doubts might well be entertained. He has to deal with a patent fact: the case of a Church learning by bitter experience to know the truth of our Lord's warning that there are those in whom the word of life is sown, who, when they have heard the word, immediately receive it with gladness, and have no root in themselves, and so endure but for a time; afterward, when affliction or persecution ariseth for the Word's sake, immediately they are offended. In the Church here addressed there had been some who, under the pressure of persecution, withdrew themselves from the Christian meetings, and forsook the assembling of themselves together; nay, the apostasy had carried off some who had enjoyed the highest consideration in the Christian community, and had given the strongest evidence of their fitness to advance its interests. Men who had not only been admitted into the Church by baptism, but who had even been partakers of the supernatural gifts of the new dispensation; who had been enlightened and had tasted of the heavenly gift, and had been made partakers of the Holy Ghost, and had tasted the good word of God, and the powers of the world to come, had fallen away. What marvel when the demon of unbelief had struck his victims in such high places, if the one predominating thought of the preacher concerning the little band who still remained faithful was, Will ye also go away?

When we thus read the Epistle to the Hebrews with an eye less to its dogmatic than its historic interest, we find ourselves, I think, in a period of the Church's history a little later than that represented in Paul's Epistles. There was no time in the Church's history when some apostasies did not occur. Even in our Lord's lifetime there were those that went back and walked no more with Him. Yet this sin was not the pressing danger at the time when the Church had not yet lost her first love, and when persecution against her had not yet been organised. Even in the first days, as we know from the Acts of the Apostles, the preaching of the Gospel was a work of danger. The missionaries were liable to be set upon by tumults of mobs, or dragged before tribunals. Yet there they had a certain amount of protection, as in the case of Gallio, in the contemptuous toleration of the Roman magistrates for a silly superstition condemned by no law. Accordingly the diseases of the Church were such as beset a state of worldly prosperity, and Paul, about to visit Corinth, dreaded that God would humble him among them, and that he must be forced to bewail many who had sinned already, and had not repented of the uncleanness and lasciviousness and fornication which they had committed. It was later that persecution assumed a systematic form, and that Christianity became an unlawful profession, so that as we learn from St. Peter's Epistle, Christian became a title of accusation, and to suffer as a Christian was an intelligible phrase. The celebrated letter of Pliny shows clearly that though trials of Christians had not formed part of that magistrate's previous experience, the thing itself was no novelty. And he conceived himself to be taking a humane view when he decided that whatever the Christian profession might be, the refusal to apostatise from it was a piece of obstinacy which might properly be punished with death. In the time of the Epistle to the Hebrews, however, the rigour of persecution had not proceeded so far against the Church addressed. Imprisonment and loss of property were the extreme punishment inflicted. Of these they had had their share. They had been made a gazing stock by reproaches and afflictions. Some of their society were in bonds, towards whom the rest fraternally exhibited compassion. The spoiling of their goods was inflicted on them, and they took it joyfully. But elsewhere the malice of their enemies had gone farther, and those to whom the Epistle was addressed could not say as these others, that they had resisted unto blood striving against sin. I am disposed to conjecture that "they of Italy," from whom in the Epistle a salutation is sent, could even then tell of the Neronian persecution, which was probably a time of trial, though less severe, for Christians all over the empire. However this may be, it seems to me that this Epistle exhibits a greater strain on Christians from external persecution, greater temptation to apostasy than the Pauline Epistles, and therefore may probably be referred to a little later date.

Though I have been discussing the Epistle to the Hebrews historically rather than with a view to draw out its doctrinal teaching for our own edification, I must not conclude without saying a few words on that point of doctrine which verses such as I have chosen for my text might seem more naturally to have suggested as the subject for our discussion. And no doubt I shall seem to be uttering a paradox if I say that the doctrine of the possibility of fall from grace, even if theoretically true, is practically false. Yet there are many cases where it is practically more important to enunciate a general proposition than to attend to the exceptions and limitations which must be taken into account if we want to bring it into accordance with strict theoretical truth.

We make practical use, with great advantage, of the theorems of theoretical mechanics, though there are no mathematical lines or circles to be found in nature, no systems of forces so simple as those which our theory contemplates. Or to take an illustration which more fairly represents what I have in my mind, we are obliged for practical purposes to lean on our understanding, to adopt the conclusions which, after weighing the arguments as best we can, seem to us most reasonable. Yet it might be objected ; to rely thus on the decisions of your own intellect is to pronounce yourself infallible. Can you deny that it is possible that you are making a mistake ; that what seems to you absurd or incredible may really be true ; that what you regard as practical wisdom may be downright foolishness ? We cannot deny it. If we were to formulate into an abstract proposition any assertion of our infallibility, we should no doubt be stating a falsehood. Yet in practice we should fall into a scepticism which would paralyse all our powers of action if we allowed any theoretic conviction of our fallibility to interfere with our taking the course which, after the best prudential calculation we could make, seemed to be the best. Thus there is a sense in which it may be said that the statement that we are fallible is theoretically true and practically false. If even yet I have not made my meaning clear let me by a different illustration come a little closer to the matter in hand. Imagine that you had to preach a wedding sermon, and that some one recommended you to address the newly-married couple as follows:—" You have promised to love each other to your life's end, and you think it certain that you will do so, but in real truth you can have no certainty whatever that your feelings will not change. Many marriages have begun as fairly as yours, and love has been succeeded by indifference, nay, by dislike and unfaithfulness." Could you reject the suggested topics solely on the ground that they stated what was not true? Could you deny that such changes of feeling as have been described do from time to time occur? Could you even venture to say that if such a change occurred it proved that the original love professed had not been sincere; and therefore that, conversely, one who was assured of his own sincerity might also be assured against the possibility of change in the future? I don't know that this can be said either; but it is certain that even if there were theoretical truth in such an address it would be practically false, and that it would be mischievous if one was cruel enough to deliver it, and the parties foolish enough to give heed to it. For why is it that true affection resents as an insult the suggestion of the possibility of its discontinuance? Is it not because there cannot be love without trust ; and trust is incompatible with doubt, the entertainment of which would very speedily bring its own justification and fulfil its own prophecies by undermining the affection it assailed. Well, whatever reason we have for trusting in the affection of a fellow-creature, we have infinitely more for trusting in the love of Christ. We may discover that we have been mistaken in our opinion of a fellow-creature, and that one on whom we had bestowed our affection was really unworthy of it. It can never happen to us to find that we have thought too highly of Him. It may happen that one on whom we had bestowed our love withdraws affection from us, and that we find it hard to go on loving without return. That disappointment can never befall our love to Christ. Men may prove inconstant, but He abideth faithful : He cannot deny Himself. What remains, then, to doubt but the frailty of our own hearts? Well, if experience of human inconstancy does not deter two human beings from exchanging pledges of lifelong affection with each other, and if we find by a better experience that their vows, made in God's sight and blessed by His Church, do receive in answer to faithful prayer, grace and strength which exalts human affection into sacred duty, which preserves it unshaken through the trials and changes of life, so that sorrow or adversity borne together only draws it closer, labour endured for the other is no toil, unkindness, even injuries received from the other find ready indulgence and forgiveness; still more may we be sure that faithful prayer will bring grace and strength to preserve unshaken our union with Christ, on which our spiritual life depends.

I do not know how to assert final perseverance as a theory. I can say nothing to encourage a backslider to trust in the memory of a dead past, and rely that his recollections of the love of former days in themselves contain a pledge of future restoration. But to those who hold fast by a present faith in the Son of God, I can confidently say, Doubt not, but earnestly believe in the faithfulness of Him in whom you trust. He will perfect that which concerneth you. He will not forsake the work of His own hands.

VIII

BOWING IN THE HOUSE OF RIMMON

"And Naaman said, Shall there not then, I pray thee, be given to thy servant two mules' burden of earth? for thy servant will henceforth offer neither burnt offering nor sacrifice unto other gods, but unto the Lord. In this thing the Lord pardon thy servant, that when my master goeth into the house of Rimmon to worship there, and he leaneth on my hand, and I bow myself in the house of Rimmon: when I bow down myself in the house of Rimmon, the Lord pardon thy servant in this thing. And he said unto him, Go in peace."—2 KINGS v. 17-19.

OF all Old Testament histories there is none with which people are generally more familiar than that of Naaman the Syrian. It is told in a chapter which has always been appointed as one of our Sunday lessons, and which as a mere story arrests attention by its graphic and lively painting of contrasted characters; while the moral and spiritual lessons which it suggests are so numerous and so obvious that perhaps no chapter in the Bible has afforded texts for more sermons, and so the details of the story are frequently dwelt on and imprinted on our memory. We have first the picture of the Syrian general, distinguished for valour, fortunate in war, high in his master's favour, honoured by his countrymen; *but* a leper. We are reminded how often the tale of human prosperity is obliged to be finished with a "but"; how the life to outward appearance the most happy has its secret sorrows, and how often from the midst of the spring of pleasures that something bitter rises which poisons their enjoyment. Then the name "leprosy" suggests a deeper meaning, as typifying that plague of sin which infects the highest as well as the lowest worldly condition; so that a man may be among his fellow men highly placed, respected, honoured, yet in God's sight a leper. The story goes on to illustrate the converse lesson, how that which is despised among men may be in God's sight of great price, by showing how the greatest benefits temporal and spiritual were brought to this Syrian household by its most insignificant member, the little slave-girl captive from the land of Israel. Here again a number of reflections suggest themselves on the importance of early education,—on the unexpected fruits that may spring up from lessons well implanted in the mind of a child; on the truth of the wise man's saying, "A word spoken in season, how good is it!" on the opportunities of usefulness which are open even to those whose worldly estate is but lowly; on the return which a single talent may make when he to whom it has been trusted uses it faithfully. Then again we have a contrast between the consternation into which the King of Israel is thrown by the seemingly unreasonable demand of his powerful neighbour that he should recover a man of his leprosy, and the calm assurance of the prophet that what was asked was no more than his God can enable him to accomplish. We have a further contrast between the programme which Naaman in his mind has sketched out of the prophet's manner of dealing with him, effecting his cure with all pomp and solemnity and due regard to the dignity of the sufferer, and what he accounts the contemptuous treatment he actually receives—the prophet not even deigning to see him, but sending him by a messenger directions to follow a mode of treatment which he pronounces quite inadequate to effect a cure. It is impossible for any illustration to set in a clearer light how foolish is the pride of rejecting a divine remedy because it seems to us too simple; and so this story has been used times without number to contrast with the simplicity of the Gospel plan the laborious schemes for their own salvation which men have devised, and to show the folly of rejecting God's ordinances because we do not see what natural efficacy they can have to produce spiritual benefit. I need not pursue the history. You will all remember how the Syrian general yields to the persuasions of his servants (whose affectionate relations with him speak well for the kindliness of his character): you will remember his gratitude when he obtains his healing, the disinterestedness of the prophet who will accept no present from him: frustrated as far as the effects on the stranger's mind are concerned by the covetousness of the prophet's servant, who cannot bear to see so fine an opportunity of gaining riches thrown away: and you will remember how vainly Gehazi tries to hide his crooked practices, and what an appropriate punishment he meets with. Great part of the charm of the story (considered merely as a story) results from the consistency with which the characters are kept up, and from the worthy way in which Elisha maintains the character of God's prophet: despising the things of earth; neither grasping its riches for himself, nor bestowing undue veneration on earthly honours. But (for in this case too there is a "but") the verses I have read as the text form an exception; and I suppose there are few who hear the chapter read without feeling here some little jar, the prophet's answer to Naaman not being such as, if we were writing the story, we should have put into his mouth.

First we have what we might call a superstitious request from Naaman to be allowed to carry home two mules' burden of Israelitish earth to build an altar to the God of Israel in his own land. We might, however, not be greatly startled at Elisha's acquiescing in this without remark, but Naaman's next request puts a greater strain on our sense of fitness. He declares his conviction that Jehovah is the only God, and his resolution thenceforward to offer sacrifice or burnt offering to Him only. But his public duty will require him when attending on his master to present himself in the house of Rimmon the Syrian divinity; and there he cannot without indecency refuse to join in the outward homage which all present offer to Rimmon. So he asks leave to be, while in his heart a believer in Jehovah, in outward appearance a worshipper of Rimmon, and while paying to Rimmon his homage in public, to atone for it at home by his private sacrifice to the God of Israel. We are inclined to smile at the simplicity of the request. Will Jehovah accept a divided allegiance? Will his prophet sanction this plan for making the best of both worlds, and declare it possible to serve both God and Rimmon? Will he not rather give directions to Naaman to act as Daniel afterwards acted, who, when living in a strange land where the worship of Jehovah was forbidden on pain of a terrible death, set his windows open towards Jerusalem and kneeled and prayed, and gave thanks before his God three times a day? Not a word of this do we hear from Elisha. Naaman's profession of belief and his reservation of promised allegiance are alike received without comment, and he is quietly dismissed with the words, "Go in peace."

The first point is one that need not delay us long. Earthen altars appear to have been a specialty of Jewish worship. At the end of the twentieth chapter of Exodus immediately following the account of the giving of the ten commandments you will find directions given to Moses that only earthen altars should be used for the worship of Jehovah; or at least that if stone altars were used they should be of rough stone, not hewn stone. Naaman would probably during his visit to the land of Israel have remarked the earthen altars, and it is not strange if in his conviction that the God of Israel was the only God, he resolved on worshipping Him exactly as he had seen His own people worship Him; and not only with an altar of earth, but of Israelitish earth.

This does not seem a very important point; but the difficulty as to the silent acquiescence in his dissembling of his faith requires more thought.

And first,—for even when we cannot solve difficulties, it is something done if we can reduce one to another, and see that two apparently different difficulties are the same,—one thing to be said about the present difficulty is that it is really one form of the great difficulty, Why did God for so many generations choose one family for His own, and leaving the heathen world in darkness confine all revelation of the higher truths respecting His purposes to the favoured seed of Abraham? So the Gentile world looked on Jehovah but as the God of the Jews in the same way that Chemosh was the God of Moab, and Rimmon the God of Syria. Even among the Jews themselves there were some who would seem to have no higher view. And such would seem to be the view expressed by Jephtha in his address to the Ammonites (Judges xi. 24): "Wilt not thou possess that which Chemosh thy God giveth thee to possess? So whomsoever Jehovah our God shall drive out from before us, them will we possess." Afterwards when it became clear to the minds of all religious and thoughtful Jews that the truth was, not that their God was greater and stronger than the gods of surrounding nations, but that theirs was the only God, and that the gods of the heathen were no gods, even then we read of no missionary efforts made by Jews to convert surrounding nations to their faith. Individual proselytes were not rejected ; but there were no systematic efforts, scarcely any symptom of a desire, to bring in foreign nations to worship by their side ; or any indication of a feeling that it was the duty of a foreigner to worship the God of Israel. So we can understand that a Jew would feel that the duty of confessing his God was to be measured by a different standard in the case of a foreigner and of one of his own nation. Daniel when in a strange land was bound to worship his people's God, and to make no secret that he did so, but how could a like duty of public confession be urged upon Naaman when the Jews had never taken any steps to teach him that it was his duty to worship Jehovah at all?

We may thus, as I have said, reduce the difficulty in the text to another larger one. But what about that? Why was the enlightenment of the world so slow? Why so gradual, and at first so partial? What need of so elaborate a scheme for the education of that people who were afterwards to be the teachers of the world? And to this we can only answer that even though we cannot explain the "why," there can be no doubt about the fact that if the God of the Bible and the God of Nature be the same we need not be surprised to find that the processes by which He works His ends are slow and gradual. Nothing in Nature is hurried. Development, evolution, have become the watchwords of modern science ; the difficulty that thinkers of the present day declare that they experience is in conceiving any kind of instantaneous creation. If the current scientific belief be well founded that this world took millions of years of preparation before it could be fitted to be the abode of living creatures, we need not be startled to hear that thousands of years were spent in the education of the human race ; that their religious knowledge was reached by no sudden spring, but followed the same laws of development, evolution, slow gradual growth, which we find to prevail in all the works of Nature. Nor is it strange that the seeds of religious truth grew up in one favoured spot, where they were guarded from injury, fenced round by that barrier of exclusiveness which prevented the nation which had been entrusted with them from adulterating them with the customs of foreign peoples, until, in the fulness of time, when their maturity had been obtained, the treasure of one people was made the property of the whole world. It is of a piece with this law of evolution that we find that favoured people itself slowly advancing from feebler to fuller light, and so we need have no hesitation in acknowledging the moral standard of an earlier age to be below that of a later one. Our Lord in His precepts refused to tolerate what Moses, on account of the hardness of the people's heart, had been content to admit; and frequently, in the Sermon on the Mount, "It hath been said by them of old time," is contrasted with, "But I say unto you." Even in the Christian dispensation we can see that its demands were not made all at once, but by degrees as they were able to bear them. I will not stop to speak of the gradual process by which the exclusive privileges of Jews were done away; but I cannot take a better illustration than the institution of slavery. It was found existing when the Gospel was first preached, and any attempt to overturn it would have revolutionised society. So no doctrine of the unlawfulness of slavery was taught. The slaves were not told that their masters had no right to their services. A runaway slave was sent back to his master. The slaves were commanded to do good service, as good when their earthly master's eye was off them as when it was on; for they were to consider their service as rendered not to their master on earth but to one in heaven. So for hundreds of years the institution lasted. Even the Church had its slaves; for when rich men bestowed their possessions on it, the Church accepted without scruple gifts of persons as well as of things. But I need not go back into the history of early times, seeing that it is comparatively lately that the doctrine of the unlawfulness of slavery has been taught among ourselves. Somewhere about a hundred years ago the well-known John Newton continued for some time after his conversion his employment as supercargo of a slave ship, and though he felt acutely the degradation of his position, counting that the trade of a jailor was not a gentlemanly one, it does not appear to have ever occurred to him that it was an unchristian one.

And yet there can be no doubt that the feeling which prevails among ourselves that it is not right to hold our brethren in bondage is the direct offspring of Christianity. The Gospel brought master and slave to partake side by side of the same love feast; nay, the Church in the very earliest times admitted slaves to the order of the priesthood, so that the master might be forced in the Church assemblies to take a lower place than that assigned to his former slave, and to partake of sacred gifts consecrated by his hands. It united master and slave as brothers with common interests persecuted by common enemies. One of the earliest authentic histories of a Christian martyrdom tells of the heroism of a female slave, suffering with her earthly masters, only subjected to more cruel tortures than they, because the law then allowed torture to be used in the examination of slaves which it was not permitted to use in the case of free persons; and it was hoped, but vainly hoped, that they could wring from her lips some testimony to the impious and immoral practices which it was currently believed the Christians in their secret meetings were guilty of. The binding master and slave together in such ties as I have described afforded the best security against the harshness and oppression which so often spring out of that relation, and implanted the seeds of a feeling which only required to be developed in order to bring about the total abolition of slavery. Such an instance as this may teach us that in judging of the conduct of men of former days we must not apply the rules and measures which it might be reasonable to employ in our own case. Christ has said to us, " He that confesseth Me before men, him will I also confess before My Father which is in heaven. Whosoever denieth Me before men, him will I also deny before My Father which is in heaven, and before the holy angels." Nothing like that was said to Naaman, and this need not perplex us even if we could say nothing more in explanation than that this is one of a number of instances in which the requirements of Christ's kingdom are more strict than the demands made in former times from others to whom less light was given.

Yet we can very well believe it to be possible that as time went on Naaman might have found strength for a confession of which at first he might not think himself capable. Perhaps every one entering on a new sphere of life, or taking up a new position, might draw back in despair if, at the outset, a detailed list were given him of all that afterwards he might find it his duty to undertake. If present duty is clear it is generally not well to try to look too far forward and speculate whether obedience to that call may not lead to further demands afterwards, no strength to comply with which is felt. If it be so that obedience to one call of duty opens the eyes to further duties, He who gives that insight will also give grace and strength to follow along the path by which He leads. And so it may very well have been that as Naaman acted on his conviction that Jehovah was the only God, and that to Him alone worship ought to be rendered, the further duty of making that conviction known to others, which, when the idea first presented itself to him, seemed beyond his strength, may have grown on him into an imperative necessity. Our merciful Lord, who will not bruise the broken reed nor quench the smoking flax, refused to put on His disciples while young in the faith burdens which the Pharisees and which John imposed on their disciples. And it is in the same spirit that the prophet sends Naaman away with his case of conscience unsolved, dismissing him without either formally giving him the permission he asks for, or formally condemning his proposed line of conduct. His faith must grow, and his duty will afterwards become clear.

I do not apprehend that any of you is likely to be persuaded by our study of the history which has been under our consideration into a belief of the lawfulness of a cowardly concealment of our convictions, or of a refusal publicly to act on .them. That, after all, is not the fault to which at the present day there is the strongest temptation. I suppose there never was a time at which there was more freedom of speech in both directions. On the one hand, the man who disbelieves not only in Christianity, but even in Theism, can publicly profess his unbelief, and try to make converts to it, not only without fear from the law of the land, but even without fear that he will not be able to retain a high degree of social consideration ; and on the other hand, the sincerest of Christians who takes the strictest view of his duties, if he boldly proclaims and honestly acts on his convictions, will only command the higher respect of those who do not share his faith. In commenting on our story, therefore, I have felt all along that I need give myself little trouble to prove that bowing in the house of Rimmon is not lawful to you; my only difficulty was to make it conceivable how it could ever seem to have been tolerated in Naaman.

One lesson we are safe in drawing from it, that of tolerance and charity in our judgment of others. We cannot do wrong in placing our own standard of duty high, but we may easily be rash in judging severely of those who permit themselves what we condemn. The error is one to which our temptation is the greater the less our experience of life. There are no so severe judges as the young. When they have fixed in their minds their code of duty, they are stern in exacting conformity with it, slow in accepting any excuse for deviating from it. And so also with the uneducated. When they are strict in their acknowledgment of duty and their obedience to it, it is usually to some conventional code they give their allegiance, and those who follow a different rule are unsparingly condemned. I should be sorry to speak in such a way as to lead you to think that the boundaries between virtue and vice were so uncertain that you could not venture to condemn wrongdoing lest haply the error might really be in your own standard of judgment. Yet instances, when a wider experience has convinced us of reasons for modifying our first rigour, are numerous enough to make us cautious to let a sense of our own fallibility temper our severity. In particular this may be said, and it has to be borne in mind, that two persons at the same point may be judged very differently according to the direction in which their face is set. One may have reached it in the progress of struggling upwards for more light; the other fallen to it from shutting his eyes to the light before him. Naaman's bow in the house of Rimmon may be but the last remaining relic of an idolatry which he is in the process of forsaking altogether; in the case of an Israelitish visitor to Syria it might be the first sinful compliance in the catalogue of those by which his allegiance to his father's God was given up. And this consideration may guard our charity in judging of others from depressing our own moral standard. It is possible that we could come to be where they are only by turning our back on the light to which they, in their way, are striving. Let us ever be careful, while we endeavour that our conscience shall be as rightly informed as we can, that our conduct do not fall below the standard of our conscience. May God's Holy Spirit so guide and rule our hearts that we may know what things we ought to do, and also may have grace and power faithfully to fulfil the same.

IX

SHAME

"Let us run with patience the race that is set before us, looking unto Jesus, the author and finisher of our faith; who, for the joy that was set before Him, endured the cross, despising the shame, and is set down at the right hand of the throne of God."—HEBREWS xii. 2.

"DESPISING the shame." These are the words to which I more particularly invite your attention. That part of our blessed Lord's trial which consisted in the shame to which He was put, must have affected Christians more forcibly in the first ages of our religion than it does in ours. For the first sufferers for Christ had to brave a trial which was not endured by the stoutest of their successors,—from the shame of the confession. In the next age, when the Christian society had been fully formed, the confessors were supported by the public opinion of their own community. They might be brought before the tribunal or cast into prison or threatened with tortures or death; but the thought most likely to occur to any of them was not, how shameful is my position, but how glorious. I suppose if we asked ourselves what kind of death is the most honourable and glorious we could not make a better answer than the death of a martyr. We honour the brave soldier who dies on the field of battle fighting for his country : yet he has done no more than risk his life, and he might reasonably have hoped to escape ; but the martyr who, with full knowledge that persistence in his confession means inevitable death, abides to the end, enduring all that his persecutors can inflict on him,—and that not in the hurry and excitement of a battlefield, but in cold deliberate choice, often made when the bodily frame has been depressed by imprisonment and other suffering,—surely performs a more difficult and therefore more honourable achievement. Accordingly the Christian martyrs were cheered by the almost worshipping admiration of their brethren at the time, and their names have held the most glorious place in the annals of the Church ever since. There was more shame then in drawing back from the confession of Christ than in remaining steadfast. Accordingly we read in one of the earliest authentic records of Christian martyrdoms that it was possible, by the aspects of the prisoners as they passed along, to discern the difference of their confessions. Those who had bravely witnessed to the truth walked joyous and radiant, so festive in their guise that some of the bystanders could hardly persuade themselves that they had not been actually anointed with perfumes; but those who had denied the faith, squalid and downcast, while the very heathen jeered at them for their cowardice.

In the New Testament, on the contrary, as is natural in the writings of men who as not having been born in the Christian Church were able to enter into the feelings of those outside that body, the disgrace of their sufferings comes out very distinctly as part of the trial which the confessors must brace their minds to endure. I take for example St. Paul's second Epistle to Timothy, and you will find that the thought is constantly recurring to him of the shame he is suffering for Christ's name, and which he has forced himself, though evidently not without some struggle, to disregard. "I suffer these things," he says (i. 12), "nevertheless I am not ashamed." He remembers gratefully of Onesiphorus that, so far from being ashamed of his chain, he had on his arrival at Rome sought him out the more diligently. He exhorts Timothy not to be ashamed of the testimony of our Lord nor of Paul himself his prisoner. And the reason of the shame is very plainly indicated in another incidental expression,

"I am suffering like a malefactor even unto bonds"; that is to say, the punishment he was bearing was that usually inflicted on criminals, and therefore suggested to all who knew of it that he too must have deserved it for his crimes. It is a very strong proof that we have in this Epistle the words of Paul himself that he shows himself so sensitive to the disgrace of his position, for in the next generation persecution for Christ's sake had become common, and the sufferers were in no danger of being confounded with ordinary criminals.

No thought could inspire more steadfastness in those called on to face this disgrace than the reflection suggested in the text that their Master had despised worse shame for their sake. No punishment inflicted on our worst criminals sounds in our ears so degrading as the punishment of the cross did in the ears of men of those days. It was the death inflicted on slaves, a class whom the freeborn scarcely regarded as their fellow-creatures. The humanity of the present day is far more revolted by unnecessary suffering inflicted on one of the brute creation than the feelings of the men who then counted for most humane would be by any tortures inflicted on a slave. If others besides slaves were subjected to the punishment of crucifixion, it was because their crimes were thought to be so bad or their condition so low that no compunction need be felt at inflicting on them the death of a slave.

In enduring the cross, then, our blessed Lord submitted to the lowest depth of earthly degradation. And He had to drain the dregs of the cup of shame deeper than any of His followers ever since has done. To scarce any of them has it happened that the trial has been all shame. If a mob cried out against them as evil-doers who deserved their fate, they still might commonly notice some present in the throng who honoured their constancy, and whose sympathy and good opinion helped them to despise the blindness of those who in their ignorance scorned and reviled them. All the early Christian martyrs that we read of could catch sight of sympathising spectators standing round the judgment seat. When Polycarp came before the tribunal he might hear the cry, " Play the man, Polycarp," ring out among the clamours of the heathen. But who was there among the crowd that stood round our Lord's cross who knew of the glorious work which His death was accomplishing? who that read the title over His head, The King of the Jews, could feel assurance to confront those who regarded it as the exposure to just derision of a vain and empty boast, and to dare to assert it as the sufferer's rightful description? He looked for some to have pity on Him; but there was no man, neither found He any to comfort Him. The shame of the cross remained for some time the stumbling-block, as the Apostle called it, in the way of those who were called to make profession of faith in the Messiahship of Jesus. How were they to own as their Saviour and deliverer him who had not been able to save himself? How proclaim him as king who had been put to open disgrace by the leading men of the nation whom he had claimed to rule?

But it might seem as if now the shame had quite passed away. It took less than 300 years from the time that the cross expressed the lowest ignominy the subjects of the Roman Emperor knew, until the Roman Emperor placed it in the standards of his army and hailed it as the sign of victory. We are under no temptation to be ashamed of the cross. We put that sign everywhere in the place of honour, and naturally, since it is the emblem of the religion professed by the most civilised and most progressive peoples of the world. And yet is shame never the terror which keeps us from owning and acting on known obligations? In the *Pilgrim's Progress* John Bunyan describes the experience of the Christian pilgrim to have been, that of all the enemies which had beset him the most shameless was Shame. No other had been so pertinacious in his assaults, so hard to baffle, so unwilling to submit to a repulse. Repeatedly has the right course been recognised, and shame has whispered of the ridicule, the censure, the disgrace that following it would entail, and the timid pilgrim has shrunk from acting on his convictions.

This allegory needs some correction which places wholly in the ranks of the Christian's adversaries that which is so often his help and supporter. If we are sometimes ashamed to do what we know to be right, still more often does the shame we shall incur scare us from turning into paths of sin from which conscience alone would have been too weak to deter us. When we meet with examples of very gross vice, it is generally when the restraints of public opinion have been weakened or removed: as men have been too high or too low or too remote to be affected by it. And there is good reason for ordinarily acting on generally accepted rules of conduct. Living as we do in a Christian country it would be a national disgrace if it were not good as a general rule to avoid everything that public opinion condemns as shameful. But yet there is no authority higher than that of our own conscience. We are cowards if any fear of disgrace from refusing tempts us to do that which our conscience condemns. If in many things the tone of public morality is higher now than it was when the Gospel was first preached, higher even than among many of those who then accepted the Gospel, it is because there have been some who have ventured to question the results which other men have received as authoritative.

Whether men own Jesus of Nazareth to be God or not, they cannot deny the greatness of His work as a moral reformer. The very form of His teaching implied a criticism of the traditional rules then accepted as authoritative : " It hath been said by them of old time . . . but I say unto you." He made a discriminating survey of the things which in His time were accounted as righteousness, and ranged them in their true proportions. Those who had been tithing mint, anise, and cummin, setting trivial and ceremonial obligations on a level with the weightier matters of the law, learned from Him the transcendent importance of those things which concerned judgment, justice, and the love of God. The secret of pleasing God was for them no longer a technical mystery dependent on arbitrary rules, but a science resting on intelligible great principles, and they were made to know that if they followed them out, they would find a sufficient reward in the praise of their Father who seeth in secret, though their good deeds might be unknown to men, or though their good might be evil spoken of.

Christians and unbelievers alike recognise that our Lord's hearers were right in revising under His direction their traditional code of morals, and though in forsaking it they lost the praise of men, contenting themselves with the approbation of God. We cannot make a higher rule of life than that which He has set us, yet it has often happened that in the practice of His disciples a lower standard than His has become so ordinary that those who have tried to raise it have incurred reproach as over-righteous, as needlessly strict, as ostentatiously setting up to be better than their neighbours.

I suppose the consciences of most of us will tell us of times when, though we felt no doubt as to our duty, we shrank from acting on our belief, because we thought we should put ourselves out of sympathy with those about us, and either expose ourselves to their ridicule or lose their good opinion or their liking. And yet we live in the society of those who are all professed disciples of the same blessed Master; whose praise, therefore, ought to follow the same rules as His, whose good opinion ought to be best earned by faithfully doing His will. And if we were really all Christians not only in name but in reality, the fear of shame which, as things are, does prevent us from doing many wrong things, or even thinking such conduct possible for us, would never be a temptation to sin, but always a motive on the side of right. I think you hardly know how much good each of you in his small way can do if he strives never to be ashamed of the right course, and always to be ashamed of the wrong one. For you are thus building up that force of opinion which is one of the most powerful rulers of life.

I recollect very well that in my young days, when duelling was common, many a man accepted a challenge, believing that in so doing he was committing a sin, and a sin in the very act of which he might be hurried into the presence of his Judge; and yet he preferred to risk his life, and, as he believed, endanger his hopes of eternal salvation, rather than be branded among his associates as a coward.

I could hardly give a more forcible example how strong is the power of public opinion; and yet I might, without paradox, complain how weak it is. For public opinion is but a bully; a tyrant to those who submit to it, a coward to those who defy it. It has terrors for the half-hearted offenders who quake under its rod, but let a man have courage to repudiate his obligations, instead of simply failing to discharge them, then if he find others to join him they are able by their countenance practically to repeal the law which had held them in bondage. If a man fails to observe the law of Christ, the mischief is seldom limited to the single act; by his example he tempts others to do the like; then with the relaxation of practical morality follows a corresponding degradation of public opinion. Men will not strongly condemn what they see habitually practised; and at length there is a risk of falling into that lowest depth of corruption, when men not only do things which the law of God condemns, but avow that they do them and take pleasure in them that do them.

On the other hand a knowledge of this weakness of public opinion may well give courage to a man tempted to be ashamed of doing what he knows to be right, or of doing what he has no cause to be ashamed of. What happened in Paul's case has often happened since. Paul had courage to say, I am not ashamed of the Gospel of Christ; I suffer as a malefactor, but I am not ashamed. And soon he found an ever-increasing number to acknowledge that he had no need to be ashamed. Nay, what was a paradox in Paul's mouth has become a truism in ours when we echo his words and say that we glory in the cross of Christ. Often does it happen that there is a widespread secret distrust of the soundness of certain popular judgments, distrust which for a time no one ventures to express, through fear of standing alone in his opinions, but which when once it finds public utterance rapidly becomes the avowed faith of multitudes. An idol is worshipped, to profane which it is believed will entail fearful penalties. Doubts of its divinity come to be entertained, yet when the first bold man ventures to smite the head of the monster with his axe, the trembling crowd expect to see him fall dead suddenly, or that other vengeance will overtake him. But when they see no harm happen him, the meanest will trample on or burn what he had once adored. Thus it happens that they who have ventured to brave ridicule or censure in the cause of Christ, constantly find that penalties most terrible in anticipation turn out little formidable in reality. And if he who has courage to confess his master before men, himself refuse to be ashamed of what he has done, the wonder or ridicule with which his conduct is first greeted rapidly pass into respect.

I feel almost ashamed to remind you of the considerations brought before us in the text; they seem to offer motives so much stronger than the necessities of our case can require. "Consider," says the Apostle in the words that follow the text, "consider Him that endured such contradiction of sinners against Himself, lest ye be wearied and faint in your minds." When we reflect what was the shame which He despised, what were the sufferings He was content to endure, it seems absurd to mention, as bearing any remote comparison, any contradiction to which we can be exposed. The words of the text were written in a time of severe persecution, under which many had denied the faith. Yet the Apostle seems to think any persecution short of the infliction of martyrdom as scarcely deserving of compassion. "For," he adds, "ye have not yet resisted unto blood, striving against sin." Yet for us no less than for them that sacrifice was offered. For us Christ bore the bitter pangs, and hid not His face from shame and spitting. "He was wounded for our transgressions, He was bruised for our iniquities." And what do we for Him? How little a thing turns us aside from following Him. Not the threat of imprisonment or tortures or death, but the fear of a jest, a contemptuous look, a silent expression of disapproval.

I have said enough as to the duty of not being afraid of undeserved shame for doing what you know to be right; but I must say a word in conclusion as to the duty of bearing deserved shame. For often does the fear of deserved shame keep those who have gone wrong from retracing their steps. Either they persevere in their course, and in spite of their conscience strive to justify it, or in the attempt to hide their misconduct they add to their sin. And yet if they would but believe it, how easy is the way by confession to forgiveness. God's forgiveness they need not doubt of obtaining, since He is ever ready to receive back repentant wanderers from His fold. And men's forgiveness is also not difficult to get when penitence is real. It is hard even for an offended person to keep resentment against one who owns that he has been in the wrong and strives to atone for his offence: so that by manly confession and willingness to accept the shame which is the deserved penalty of wrong-doing, the shame is quickly made to pass into honour. Take care then lest what keeps you back from confession may not be despair of finding love and forgiveness after confession, but the knowledge that confessing your sin without forsaking it would be a mockery, and that you cannot yet resolve to abandon it. If so, beware lest in shrinking from shame you fall into deeper shame. Does to lose the praise of men seem terrible to you? What is it to lose the praise of Him whose praise only is worth having? What will it be when those who sleep in the dust of the earth shall arise, to wake to shame and everlasting contempt? What will it be, if in the day when the secrets of all hearts shall be made manifest, He whose name you have been ashamed to confess before men, and whose will you have despised and refused to obey, is ashamed of you?

X

THE DENIAL OF PETER

"When Jesus beheld him, He said, Thou art Simon the son of Jona: thou shalt be called Cephas, which is, by interpretation, a stone."—JOHN i. 42.

THE text relates at full length what St. Mark and St. Luke had briefly indicated in the words "Simon He surnamed Peter," "Simon, whom He also named Peter." We learn thus that the name Peter, by which we habitually know the Apostle, was not his original name, but a title given him by his Master. And we learn further, that this title was not (as a reader of St. Matthew's Gospel might possibly imagine) given at a late period when the ardent disciple, outrunning the rest in his discernment of his Master's true character, had done something to merit a title of honour. We are told that it was conferred on his very first enrolment as a disciple. It expressed then the view of his character taken by Him who could discern the hearts, who knew what was in man. This disciple was a Rock-man.

What should we expect from such a title? Firmness, steadiness, stability. We should expect to hear of a calm resolute man on whom implicit reliance might be placed, who would be sure to stand unshaken, however others wavered. But I suppose this would be the last epithet that a student of the life of Peter would apply to him. We find him ardent, eager, impulsive, but easily discouraged. The relation which St. Matthew gives of Peter's walking on the sea affords a really typical representation of this Apostle's character. To see his Master, to long to be with Him, to scorn danger, to feel confident that in his Master's presence he must be safe; all this is his first impulse. But when he actually feels the strength of the boisterous wind, and the tossing of the raging waves, his courage suddenly gives way. And all through his life we have these alternations of confidence and failure. Among the Apostles he was bold to make the first confession of belief in the Messiahship of Jesus, and so was rewarded with the promise that on this Rock Christ would build His Church. Yet immediately after words of commendation so strong that they have given rise in the Christian Church to the very loftiest ideas as to the extent of the privileges conveyed, Peter incurs an equally strong rebuke, and is addressed by his Master in the words "Get thee behind Me, Satan, for thou art an offence unto Me." A later history equally presents to us an alternation of confidence and cowardice. He tells his Lord: "Although all men shall be offended because of Thee, yet will I never be offended. Though I should die with Thee, yet will I not deny Thee. Why cannot I follow Thee? I will lay down my life for Thy sake." The hour of trial comes, and at first his faith is strong. There are but two swords in his little company, and a great multitude armed with swords and staves comes against them. Yet he hesitates not to draw his sword and strike in his Master's defence. But when his Lord disowns his resistance, and does not, as he had expected, supernaturally render it effective, his courage sinks at once. He sees Jesus led off by His enemies, to all appearance a helpless captive, and he follows in painful anxiety to see what the miserable end would be. Then all of a sudden he finds that he has brought himself into danger, and the lie springs to his lips by which he hopes to escape. And having once involved himself in denial, the pertinacity of those who recognised him forces him to plunge deeper and deeper down the path of shame.

A still later history displays the same unsteadiness of character. The question which then agitated the Church was the throwing down the barriers that separated Jew and Gentile. Peter goes down to Antioch, the city where first Gentile converts, in any considerable numbers, had been added to the Church. He rejoices in the triumph of the faith, and his warm sympathetic nature expands in manifestations of friendship towards his new brethren. But there come down emissaries from the parent Church at Jerusalem, men bigotedly attached to the law of their fathers, and Peter dreads to lose caste by letting himself be seen by them eating at the same table with the uncircumcised and unclean, whose society a strict Jew had always regarded as pollution. So he draws back in alarm, and resumes his Jewish exclusiveness.

Thus the character of Peter is consistently painted all through the New Testament. There is much to love, much to admire, in his eager impulsiveness, his quick sympathies; but surely, one would say, firmness and steadiness are not the qualities he displays: Rock is not the name by which we should think of describing him. How is it then that this was the title which He who could see the heart bestowed on him?

I believe that by this very title our blessed Lord showed that He really did possess the power of reading men's hearts. Superficial observers could detect the impulsive unsteadiness of Peter's character; at one moment crying out, as we are told in a history related by St. John, "Lord, Thou shalt never wash my feet," the next moment, "not my feet only, but also my hands and my head." We may be sure it would not have been difficult, on a short acquaintance with Peter, to discover in him inconsistencies of conduct. But our Lord discerned beneath the shifting sands of changing emotions the firm rock of an honest and true heart. We know that Peter's love to his Master was genuine, for, with respect to this, he did not fear to challenge the eye of the All-Seeing. "Lovest thou Me?" his Master asked, and he replied, "Lord, Thou knowest all things; Thou knowest that I love Thee." Just as in the stormy seas a projecting rock may for a time be buried out of sight by the billows that wash over it, yet in a little while they sink, and the rock is seen unshaken; so, though the waves of panic terror covered up for a time the rock of Peter's faith and love, yet, though hidden from sight, it was still there, and remained to serve as a foundation for the fabric of his subsequent apostolic labours.

 The very character which made Peter capable of strong affection, made him specially liable also to the assaults of temptations such as those under which he succumbed. That rash speech by which he incurred rebuke so soon after the promise that his confession should be made the foundation of the Church's faith, was prompted by his love for his Master. To be told that the leader on whom all his hopes were fixed was to go to Jerusalem, not to be recognised as king, but to suffer many things at the hands of the chief priests and scribes and elders, and be killed, was so inexpressibly shocking to him that he absolutely refused to believe it, even on his Master's word, and cried : " Be it far from Thee, Lord ; this shall not happen to Thee." Little did he then understand that to reject the cross was to reject the salvation of the world. Little did he know that he was making himself an instrument in the tempter's hand, who tried to shake our Lord's human soul by setting before Him the shame and sorrow which lay on His path, and the cruel shock and disappointment which an event so contrary to their expectations would give to the hopes of His followers.

And Peter's other temptations owed all their force to his strongly sympathetic nature. There are some to whom it costs nothing to be out of harmony with those who surround them. They will take the course which to them seems right, regardless of the disapprobation they may meet with. It costs them no pain to express a difference of opinion. They will blurt out their censures, and little care whose feelings they may wound. You might imagine that it would be a man of this stamp who would be chosen for the chief preacher of a new religion, one who could force its truths on unwilling ears, protesting against every form of wrong with the plain-spoken boldness of Elijah or John the Baptist. But such was not the instrumentality which it was our Lord's will to adopt. Peter was, as I have said, of a peculiarly sympathetic character. He readily entered into the feelings of those around him, and could not set himself in opposition to them without pain. Thus when he goes down to Antioch, to the Church of Gentile believers which St. Paul had collected, he quickly recognises the love which they all bore to their common Lord, and gladly owns them as brethren. But when his Jewish brethren come to the same city it is equally repugnant to him to wound their feelings by setting at nought the traditionary restrictions which had served to keep the worshippers of the one true God from being debased by too intimate association with idolatrous heathen.

And so likewise we may attribute his denial of our Lord not so much to sheer cowardice as to the facility with which he received impressions. Think how his heart must have sunk within him as he mixed in the crowd of the chief priests' attendants, and heard the language in which they spoke of the capture that had been made; as he saw that it was the undoubting belief of all that an impostor had been exposed, and his powerlessness to deliver himself made manifest to everybody; as he heard their expressions of contempt or pity for the miserable followers who had blindly put their trust in this leader, but had run away when the moment came for testing his pretensions. Even if the protest could have been made without personal risk, what resolute independence of spirit, what reliance on past convictions, it would have needed for the solitary disciple to tell the unfriendly circle, "You are all wrong. My Lord is all we ever believed Him to be; the triumph of His enemies is only apparent; and this moment, if He pleased to do so, He could deliver Himself from their hands." It is not only that Peter had not courage and presence of mind on the spur of the moment to say this, but it is likely that he hardly ventured to think it. The apparent failure of all his hopes may well have paralysed his faith; but yet his love remained to add bitterness to the shame of his denial. Whatever Jesus was, Peter loved Him. He had promised an adherence not to be loosened by worldly adversity,—" I will go with Thee to prison and to death,"—and when the moment of trial came he failed. No wonder that an agony of contrition and shame seized him when his Master's look in an instant revealed to him how little he had known his own heart, or judged of what baseness it was capable.

But Peter's love shone out in full strength when the miracle of the Resurrection rolled all the clouds of doubt away. The Gospel history tells of one appearance of our Lord to Peter separately, the details of which are not recorded. But St. John tells of another appearance of our Lord to the disciples as they were fishing on the lake of Tiberias, and he records the characteristic trait that as soon as the disciple whom Jesus loved had made Peter understand that the stranger on the shore was his Lord, he waited not for the ship to be brought to land, but dashed into the water to get near to Him. Once his faith had been confirmed his love kept him steadfast to brave the threats of power. When rebuked by the high priest in the name of the Jewish council his answer was, "We ought to obey God rather than man"; and when beaten for his preaching of Christ he departed from the presence of the council rejoicing that he had been counted worthy to suffer shame for the name of Jesus.

There is one service which I believe St. Peter's

love of his Master has rendered to the Church, and which I think is not generally understood. I mean that I believe it to be Peter's loving memory which has preserved for us many of the words and deeds of our blessed Lord. If you read attentively the first three Gospels you cannot fail to notice that there are several narratives and discourses which are found in almost identical words in all three. Now, if three different companions of our Lord had independently related occurrences which they had all witnessed, they would no doubt tell the same story in substance, but there would be sure to be differences in their way of telling it, so that it is rational to believe that where the three evangelists agree in words as well as in substance, it is the narrative of one and the same witness that comes to us through the three channels. A very early Church tradition relates that St. Mark was an intimate companion of Peter, and that in Mark's Gospel we have recorded for the permanent instruction of the Church the things that that Apostle used to tell about his Master's life. There are many minute touches in that Gospel which have convinced even sceptical critics that they must have come from an eye-witness. Renan, for instance, says, "Mark is full of minute observations, which, without any doubt, come from an eye-witness. Nothing forbids us to think that this eye-witness, who evidently had followed Jesus, who had loved Him, and looked on Him very close at hand, and who had preserved a lively image of Him, was the Apostle Peter himself."

I think that even if no early tradition had preserved this account of the matter, thoughtful criticism would have led us to the same result. Take the very commencement of the Gospel. The whole of the first chapter of Mark is occupied with a detailed account of one day of our Lord's ministry. It was the Sabbath which immediately followed the call of Simon and Andrew, John and James. We are told of our Lord's teaching in the synagogue, of the healing there of a demoniac, of the entry of the Saviour into Simon's house, the healing of his wife's mother, and then in the evening, when the close of the Sabbath permitted the moving of the sick, the crowd of people about the door seeking to be healed of their diseases. In whose recollections is it likely that that one day would stand out in such prominence? Surely we may reasonably conjecture that the narrator must have been one of those four to whom the call to follow Jesus had made that day a turning point in their lives. The narrator could not have been John, whose authorship is claimed for a different Gospel, nor could it have been Andrew, who was not present at another scene described in this Gospel, and where the traces of an eye-witness are the strongest: I mean the narrative of all that followed the descent from the Mount of Transfiguration. There remain then only Peter, and James the son of Zebedee, and we can hardly doubt that it was the former who has recorded for us the words which he spoke at that scene of the Transfiguration, while heavy with sleep and scarce understanding what he meant by them. I believe that we should not now possess so much knowledge of the words and deeds of our blessed Lord if the Holy Spirit had not used as His instrument for the edification of His Church the loving memory of this Apostle, and thus that it was not only by those labours of Peter's of which we have direct knowledge, but also by a work which we seldom associate with his name that Peter's love has been a foundation of the Church's faith.

But my object has been to speak rather of Peter's failures than of his successes. It is his real love for his Lord which makes his fall so full of practical warning for us. If I had chosen now to speak about the treachery of Judas Iscariot I should scarcely have been able to make you feel that you could ever be capable of sin like that. You might pronounce him to have been a mere hypocrite who had never really been a sincere disciple: who had merely followed Jesus for the sake of the dishonest gain he could make as treasurer to the little community; and who lightly abandoned Him when it seemed that a greater gain could be made by deserting Him. Many have thought that this is not a true representation of the character of Judas; concluding from the anguish of his remorse that his heart was open to loftier motives than the sordid love of gain.

But, however that may be, if you believe yourself to be conscious of real love to our Lord such as you cannot think that Judas ever had, can you equally flatter yourself that your love to Him is warmer than Peter's, and that you are more exempt from danger of fall than he? To himself how impossible it seemed that he could deny the Master whom with all his heart he loved, and yet how unlike was his actual conduct to what he had planned and resolved it should be. Does it never happen to you that by the gusts of sudden temptation firm resolves are unexpectedly blown away? You lose your presence of mind, and almost before you know it the temptation has triumphed to which you had thought yourself incapable of yielding. Sometimes the insignificance of the trial to which you are exposed may constitute part of its danger. You might think that you could stand firm if brought before the tribunal of a heathen persecutor and offered your life only on condition of your denying your faith. But that is not the task imposed on you. Nothing may be required of you but to give faithful utterance to the convictions of your heart, when you incur no danger by speech, but merely put yourself out of sympathy with those with whom you are associating. A scoff at your faith is uttered; an impure story is told. You feel that some words of protest are demanded of you, and yet you are silent and let it appear as if you took pleasure in that from which you can find no word of dissent. Or your temper may be tried, and you speak unadvisedly with your lips as one ought not to speak who professes to follow Him, who, when He was reviled, reviled not again. To tell a lie you not only believe to be a sin, but also to be dishonourable and ungentlemanly; and yet does it never happen to you to slip into untruthfulness to avoid some trifling loss or escape some small inconvenience? and though the untruthfulness may be but petty, perhaps the temptation to which you yielded was quite as insignificant.

And in this and many another case where you fail at the right moment to say the right word or do the right thing, the shame of owning your fault may lead you like Peter to try to cover sin by the addition of other sin. How often after we have ourselves perceived that we have been in the wrong does unwillingness to acknowledge this keep us silent; and often induce us to be consistent in going on in a wrong course rather than incur the humiliation of retracing our steps! I might speak of many other forms of temptation through which men slide into actions of which they had thought themselves incapable: how, for example, men who really desire to be generous will find themselves doing things which they cannot deny were selfish, not to say mean or shabby.

We manage to keep on good terms with ourselves because we judge ourselves not by our actions but by the good feelings of which we are conscious, and the good principles which we attribute to ourselves.

In judging others we do well charitably to remember that the man may be better than his conduct. One would have greatly erred who had supposed that Peter did not love his Lord because he denied Him. But when we judge ourselves we must bear in mind that the good feelings and good principles which are not strong enough to keep us from sin are apt to wear away under the corroding influence of the deceitfulness of sin. If these feelings are real they will exhibit their existence by the force of recoil which they produce. An elastic spring will yield to sudden pressure, but if it be not broken it starts back again: it contains a power of reaction. In the Peter of the Acts of the Apostles we find no disposition to be ashamed of his Master, no disinclination to brave suffering for His sake.

And what awoke Peter's slumbering conscience? The look of Jesus. Jesus turned and looked upon Peter. Who can venture to put into words all that that look conveyed to the mind of the Apostle? Your thoughts would outrun me if I attempted the description. Could we but see that look directed on ourselves, how would it shame our cowardice and rebuke the coldness of our love! And why do we see it not? It is because in the deadness of our faith we turn our eyes away from Him. The Apostle directs us to run with patience the race that is set before us, looking unto Jesus. If we strove to keep ever before us the thoughts of what He has done for us, and of what He has asked us to do for Him,—even to follow in His steps and to imitate His holy example,—there would be ever present in our hearts a force which, even though at times overmastered by sudden temptation, would be strong for reaction and restoration.

God grant, brethren, that the fatal words, "too late," be not stamped on your repentance. Sorrow for sin is sure to come: for sin must always be followed by sorrow. But may yours be that godly sorrow which leadeth to repentance. May yours be the sorrow of Peter whose bitter weeping was the beginning of a happier life—who sowed in tears what he should reap in joy—not the sorrow of Esau who, when he came too late to value what he had despised before, found no place of repentance though he sought it carefully with tears.

XI

CHARITY AND LOVE[1]

"And now abideth faith, hope, charity, these three; but the greatest of these is charity."—1 CORINTHIANS xiii. 13.

In the Revised Version it is: "But now abideth faith, hope, love, these three; and the greatest of these is love."

ONE of the features which distinguishes the new version from the old is that a different rule is followed with regard to the translation of the same Greek by the same English word. This is not a thing that is always possible to be done consistently with faithful translation; for it constantly happens that corresponding words in different languages do not so completely correspond, but that the meaning of one somewhat overlaps that of the other, so that often two words in one language must be used to express all that is meant by one word in the other.

But King James's translators of set purpose disregarded any attempt to preserve uniformity of rendering in this respect, and without any neces-

[1] Preached on Quinquagesima, 1882.

sity, but from mere love of variety, translate the same Greek word differently even when it recurs within a verse or two. In their Preface they defend this method of theirs, and altogether repudiate the notion that they were to be tied up if they had translated a word "journeying" in one place not to render it "travelling" in another; if one where "think" never to translate "suppose"; if one where "pain" never "ache"; if one where "joy" never "gladness." "Thus to mince the matter," they say, "we thought to savour more of curiosity than of wisdom, and that rather it would breed scorn in the atheist than bring profit to the godly reader. For is the kingdom of God become words or syllables? Why should we be in bondage to them if we may be free?—use one precisely when we may use another no less fit as commodiously?" And they give other reasons which I need not delay to quote.

There is no doubt that King James's translators, than whom no men understood the genius of the English language better, made their version much more agreeable to the ear by the variety with which they enriched their language; for the simple taste of earlier times had taken no offence against the constant repetition of the same word in a narrative, which English writers have generally thought it an elegance to avoid. But there is a grave inconvenience from the course followed by King James's translators, namely, that it has made the English Bible inadequate for a very profitable way of studying the Bible. One of the best commentaries on Scripture is Scripture itself. To compare one passage with another is often the best way of throwing light on the meaning of both. Now the similarity of two passages is often disguised when the same Greek word is made to wear different English dresses in the two places; and on the other hand the English reader is sometimes put on a false scent when he thinks he has found the same word used in two different texts, when in truth the Greek words are different. For these and other reasons, the late Committee of Revision decided that they would aim at rendering as far as they could the same Greek word by the same English. And this gave rise to one of the first complaints that was made against their work. When their version was compared with the old one, it was found that in many a familiar text a word had been changed for another of very nearly the same sense; whereupon an outcry was made against such needless tampering with the venerable translation to which we have been all accustomed. " We can understand that King James's translators should be corrected if they had made a mistake, but why alter their work gratuitously when the sense is not in the least improved?" You may take for granted, as a general rule, that when you find the new version differing from the old by a verbal change which does not affect the sense, the reason of it has been in order to preserve uniformity of rendering the same word in different places.

I have no doubt it was not without some pangs of regret, and possibly not without some differences of opinion among themselves, that the late revisers found that the application of their rule obliged them to cast out of their New Testament the familiar name of one of the three theological virtues, faith, hope, and charity,—a name consecrated by Church use, as for example in the Collect for this day, which, though one of the latest of our Collects, being only a composition of the Caroline revisers of the Prayer-Book, well bears comparison with the most beautiful of the prayers that have descended to us from the ancient Church. Yet if the rule of uniformity of rendering is to be followed, the case is one that admits of no doubt.

The noun ἀγάπη and the verb ἀγαπάω are of constant occurrence in the New Testament. In the rendering of the verb our translators appear to have found that they had no choice, and uniformly translate "to love." "Love" is also their ordinary rendering for the noun, but in some ten or twenty places beside the chapter of the text they introduce the word "charity," without any apparent reason for the preference in these passages, but merely because one of two words which they regarded as synonymous being, according to their principles, equally at their disposal, they took one or other as the suggestion of the moment prompted.

In introducing the word charity into this chapter, King James's translators adopted an innovation on the current practice of English printed Bibles: Tyndale's, the first of them, had "love"; so had Cranmer's; so had the Bishop's Bible and the Geneva Bible. It was the Rhemish or Roman Catholic New Testament that introduced the word into English printed Bibles, deriving it naturally from Jerome's Latin Bible, whence that translation was made. In the adoption of the word by King James's translators they may have been influenced by the opinion of Lord Bacon expressed a few years before. He says, "I did ever allow the discretion and tenderness of the Rhemish translation in this point, that finding in the original the word ἀγάπη and never ἔρως, do ever translate charity and never love, because of the indifference and equivocation of the word with impure love." In the words I have quoted, Bacon's "never" is too strong a description of the practice of the Rhemish translators. They sometimes translate

P

love, but more usually "charity," and that in many passages where the word does not occur in the Authorised Version. Even the saying "God is love" becomes "God is charity." The reason given by Lord Bacon was doubtless that which influenced St. Jerome in his appropriation of the word "caritas" to Christian use. In the Latin language "amor" had to do duty as an equivalent both for $\dot{a}\gamma\dot{a}\pi\eta$ and $\xi\rho\omega\varsigma$, and from its use in the latter capacity had doubtless become in the mind of Jerome and that of his readers so tainted with sensual associations as to seem to him unfit for sacred purposes. It would grate on Christian feeling if St. Paul's noble encomium on charity were made to read like a hymn in praise of one of the least respectable of the heathen deities. So it was necessary to find a word which might express "heavenly" as distinct from "earthly" love, and St. Jerome found that he could do no better than take the word "caritas," literally "dearness"; or I suppose we might translate "affection," and distorting it a good deal from its classical use, make it, in all cases where heavenly love is meant, take the place of "amor."

From Jerome's Vulgate the word charity passed naturally into popular language. Although in pre-Reformation times a sermon was not regarded, as it very commonly is now, as an essential part of every religious service, yet vernacular sermons were common enough, and these were necessarily preached by men whose own knowledge of the Bible had been exclusively derived through the medium of St. Jerome's Latin. Hence the word charity became early part of our language. It is, in fact, one of three or four of the earliest words which we have in common with French. It was used by Wycliffe before the invention of printing, in his translation made from the Vulgate. It is used by Chaucer and other early writers. And I am inclined to believe that the popular limitation of the word to almsgiving took its origin in the frequent use of this word in appeals of preachers asking either for money on behalf of some good work, or for prayers on behalf of the souls in purgatory. The common exordium was, "Good Christian people, we pray you of your charity to give so and so."

If the word charity had been only introduced into our language by the Rhemish translators, we may safely say that King James's translators would not have adopted it; for in their Preface they criticise severely the Latinisms of the Rhemish translation, and perhaps not altogether in the spirit of that charity of which we speak; for they pronounce these words "Azimes," "Holocaust," "Prepuce," "Pasche," and a number of such like, "whereof their late translation is full," as introduced "of purpose to darken the sense, that since they must needs translate the Bible, yet by the language thereof it may be kept from being understood."

But an opposite extreme which King James's translators claim to have avoided was "the scrupulosity of the Puritans, who leave the old ecclesiastical words and betake themselves to other, as when they put 'washing' instead of 'baptism,' and congregation' instead of 'church.'" The use of the word love instead of charity in Tyndale's translation was part of this systematic avoidance of ecclesiastical words. He translated "congregation" instead of "church," "washing" instead of "baptism;" "favour" instead of "grace," "elder" or "senior" instead of "priest," and so on.

It was this feature of Tyndale's translation which most provoked the dislike of the Church rulers, for it would be unjust to them to believe that the hostility Tyndale encountered was entirely due to unwillingness on the part of the Church authorities that their people should be made acquainted with the Bible. They supposed that they could discern in this characteristic feature of his translation a desire to undermine the attachment of the people to the Church, and a wish to detach her doctrines from their foundation of

Scripture proof. Accordingly this characteristic of Tyndale's translation was vehemently assailed by Sir Thomas More, who having discussed separately Tyndale's use of the word "congregation," not "church"; "elder" or "senior," not "priest"; "favour," not "grace," treats of this question between the words love and charity, on which occasion everything was said on both sides that can easily be said if the dispute is renewed at the present day. King James's translators aimed at a mean between Papistical obscurity and Puritanical scrupulosity, and desired, as they said, "that the Scripture might speak like itself as in the language of Canaan, that it may be understood even of the very vulgar." It was in conformity then with their system to bring into the Bible the ecclesiastical word charity, of the popular use of which long before their time it is easy to give abundant proofs. A student of our language might examine with advantage the uses of the words charity and charitable in Shakespeare, who employs them so often that it would be impossible here to comment minutely on what we learn from him as to the extent to which these words had then worked themselves into popular language. But we have plainer evidence in our Prayer-Book where, in the baptismal office, in a prayer dating from 1549 the phrases "stedfast in faith, joyful through hope, rooted in charity," show that while the three Christian graces were in the Bible faith, hope, and love, they were in ecclesiastical language, as well as in popular speech, faith, hope, and charity.

The word charitably occurs even in Tyndale's translation : in the passage in the Epistle to the Romans, " If thy brother be grieved with thy meat, now walkest thou not charitably." The Greek is κατ' ἀγάπην, and the Revised Version is " Thou walkest not in love."

We find very early instances of that use of the word charitable which would make it indispensable to the English language even though driven out of the Bible, I mean as expressing the disposition which refuses to judge harshly of others, which puts the best construction on their doings, and delights to speak as much good of them and as little evil as it can. The usage no doubt springs out of St. Paul's " Charity thinketh no evil," yet if we limit the word charity to this we commit an error the same in kind as if we limit it to almsgiving : we forget that the amiable characteristics to which I have referred are mentioned by Paul as only one part of the ways in which manifestation is made of the spirit of Christian love.

The history then of the English word charity being as I have stated, the late revisers had to consider whether they ought not to retain it in their version. It is, as I said in the beginning, no uncommon occurrence that a Greek word should have in English more equivalents than one, and that it would be more suitable in translation to use sometimes the one, sometimes the other. The word charity has a real place in our language which entitles it to be regarded as in many cases the best equivalent to the New Testament ἀγάπη: not only as denoting, as I have already said, heavenly love as opposed to earthly, but also as denoting a feeling more diffusive, less intense than that strongly personal attachment to which we give the name of love. Yet if anything like uniformity of rendering were to be preserved, the effect of retaining the word charity would be to banish the word love from great part of the New Testament. This might be a small inconvenience if it were not that charity has in English no corresponding verb. And there is a number of passages where the relation of verb to noun in the sentence is so close that it would be highly unsuitable to translate them by unrelated words. For instance in the two sayings which occur within a couple of lines, " He that loveth another hath fulfilled the law," and " Love is the fulfilling of the law." Even the Rhemish translators here felt that the same word must be used, and so they do not introduce the word charity into the latter passage. Also the phrase "the love of God" (whether subjective or objective) could not be replaced by the "charity of God." Thus you see that the late revisers found themselves compelled either to give up in this case their general principle of uniformity of rendering, or else, if they used only one English word for ἀγάπη, to decide that that word must be love. I own I rejoice that it was not in their power to expel the word charity from the English language, where it now has a place of its own which no other word could supply, and I am glad also that its sacred use should retain the sanction of that which, as far as I can see, must for many years continue to be the authorised version, and for very many years after that must retain its hold on the affections of the people.

Yet several advantages will spring from the liveliness which the circulation of the Revised Version will give to the general knowledge of the fact that in Scripture use the words Charity and Love are identical. When it was alleged as a reason for banishing charity from the English New Testament that the word in popular use was limited to the sense of almsgiving, it was answered with a great deal of truth that there were comparatively very few who did not know the true Scripture meaning of the word, that those who did not know it could easily be made to know, and that no one would be in danger of mistaking it for almsgiving who read the earlier verse of the chapter from which I have taken my text, "If I give all my goods to feed the poor, and have not charity, it profiteth me nothing." Yet the inconvenience of having a technical word to denote the Christian grace is that with our usual readiness to pare down a command to the standard at which fulfilment is not too burdensome, we have banished from the word charity all that intensity of feeling which belongs to the word love. If you think that the two words are really synonymous in the mind of an educated person who knows that they are only different translations of the same Greek word, compare the words in the verbal form. Is the requirement of the Catechism to "be in charity with all men," exactly the same thing as our Lord's command, "Thou shalt love thy neighbour as thyself"? One sees at once how negative our conception of charity has become; how little more is implied by being in charity with a man than the absence of malice and hatred towards him, or of any desire for his injury. Just, then, as by reviving the ink of some ancient writing we make that easy to be read which before had been just possible to be deciphered, so I think the circulation of the Revised Version will give quite a new life to men's knowledge of the fact that St. Paul's precept of charity is but the republication of our Lord's summary of the ancient law, "Thou shalt love the Lord thy God with all thy heart, and with all thy soul, and with all thy strength; and thou shalt love thy neighbour as thyself."

Another incidental advantage will be our increased perception of the unity of Apostolic teaching on this subject. We familiarly think of St. John as the Apostle of Love, and perhaps do not know how much our disposition to look on the inculcation of this grace as a specialty of this Apostle arises from the fact that both in the fourth Gospel and in his Epistle our translators have translated ἀγάπη not by charity, but by love. For surely if this thirteenth of Corinthians had been rendered in the same way we could not have failed to see that love has as prominent a place in the system of St. Paul as of St. John. Or take another passage from the Epistle to the Romans, to which I have made partial reference already. "Owe no man anything, but to love one another: for he that loveth another hath fulfilled the law. For this, Thou shalt not commit adultery, Thou shalt not kill, Thou shalt not steal, Thou shalt not bear false witness, Thou shalt not covet; and if there be any other commandment, it is briefly comprehended in this saying, Thou shalt love thy neighbour as thyself. Love worketh no ill to his neighbour; therefore love is the fulfilling of the law." In other words, the one commandment of love sums up all the commandments of the second table of the Decalogue, for they all but forbid in some form or another working ill to our neighbour, and if we love him we cannot desire to work him ill. That we have harmony here between the teaching of St. John and St. Paul arises from the fact that both are but echoing the teaching of their Master; for St. Paul, who was not a personal disciple of our Lord, nowhere more distinctly shows himself to have possessed a traditional knowledge of His teaching than here, where there is a plain reminiscence of our Lord's answer to the question "Which is the great commandment of the law?" The same position is given to love in the Epistle of St. Peter, whose exhortation is, "Above all things, have fervent love among yourselves."

One advantage resulting from the familiarisation of men's minds with the knowledge that charity means the same thing as love, will be the dispelling of the notion that theological virtues are something quite different from those graces which in common life men count as virtues. It was a deep-rooted heathen idea that if men only knew the right means they might conciliate the Divine favour notwithstanding that they were violating all their obligations to their fellow-men. And surely we cannot say that Christian teaching has always escaped the danger of inculcating the special virtues necessary for gaining the Divine favour as so much more excellent than the fulfilment of homely human duty, that the latter ran the risk of being dropped out of the scheme altogether. The word love binds together our duty towards God and our duty towards our neighbour in a way that the word charity does not. At least when on a memorable occasion martyrs in Mary's reign were forced to listen to a sermon before their execution, and when the preacher chose for their edification the text, " If I give my body to be burned, and have not charity, it profiteth me nothing," I think that if the word in his Bible had been Love, a man consigning another to the flames would scarcely take that occasion to boast that he was full of the grace of love, and that his victim was not.

In a lately published work[1] a conversation with Wordsworth is reported, in which the poet owned that he had had some difficulty in accepting St. Paul's exaltation of the grace of Charity over Faith,—Faith which, according to his conception of it, gave men a perception of higher truths than his

[1] *Caroline Fox's Diary.*

understanding was capable of arriving at, and elevated him to a loftier region. And surely no Christian can disparage the excellence of faith or the importance of the truths which it reveals. But the nature of the truths which Christian Faith at least makes known is such that it is impossible to conceive that grace as separated from Love. We cannot imagine any one as merely revelling in solitary contemplation of these truths. Indeed the solitary enjoyment of knowledge of any kind is almost inconceivable to us. We can hardly think of a man as acquiring knowledge without the wish to impart it. But as for the truths which Christian Faith makes known to a man, if they have not elevated and drawn out his love both toward God and toward his brethren he has learned them in vain. If faith were nothing more than a higher kind of knowledge, it would be after all but a poor thing. Some small improvement in man's senses, or some little increase in his brain-power, might make him capable of knowing without effort all that now it is some only of the more highly gifted of our race who can with difficulty discern. And yet is such increase of knowledge the thing that for his happiness man has most reason to desire? If a man at the close of life asks himself what are the best things God has given him here to enjoy, I am persuaded he will not think of the knowledge he has acquired or the earthly honours he has won. If he knows the truth, the best things he has had are the love he has received and the love he has given. And if he hopes that this life has not been his all, and has faith that God will give him good things hereafter, it is for the enjoyment of love more perfect that he looks,—his own love purified from the alloy of selfishness that has debased it here, and love given back to him in fullest measure by others whose love has been in like manner made perfect. And so we may own that if "now abideth Faith, Hope, Love, the greatest of these is Love."

XII

CHARITABLE BELIEF[1]

"Charity believeth all things."—1 CORINTHIANS xiii. 7.

IT is common to hear the Roman Catholic doctrine of exclusive salvation in the Church of Rome condemned as a most uncharitable doctrine. What want of charity, it is said, for men to believe that all who do not cast in their lot with them must perish eternally. The same doctrine "outside the Church no salvation" has been held and is held by many who do not understand "the Church" as limited to mean the Roman Church. And here again the same objection arises, What about virtuous heathen who lived before our Lord's coming? What about virtuous heathen at the present day? Must we believe that there are none? Well, what about Quakers and other Christian, or nominally Christian, people who live without the use of those sacraments which our Church pronounces to be generally necessary

[1] Preached on Quinquagesima, 1887.

to salvation? Is it not gross want of charity to believe that such cannot be saved? I have heard the same epithet "uncharitable" applied, though with less apparent reason, to the opinion that members of our Church stand in a position of spiritual advantage over members of dissenting communities. Thus I have heard it called uncharitable to believe that a clergyman of our Church stands on any higher level than the minister of one of these communities.

When it comes to this we must be conscious that there has been some abuse of language; and a doubt arises whether it is correct to apply the word charitable to beliefs at all, the important question being not whether a belief is charitable but whether the thing believed is true. With regard to the things of this life there is no want of charity in believing that some other men are in a less advantageous position than ourselves. Would it not be absurd to call it uncharitable to believe that civilised nations have material advantages over savages? On the contrary, does not that belief often elicit evidence of the highest charity when it prompts men to make benevolent efforts, and even sacrifices, in order to raise the condition of those whom they believe to be in an inferior position to themselves? Of such efforts some of the strongest and noblest examples are missionary efforts. And thus to go back to the example I first took, those who hold the most extreme doctrine of exclusive salvation can easily repudiate the name uncharitable applied to their belief if it is supposed to imply that those who hold it are uncharitable persons. As I have just said, the important question is not whether a belief is charitable, but whether it is in accordance with truth. Suppose this doctrine of exclusive salvation to be true, then it is the highest charity to proclaim it loudly in order that those who are outside the true Church may be made sensible of their peril and induced to fly into the place of safety. Suppose you saw a man sleeping on the brink of a precipice, which would be the charitable course, to allow him to slumber on, or to awake him, it might be from the pleasantest of dreams, and bring him into security? When men have given up ease and comfort, all the delights of domestic affection, all the happiness of civilised life, have endured toil and privation, and at length, as so many have done, have spent out life itself in efforts to make the Gospel known to lands which it had not reached, call them if you will mistaken enthusiasts, fanatics, but at least do not say that the belief which has in so many cases inspired all their exertions, the belief but for which they would never have cared to leave their homes, was uncharitable.

Suppose it to be said that there is something uncharitable in the frame of mind which disposes a man to believe such a doctrine, might it not be retorted that on the contrary want of charity is indicated by the frame of mind that is disinclined to believe it? Suppose an organised effort were being made for the relief of distress said to prevail in a certain locality to an exceptional degree, which would show most charity, the man who gave ready credence to the story and, acting on his belief, joined heartily and liberally in the projected plan of relief; or the man who at once declared that he was sure it was impossible there could be any such misery, that no doubt the people in question were very comfortable in their own way, and that it was quite unnecessary for him to trouble himself about them?

In the Church of Rome there are beliefs said to be pious which it is accounted meritorious to hold. If of two opposing opinions one seems, according to the conceptions of our day, to attribute more honour to God or to the Blessed Virgin than the other, then it is held to be a right thing to adopt it, even without evidence, or it may be in opposition to a preponderance of evidence. This notion of beliefs to be held not on the ground of evidence, but of their supposed piety, has a close affinity with the idea that we can safely declare a doctrine to be untrue merely because it represents the condition of others to be in some respects worse than we in all charity could wish it to be. It might seem to follow from what has been said that piety or charity have nothing to do with belief which ought to follow the preponderance of evidence, no matter though we could wish the facts to have been different from what evidence exhibits them. But there is another aspect of the case which needs to be presented.

In the first place, it is plain enough that whether or not charity ought to affect belief, belief can affect charity. Take the doctrine of exclusive salvation about which I commenced by speaking, there is no doubt that in some cases it has inspired exertions evidencing the highest charity; but has it not in other cases killed brotherly love towards persons supposed to be the object of God's extreme displeasure and wrath, and whom, therefore, all who loved God ought to hate as though they were their own enemies? When such persons added to their guilt by endeavouring to propagate their opinions, thus doing work infinitely more pernicious than if they disseminated poison for the body (inasmuch as they made all whom they could succeed in seducing from the fold of the true Church their partners in eternal condemnation), no severity was thought too great for the suppression of such wickedness; and if the worst tortures the Inquisition ever invented were employed, pity for the sufferer was quenched by indignation at the atrocity of his crimes. Even when a heretic's sufferings were incurred in consequence of his resolute profession of the faith held in common by all who bear the name of Christ, they have not commanded orthodox sympathy; and a pious and amiable ecclesiastical historian records the death of a heretic martyr with the remark that thus his soul passed from temporal torments to the never-ending torment of the other world.

It needs little proof that belief affects feeling, and it needs little more that feeling acts on belief. Granted that, belief ought to be founded on evidence, but in judging of evidence feeling plays its part. The mind cannot but form its canons of probability, determining what is to be received as credible and what not. Our judgment as to testimony with regard to what in a particular instance has been done must be affected by our opinion of the characters of the persons referred to,—an opinion which must influence our judgment as to what they are likely to have done.

All this will appear more clearly if we follow out the more obvious thoughts which the words of the text suggest. When we hear the words "Charity believeth all things," we naturally think of it as a rule for judging of the conduct of our fellows; and when we say "all things" we of course take it to mean "all good things"; we mean that we are always to think as well of them as we can; to be ready to believe everything to their advantage, nothing to their discredit. Evidently a cynical man of the world might easily assail this maxim on the score of truth; he would say that his experience had taught him to take a very different view of what might be expected from men, and that if "Charity believeth all things" it must believe a pack of lies. And yet judge of the matter on the score of truth alone, and whose views do you suppose would approach nearest to the reality of things? those of him who regarded other men as actuated solely by motives of self-interest, and as ready to take advantage of him whenever it might appear to them they could do it with impunity, or of him who was willing to give them credit for generous and grateful feelings, and was apt to trust them extensively and boldly? That such a man as the latter might from time to time be deceived in his expectations is very possible; but far more often would his confidence be rewarded; and he would find that through the hearty co-operation of trusted allies he was able to accomplish far more than any suspicious solitary man could have done. How can you know the real truth of anything? By viewing it from the outside and from a distance, or from within? whether are you more likely to know the real truth of others, by shutting yourself up in your own personality, and taking cognisance of them only as their actions seem likely to hurt or benefit yourself, or by throwing yourself into their feelings and trying to see with their eyes, and view things as they do? Actions of theirs which might otherwise have seemed unintelligible or perverse then become obvious and natural. The modern student of history feels that his views are truer than those of his predecessors, if they have but depicted the external appearance of the facts, while he has endeavoured to realise the state of mind of the agents, and to comprehend their motives. Plainly, sympathy confers insight ; and what such key to sympathy as love? How natural is it to take the side of one for whom we feel real friendship, in any controversy in which he is engaged ; how natural to see with his eyes, and accept as correct his views on the questions in dispute; how ready are we to resent an injustice done him or an indignity offered him as if it were done to ourselves,—perhaps more, since we can give free expression to indignation at affronts offered to a friend to which in our own case we might think it more dignified to submit in silence. Possibly love to a friend may mislead us, making us if more than just to him, less than just to others to whom his interests are opposed. That objection does not lie against charity, a word which though it came into our language as an equivalent for ἀγάπη love, has now a special meaning of its own, denoting a feeling more diffusive than what we call love, and therefore less liable to degenerate into injustice. But whether the feeling be called love or charity, in either case it denotes a power of sympathising with others and entering into their feelings, and so confers a power of insight which the isolated self-contained man does not possess. Ill then is he justified in rejecting its revelations as inconsistent with truth, or in imagining that his harsh uncharitable judgments correspond more accurately with the reality of things than the views taken by one who can see both sides of each question; and even in the case of actions which he must condemn, can acknowledge the strength of the temptations which in some degree excuse them, or the force of the arguments which had seemed to the actors sufficient to justify them. In fact it is so plain as hardly to require argument, that the better we know any one's character the more correct judgment we are likely to form as to what he is likely to do or as to what in any particular case he has done; and it is equally plain that we know any one's character the better the more we can succeed in putting ourselves in his place and throwing ourselves into sympathy with him; and again it is equally plain that love is the best key to such sympathy, so that the judgments which love prompts are likely to be not only the kindest but the truest.

But though love teaches us to correct many harsh judgments, and enables us to discover in those whom we might on a hasty glance have pronounced to be wholly bad, some redeeming qualities, and some excuses for their bad actions, I do not pretend that in every case the better we know a man the more we shall find to approve of in him. That is not true of ourselves. Indeed, self-knowledge is commonly the best guide to charitable judgment of others, for we are severe on their faults when we are blind to our own; and if we have escaped sins into which they have fallen, and to which our own temptations have not been so strong, we forget lapses of our own in other directions not a whit more excusable. But however that may be, since it is by no means true that all men are equal in virtue or moral goodness, it follows that a true judgment of others cannot always be a favourable one. In that case certainly charity does not oblige us to shut our eyes to facts. Ill were it for the world if it were our duty to suppress that indignation against wrong-doing which constitutes the moral strength of a community, and the fear of the expression of which is the greatest deterrent from vice. It is a spurious charity which imagines the line separating right and wrong to be so indistinct that it is never safe to pronounce a verdict, and when a crime is committed has no courage to call it a crime. If the moral sense of a community is to be strong enough to exercise an overmastering influence on every member, it must speak with no uncertain sound. Pleas of excuse, if offered in mitigation of punishment, may be judged of with all leniency, but no tenderness towards the offender ought to be permitted to obscure our discernment of the difference between right and wrong.

What has been said on the subject of charity in judging of the acts of other men, may now be used to throw light on the question I began by considering, namely the principles on which we can form opinions as to the rules of the Divine government of the world. It may be urged that it now appears that it is an error to speak slightingly of pious beliefs, as if our belief ought to rest solely on evidence and not on our notions of piety. It has been seen, it may be said, that in judging of evidence how any man has acted, our opinion of his character forms an important factor. There are some men of whom we think so highly that we should be very slow to accept evidence purporting to show that they had acted unhandsomely or ungenerously, not to say basely. Must it not in like manner be the best key to correct judgments as to the Divine government of the world that we should judge rightly of the character of God ? Then we shall best know what evidence as to His actions we ought to admit. A pious belief, it may be urged, is no more than a persuasion that the Divine acts will always be such as might worthily proceed from a Being of perfect excellence. There is nothing more unreasonable in being easy in accepting evidence attributing to God acts of such a character, and slow in receiving evidence of acts of a contrary character, than there is if, in the case of a fellow-creature whom we love and trust, we reject with contumely slanderous stories impeaching his character, and readily believe what is consistent with the goodness we have always observed to mark his conduct.

This argument would be sound if it were

really as easy for us to judge of the acts of God as of those of one of our fellow-creatures. But it requires only a little knowledge of the history of religions to teach us how precarious is the method of beginning by forming conceptions of the character of God and then taking for granted that facts must correspond to these conceptions. In the old heathen religions, the gods were thought of as differing only from men in being immensely stronger and more powerful. They were thought of then as acting as men would act who possessed unlimited means of gratifying their passions. In process of time even heathen minds found the Homeric conceptions of the divinities to be revolting to them, and it was recognised that it was not enough to attribute to the gods superior physical power; but that there were some moral weaknesses which must be left out by any one who would form worthy conceptions of the Deity. Still the predominant feature of the conception of God which passed on even to Christian minds was that of an autocrat; no doubt not an autocrat who used his power in a way which a cultivated moral sense condemns as disgraceful in an earthly ruler, but still an autocrat, subject to those more subtle forms of weakness which result from the precarious character of the best-established earthly sway.

With every human authority it must be a leading object to provide for the maintenance of its own power. And as power depends largely on public opinion a ruler is not safe if he neglects to take care that his authority shall be recognised throughout his dominions; rebellion must be put down with a high hand; all expressions of dissatisfaction discouraged; praises and adulation warmly received, not merely because they are gratifying to the ruler's vanity, but because the state of feeling which prompts such language is really necessary to the stability of the throne. A moment's thought convinces us that we are misled by a completely false analogy if we attribute the jealousies prompted by the precariousness of earthly rule to the possessor of sovereign omnipotence whose will must prevail whether men accept it or reject it, and whose glory can receive no augmentation from human praises. It would be an ungrateful task if I were to enumerate the errors disfiguring Christian schemes of theology which have had their source in the conception that God is a Being whose dealings with His creatures are mainly governed by the desire to display His power and, as it has been said, to promote His own "glory."

We can study errors of this kind with more impartiality if we examine how they have operated in a case in which we are not ourselves infected by them. In the Roman Catholic Church pious opinions are not only those which are supposed to prove their truth by their being more honourable to God than the reverse, but also those which similarly prove their truth by their being honourable to the Blessed Virgin. We certainly have no desire to withhold any honour that is her due from one on whom God was pleased to bestow the highest earthly honour, that of being mother of our blessed Lord. But when we look into the beliefs which gained acceptance because supposed honourable to her, and the tales which those beliefs caused to be willingly received as credible, we cannot but feel that they are not honourable to her but deeply degrading. Those who have wished to exalt her material dignity by acknowledging her as Queen of Heaven have represented her as swayed in the exercise of her sovereignty by a caprice and vanity which would be disgraceful in an earthly queen. Those who are familiar with the stories to which I refer know well how she has been represented as greedy of personal adulation, anxious only that sinners should put themselves under her patronage, resentful against those who neglect her, but resolute to use her influence with the Divine Judge in order that those who have sought her favour, even by paying her comparatively trifling compliments, shall suffer no eternal injury, no matter what breaches of the Divine law they may have been habitually guilty of. We can clearly see that even if we were to admit that an opinion is pious in proportion as it does honour to the Blessed Virgin, the teaching of which I speak is not really pious; and that those who thought to do her honour were really her slanderers. But then the reflection occurs, May it not be equally true that those who have thought to do God honour by exalting His power, and dwelling too exclusively on the advantage of paying Him homage, may really have given a representation degrading to His character? At all events we see how fallible a guide is the mere piety of a belief about God unless there be direct evidence for the actions we attribute to Him.

Something of the same kind may be said about charitable beliefs. Undoubtedly charity towards men has done much to correct and elevate our conceptions of God. In the early polytheistic systems, a God was the tutelary defender of the family or the nation or race. His function was to protect his clients, right or wrong; to those outside his patronage he owed no duties, and was not expected to show any tenderness. In cultured heathenism there grew up a worthier conception of God, which was confirmed and enlarged by Christianity, thinking of Him as one who has in every race of men subjects whose homage He accepts and rewards. But yet in cultured heathenism there prevailed an aristocratic theory of religion, which also passed on into Christianity, which, if it did not limit God's favour by tribal or family distinctions, yet practically regarded God's love as only exhibited to a certain aristocracy of the human race. The contempt which the Grecian philosopher felt for the vulgar had its counterpart in the pride of the Jewish rabbi who exclaimed, "This people which knoweth not the law are cursed." When men of thought and culture embraced Christianity it was painful to them to think that they must put themselves on a level with the common herd, over whom they regarded themselves as elevated by the original bounty of nature. They had been from their birth "pneumatici," endowed with a spiritual nature not possessed by the merely carnal, who were doomed to annihilation on the dissolution of their bodily frame, or the "psychici" who could at most aspire to a position in the future world immensely below their own. The particular theories to which I refer, in process of time died out. But other theories replaced them which owed much of their acceptance to the readiness with which men will receive doctrines which represent themselves as the special favourites of Heaven. It costs men little to believe that those who are bound to themselves by no ties of love or sympathy should equally be disregarded by the Supreme. But Christianity had revealed God as a Father, the Father of all, whose tender mercies are over all His works, and who has made of one blood all nations of men. This conception of God has produced great practical results, inspiring Christians with zeal to make efforts for the elevation and enlightenment of depressed races of men with whom they had no tie of close kindred or even of neighbourhood. But working for others is in itself enough to produce sympathy with those on whose behalf we labour; and as our sphere of love for others is enlarged, it is inevitable that theories also should be affected as to the dealings of God with His creatures whom we are persuaded He loves with love far greater than ours. Thus it would appear that there is a legitimate place for charitable beliefs. The judgment we pass on evidence as to the dealings of God must be influenced by the conception we have formed as to the character of God; and as our charity, that is our love to others, increases, so is our belief in God's love heightened, and our disinclination to think of Him as doing anything inconsistent with love.

But here again we are bound to keep in mind man's inability to judge of the Divine plans, or to pretend that he can measure the attributes of God. There are in fact two ways in which God reveals Himself to us, showing Himself to us in different aspects, both of which we know must be true, and yet which we cannot always reconcile with each other. There is God as He reveals Himself in the study of physical nature, One working by fixed laws which will make no allowance for ignorance or oversight, but will exact their penalty to the full if they are violated ; One who places His creatures in positions of unequal advantage, and permits the weaker to be crushed out by the stronger ; whose rule is reward for the obedient, punishment for the disobedient, without any allowance for circumstances which might seem to make disobedience excusable. And there is God as He reveals Himself to our moral nature ; for we cannot imagine that He who has given us that nature should Himself be without the qualities which he Has taught us to approve and love. He must then be One who hates injustice, who does not willingly afflict, One who if experience did not teach us to the contrary we might imagine would be too loving ever to inflict punishment. We shall certainly be misled ourselves, and shall mislead others, if we allow our minds to dwell on one of these aspects of God to the exclusion of the other. Painful as it is to us to inflict suffering ourselves, or to see others suffering, we shall find ourselves preaching peace when there is no peace if we venture to contradict the experience of the wise man, " Though a sinner do evil a hundred times, and his days be prolonged, yet surely I know that it shall be well with them that fear God, which fear before Him : but it shall not be well with the wicked, neither shall he prolong his days, which are as a shadow ; because he feareth not God." The whole experience of the world cries out against us if we venture to comfort the sinner with the assurance that if he continues in his sin God will be too merciful to punish him, and it must be well with him at the last. Our belief in the mercy of God teaches us a different exhortation. " As I live, saith the Lord God, I have no pleasure in the death of the wicked ; but that the wicked turn from his way and live : therefore turn ye, turn ye from your evil ways ; for why will ye die, O house of Israel ? " " I have no pleasure in the death of him that dieth, saith the Lord God ; therefore turn yourselves, and live ye."

XIII

SLAVERY[1]

"Whatsoever ye do, do it heartily, as to the Lord, and not unto men; knowing that of the Lord ye shall receive the reward of the inheritance: for ye serve the Lord Christ."—COLOSSIANS iii. 23, 24.

THE circumstances of this pulpit suggest to the preacher, and sometimes impose on him, a treatment of his subject different from that which would elsewhere be suitable. In congregations, scarcely any of whose members has been disquieted by difficulties as to the authority of Revelation, and who have had little occasion to consider objections, either for the purpose of satisfying their own doubts or those of others, the preacher finds sufficient employment in interpreting Scripture, in eliciting from it the doctrines which Christians ought to believe, and in enforcing on them the duties which they ought to practise. In this place, however, one cannot always shut one's ears to the noise of controversy. In addressing an

[1] In deference to the opinion of a friend, this sermon is included in this collection, though preached so long ago as 1864.

audience, many of whom must expect hereafter to be called on to reply to objections which assailants of our faith have raised, the preacher's duty is not always completely discharged by the exposition of a text, and the drawing from it its practical lessons. Where the moral teaching of part of Scripture has been censured as erroneous or inadequate, it becomes necessary to notice such objections, and to examine their validity. The passage chosen for my text conveys teaching to which it might be imagined that no objection could be made. Few parts of the Bible are more thoroughly imbued with the practical spirit of Christianity—a religion which worships God less by pompous rite or solemn sacrifice than by the constant recognition of His presence. The religions of old might be dissevered from the business of daily life. By costly offerings and the payment of other honours to the gods, the reputation of great piety could be acquired, though the character was disfigured by dishonesty, deceit, impurity. Christianity has instituted a worship of God, performed not in occasional rite, but in the discharge of daily recurring duties; it has instituted a sacrifice nobler than that of costly hecatombs, the sacrifice of self. In the text, and other passages of Scripture, the Christian's daily work is consecrated. Every task which men impose is to be done heartily, not in order to please men, but to gain the commendation of a greater Master, who promises a higher reward than any earthly prize. The work of one whose religion is of this practical character will not be eye service; it will not be performed showily and ostentatiously,—done well when praise can be earned by it, and slurred over when shortcomings are likely to be unnoticed; but all will be discharged conscientiously as in the sight of Him before whom all things are naked and open. And the reward of his work depends not on the construction which men put on it, is not liable to be lost by their neglect and injustice, not even by his own want of ability to bring to a successful issue labours to which he has earnestly devoted such powers as God has endowed him with, but will be given him by One who knows his strength and his weakness, and who will graciously accept imperfect services if heartily rendered in obedience to His command. The rule of conduct then given in the text, if considered as a general rule for Christians, must commend itself to the approval of all as one which, if followed, must increase both the usefulness and the happiness of those who act by it.

But it is objected that this rule, however excellent in general, was not the advice which the Apostle ought to have given to the particular class whom he was addressing in the part of this Epistle from which the text is taken. The text is taken from one of those practical parts of St. Paul's Epistles in which he deduces from the general principles of the Christian religion rules of conduct for persons in every condition of life: rules of conduct for husbands and wives, parents and children, masters and *slaves*. What is complained[1] of is that in dealing with this last class, the Apostle omits to teach that the whole relation connecting them and their masters is unchristian and immoral: he does not command the masters to manumit their slaves; he does not teach the slaves that their masters' claims on them are founded on robbery, and are only to be regarded when the superior strength by which they are enforced cannot be resisted. Paul and Peter, complains Mr. Francis Newman, deliver excellent charges to masters in regard to the treatment of their slaves, but without any hint to them that there is an injustice in claiming them as slaves at all. On the contrary, Paul directs the slaves to obey their masters cheerfully, and render them service conscientiously and ungrudgingly; to count their masters worthy of all honour; if they have believing masters, not

---

[1] The complaints referred to were contained in a section of Mr. F. H. Newman's *Phases of Faith*, a book much read at the time this sermon was preached.

to be tempted by their equality of Christian privileges to despise them: while again Peter directs them to be subject not only to the good and gentle, but also to the froward, and if they suffer wrongfully to think on the wrongful sufferings which Christ endured, and bear it patiently. St. Paul indeed on one occasion[1] uses language the ambiguity of which leaves it doubtful whether he would recommend slaves to accept their freedom even if it were offered them. In any case they were not to care for their servile condition. In the most essential point they were on an equality with their masters. If the slave were a believer, he was a freeman in Christ; while his master could have no greater glory than if he could boast with truth that he was Christ's servant.

There can be no doubt as to the practical wisdom of the course adopted by the preachers of Christianity. Counting, as they probably did, the majority of their disciples among the poor, and no small number among this despised order of slaves, whatever teaching they gave this body must have speedily made itself felt in practical consequences through multitudes of households. Had the Apostles taught the slaves to think lightly of their masters' claims, they would have at once arrayed against their religion all the prejudices and all the

---

[1] 1 Corinthians vii. 21.

interests of the rich. They would have really deserved the title of men that turned the world upside down if they gave countenance to servile insurrection. And the persecution against them, which was often bitter enough when proceeding merely from the wantonness of popular dislike and wounded religious feeling, would have been so formidable as, humanly speaking, to be irresistible if urged by the spite of powerful men who had personal injuries to avenge, and if supported by the moral indignation which would be felt against men who were undermining the whole fabric of society. By their actual teaching on the other hand, they doubtless dissipated prejudice and gained converts in the wealthier classes. One of the motives urged on the slaves in order to deter them from misconduct is the discredit which their ill-doing would bring on their religion. They were to please their masters well, and show them good fidelity, that they may "adorn the doctrine of God our Saviour in all things," and in order "that the name of God and His doctrine may not be blasphemed"—may not be evil spoken of. And no doubt in many a household the attention of the master must have been arrested by discovering that a worthless slave had become profitable; that one who before had been untrustworthy, doing his work with eye service, had become scrupulously conscientious in the discharge of his duty, performing his service with good fidelity. We may consider it to be certain that such a change must have frequently occurred. One of the reasons why slave labour has been pronounced to be economically wasteful is that it is as a general rule reluctant labour. It can be relied on only as long as, and as far as, the slave works under the master's eye. The slave has no motive for doing more than he can help, or for improving his capacities of work. His master's interest is not his. And though the attachment of slaves to kind masters may have caused exceptions to the general rule, we can scarcely doubt that the masters in those days must have had frequent occasion to complain of the laziness, self-indulgence, and dishonesty exhibited by their servants whenever they seemed to have a prospect of impunity. But the conduct of such servants must inevitably have altered under the influence of a new motive, namely, passionate zeal for a newly-embraced religion,—a religion which must have had peculiar attractions for men in their despised condition, because it taught that God was no respecter of persons, and that in Christ all distinctions of nation or of social condition are done away. This religion which placed them on a footing of perfect equality with the freemen who were members of it, still made it their duty to show good fidelity to their own masters, and it is likely that with the view of commending to others the faith which they loved, they would heartily fulfil this duty urged on them by their religious teachers. The change of conduct produced by this new principle of action must in some instances have been astounding, and in many quite striking enough to arrest the attention of the master. The contempt would thus be dissipated which he would otherwise have felt for the miserable superstition of his wretched servant; for he would be forced to own that a belief of whose beneficial influence he had practical experience must have something in it which deserved to be attended to. Thus the institution of domestic servitude afforded connecting links by means of which Christianity could more easily pass from the inferior to the governing classes of society; for when it was once embraced by the lowest member of a household, his exemplary life might cause the leaven to spread until the whole was leavened.

Christianity, however, would have no cause for triumph in any success obtained by a compromise of principle. If she made progress in any age by conniving at wrong, by abstaining from denouncing the selfish greed of the wealthy or the tyranny of the powerful, she must pay dearly for her temporary victory by forfeiting the respect of subsequent and more enlightened ages. We must ask then, Has the course taken by the preachers of Christianity in respect of the institution of slavery inflicted this lasting discredit on the religion? In the first place, it will be admitted by all that it was not worldly policy which inspired the teaching of the Apostles on this subject. They sought not to please men; they disguised no doctrine of the Gospel through the fear of offending men. The course they took in this matter certainly did tend to the furtherance of their religion, but no one, I think, accuses them of having, for the sake of this advantage, knowingly kept back important moral truth. Their instructions to this class of their disciples flowed naturally from the other parts of their system of doctrine. Their morality was not only on the level of the age in which they lived, but very much above it. Mr. Newman tells us that no Christian of those days seems to have suspected that slavery as a system was essentially immoral. It is understood, then, that there is no charge against the first preachers of Christianity of wilful reserve of what they knew to be truth. The charge is not against them, but against the Divine inspiration which they claimed. The objection is, that if God had inspired them and commissioned them as teachers, He would not have allowed them to content themselves with giving good advice to masters to treat their slaves humanely; He must have made them aware of the essential iniquity of the whole system of slavery, and could not have permitted them to acquiesce in it even for a season.

But in the second place, I would observe that it must also be granted that the teaching of Christianity is, in principle, hostile to the system of slavery; that it undermined it and led to its overthrow. One of the primary doctrines of Christianity is that God is no respecter of persons, and that all are equal before Him. When Christianity burst through the barrier of hatred and prejudice which separated Jew from Gentile, it levelled at the same time every other social distinction. In our careless reading of the Bible we scarcely think what a social revolution was implied when an apostle wrote the words, "By one Spirit are we all baptized into one body, whether we be Jew or Gentile, whether we be bond or free." Or again, "As many of you as have been baptized into Christ have put on Christ. There is neither Jew nor Greek, there is neither bond nor free, there is neither male nor female: for ye are all one in Christ Jesus." The strongest barriers which separated nation from nation and class from class are here thrown down. And this was no mere verbal acknowledgment of unity. It was not that masters and slaves, nominal professors of the same faith, worshipped the same God in congregations apart from one another. The pressure of persecution from common enemies drew them closely together. Master acknowledged slave as not now a servant, but above a servant, as a brother beloved. In one little assembly they met together, they gave and received the kiss of peace, and shared with each other the memorials of their Saviour's dying love. When masters and servants were bound together by such bonds as these, cruel treatment was out of the question, and manumission was a mere question of time.

It has been objected that though the genius of Christianity was undoubtedly hostile to slavery in the case I have supposed, namely, where the slave was a Christian and a brother, it claimed freedom not for men but only for Christians; and the writer from whom I quote argues elaborately against the doctrine that pagans have not human rights. But it must be borne in mind how much was implied when Christianity opened its arms to the servile class. The slave, though a pagan, could not be considered by his Christian master as a chattel. He was a man: one capable of Christianity, one included in the Saviour's command to preach the Gospel to every creature, one whom it was the master's duty to win over, if he could, to the service of Christ. And in point of fact we know that slavery, which was universal over the civilised world when Christianity was first published, did gradually, though it must be owned very slowly, disappear under her influence. As Christians gained civil power, the harshness of bondage was mitigated, manumission was encouraged, and was placed by Constantine under the special superintendence of the clergy. As years went on, ecclesiastical influence was strenuously exerted against all forms of serfdom, so that there can be no doubt that it was in the name of religion the fetters of the slave have been struck off in some of the principal countries of Europe. Some thirty or forty years ago, no doubt would have been entertained of the opposition between slavery and Christianity. Where slavery was retained, it was either among men who made no pretensions to be governed by the restraints of religion in their conduct, or else as a necessity felt to be painful, and hoped to be only temporary. But when zealous men insisted that emancipation should not be a mere dream of the future, but that some practical steps should be taken towards effecting it, then, under the pressure of controversy, the slave-owner became bolder. It was discovered that slavery was an institution, in itself desirable as most conducive to the material prosperity of certain countries and to the education and civilisation of inferior races. It was urged that slavery, so far from being formally condemned by the Bible, was throughout sanctioned by it : that the patriarchs, Abraham and Isaac and Jacob, were slaveholders ; that the Jewish code of laws contained provisions legitimising slavery and regulating the control of master over his servant ; that neither our Lord nor His Apostles ever intimated that the system of slavery, which they found existing in the society of their day, was morally wrong ; that a fugitive slave was sent back by St. Paul to his master, and that all the Christian teachers exhorted their converts of servile rank quietly to obey their earthly masters. Nothing was more startling to those who were carrying on a crusade against slavery in the name of religion than to see the venerable authority of Scripture alleged against them, and to find themselves challenged to produce a single text where the institution of slavery was in terms condemned. And then it came to pass that benevolent men, not able to meet this challenge to their satisfaction, disappointed with the Bible for its lukewarm or doubtful advocacy of the cause of humanity, were shaken in their faith in the Divine authority of the Book. They felt that if it were true that the Bible sanctioned a system so full of wickedness as the rapine and murder springing out of slave-hunting in Africa, the horrors of the middle passage, the occasional acts of cruelty or tyrannous lust (some instances of which are inseparable from the exercise of irresponsible power), the degradation of the enslaved race who were treated as having no more rights against their master than any other of his domesticated animals, the attempt to keep that degradation permanent by denying them education: many benevolent men felt, I say, that if the Bible sanctioned such a system as this, it would prove, not that these things were right, but that the Bible did not come from God.

The opponents of Revelation then caught up and used the objection. I have already mentioned the name of Mr. Francis Newman as having urged this among other instances of the moral imperfection of Christianity. More recently the feelings of another student of the Mosaic code[1] have been shocked by laws on the subject of slavery: the law, for example, which gives no right to a servant on recovering his freedom to claim also the freedom of a female

[1] Bishop Colenso.

slave who may have been given him for his wife, or of the children whom she may have borne him, and the law which inflicts no penalty on the master who may have caused the death of his slave by immoderate punishment, provided that some interval of time has elapsed between the punishment and the death.

From these objections I feel much more solicitous to vindicate the Apostles' precepts than the ordinances of the Mosaic Law. Moses was not only a religious teacher but a civil legislator. His books contain not only the Jewish religion, but their code of civil and criminal laws. The seventh Article of our Church declares that the law given from God by Moses as touching ceremonies and rites does not bind Christian men, and that the civil precepts thereof are not of necessity to be received in any commonwealth. And I make no difficulty in admitting that certain things which we find in the Old Testament were permitted to the Jews, would not now be considered as reconcilable with Christian morality. I may mention in addition to the regulations concerning slavery already quoted, freedom of divorce, polygamy, severity in the usages of war, if not directly sanctioned by the law, at least practised by pious kings, and recorded without any reprobation by the historian.

Our Lord Himself has given us the explanation of this laxity. He has taught us that the morality of this code was not the highest possible, but the highest which the Jewish nation was then capable of receiving. "For the hardness of your hearts Moses wrote you this precept."

And yet there can be little doubt but that that Jewish code, some of the imperfections of which suggest difficulties to the mind of a Christian reader, was felt to be, in moral elevation, far above any previous legislation. The Jewish law-giver could, with well-founded confidence, put the challenge, "What nation is there so great that hath statutes and judgments so righteous as all this law which I set before you this day?" This very law concerning slavery which has just come under our discussion, I have no doubt struck those to whom it was given as remarkable for its humane care of the slave. The novelty then, no doubt, was that a master should be called to account at all for his treatment of his slave. The law did not permit the master, as he may have fancied he had a right, to do what he would with his own. If by a blow to a slave he struck out a tooth, he was compelled to give him his liberty in compensation. If he killed him, vengeance must surely be taken. And I see no reason to doubt that Jewish commentators are right in understanding the word to denote that the same vengeance for blood was to be taken as if the sufferer were a freeman. Let this legislation be judged not by a Christian standard, but let it be compared with that of nations far above the Jews in civilisation. How many centuries of Rome's greatness elapsed before the law gave protection to a slave against his master! I could tell of many laws, some of them cruel enough, to protect a master against his slaves. I might refer to the law which made slaves responsible for the life of their masters, and ordained that in case of the murder of a master all slaves within a certain distance should be held to have had it in their power to prevent it if they would, and which put all to death, once as many as four hundred at a time, without inquiry as to their guilt or innocence.[1] And I might refer to the anecdote told by Cicero of the rigorous enforcement of the rule that forbade slaves to carry a weapon; how when a shepherd slave had slain a mighty boar and expected praise and reward, he was sent to crucifixion because the deed convicted him of having been in possession of a hunting spear.[2] How many centuries of Rome's greatness passed before that Edict of Antoninus which in the case that a master causelessly put

[1] Tacitus, *Annal.* xiv. 42.   [2] *In Verr.* Act II. v. 3.

his slave to death, inflicted on him the same punishment as if he had injured the property of another. And possibly it is not quite reasonable to complain that the judicial processes of rude, and at the time nomade tribes, were inadequate to determine points on which we, with our more complicated methods, can venture to pronounce; that they did not undertake, by a lengthened investigation and the examination of medical witnesses, to decide whether a death following an injury, after some interval, were positively caused by that injury, and that when the sufferer was a slave, the law was content with the presumption that the master would not wilfully destroy what he had bought with his money.

As I have said, we are in no way concerned to maintain that the Jewish code was absolutely the most humane possible, and the most rigorously equitable, if there are reasonable grounds for thinking that it was relatively the best, having respect to the time when and the people to whom it was given. Our acknowledgment that the laws of Moses do not of necessity bind every Christian commonwealth is in fact an admission that in different times, and under different circumstances, other laws may be better than these. I am therefore content to vindicate Christianity from the imputations which have been cast on it, without endeavouring to maintain that the Mosaic code contained that recognition of the perfectly equal rights of all men before God which Christian teaching has made so familiar to us. As Christians we have no difficulty in ascribing, not indeed error, but incompleteness, to that earlier revelation which we now know was intended to be largely supplemented by a further declaration of God's will.

I suppose it might be maintained that the apology which has been made for defective teaching in the Jewish code might also apply to the teaching of the Apostles. Supposing, what I do not admit, that our morality has risen above the level of their teaching, it may be said that they will be excused if their teaching were the highest which the men of their day were capable of receiving. I do not admit, I say, that we have risen above the moral teaching of the Apostles, because I do not hold that the revelation of God's will made in the Gospel was intended to be succeeded by any other destined to supplement its imperfections. If the moral tone of society be in any respects more elevated among us than it was in the first century, the cause is ultimately to be referred to the teaching of the Christian preachers. If, for instance, the dislike of slavery be greater with us than with them, the reason is, not that we have received any new revelation of the will of God, but only that we have more thoroughly apprehended all that was involved in what the Apostles taught of God's equal regard for all His creatures, and in our Lord's precept to do to others as we would that they should do to us. But still it would go some way towards justifying the Apostles for omitting to enforce a precept if it could be shown that the insisting on it would have caused the general rejection of the religion, and would have had pernicious effects on the conduct of those even who received it. I have already shown that if we admit the truth of the doctrine that slavery, in any form and under any circumstances, is absolutely unlawful, we must still confess that the minds of men in the first century were not ripe for this truth ; that a religion that inculcated it would be met by opposition apparently insurmountable ; and that the preaching of this doctrine might justly be deemed pernicious if it led to servile insurrection which, whether it succeeded or failed, would be likely to cause worse evils than slavery itself.

Mr. Newman, indeed, contends that the preachers of Christianity might, without any fear of dangerous consequences, have taught the absolute unlawfulness of slavery as part of their religion. He urges that the Quakers in America refuse to hold slaves, and teach that slave-holding is essentially immoral, and yet that these doctrines have caused no political convulsion. This, indeed, was written a few years ago, and perhaps would not be so confidently repeated now. He argues that if Peter and Paul and James and John had done as these Quakers, the imperial administration would have looked on it as a harmless eccentricity of the sect, and not as an incentive to sedition. The Romans, he says, practised fornication at pleasure, and held it ridiculous to blame them. If Paul had claimed authority to hinder them, they might have been greatly exasperated; but they had not the least objection to his denouncing fornication as immoral to Christians. Why not slavery also?

It is very strange that a writer, by no means wanting in acuteness, should not have seen the obvious answer to this question. The doctrine of the essential immorality of slavery bears a very different aspect when it is preached to slaveholders and when it is preached to slaves. It might be, no doubt, but a harmless eccentricity if the members of the new sect determined that they would give liberty to all their slaves. But since we have good grounds to think that there were far more poor than rich among the Christian converts, and that there were found among them many of the servile class, to teach the absolute immorality of slavery to men like this would be felt to be no harmless eccentricity. If the Quakers in America merely refused to hold slaves themselves it might be regarded as a harmless eccentricity; but if they proceeded to propagate abolitionist doctrine among the slaves, it would have been resented as an incentive to sedition. If St. Paul, instead of sending Onesimus back to his master, had told him that he was perfectly right in running away, who can doubt what practical inference the multitude of Christian slaves would draw, and that the example would be imitated as far as they dared? Now, the question is not whether it was a good thing that slavery should be abolished, but whether this would have been the right way to proceed to abolish it.

I have said that if the Christian preachers had inculcated the absolute immorality of slavery under all circumstances, it would have been regarded as an incentive to sedition; but the seditious tendency of such teaching is even stronger than might have been supposed. For what was the whole Roman empire at that time but one vast system of slavery! Tacitus describes the assemblage of the nations subject to Rome as one great "famulatus orbis terrarum;" each nation being held by the ruling state in bondage as severe as a household slave under his master. But the citizens of the ruling state itself were then in no better condition. The word despotism, by which we describe the nature of the authority that was exercised over them, implies that their relation towards their ruler was that of slaves to a master. It was in vain that Augustus professed his dislike of the title Dominus. His successors for the most part did, without any restraint save what the fear of assassination might suggest, give free indulgence to their cruelty or their lust, and acted as if they counted not their subjects to have a right to property or liberty or life when it was their will to take them. If it was the duty of the Apostles to teach that no human being is justified under any circumstances in being the δεσπότης of another, the doctrine of the immorality of slavery must have drawn as a corollary the immorality of the whole system of government which existed at the time. It would have been the duty of the Apostles to teach, as part of their religion, a republican theory of political philosophy. It would have been their duty to declare themselves irreconcilable enemies of the then ruling powers, and to invite all the assaults which would have been suggested by the terrors of a government concerned to put down a sect openly conspiring against its existence. Humanly speaking, then, we may say that if the Apostles had preached the doctrine which it is asserted they ought to have preached, the first sparks of their religion would have been trampled out before it ever could have spread.

But then, it may be asked, Does not the view here taken represent the Apostles if not as designedly holding back a truth which they ought to have published, at least as left by God in ignorance of it? And is it not incredible that if they were truly inspired by God such ignorance could have existed? Can we conceive God as conniving at essential immorality? And if it is to be granted, as it apparently must, that the publication of the truth would have excited such opposition as would, humanly speaking, have been insurmountable; still what is impossible with men is possible with God. And we ought rather to expect that He would work a miracle than that He would give even a temporary sanction to wrong. We cannot, then, wholly evade the question, Is slavery essentially immoral in the same way that fornication and lying and evil speaking are immoral? Is it absolutely impossible for a Christian under any circumstances to have anything to do with slavery? and ought the new converts, on coming to a knowledge of the truth, to have at once abandoned slaveholding in the same way as they abandoned the other evil practices of which I have spoken, and which were admitted by heathen without scruple?

Now it is a difficult thing, though one is sometimes obliged to do it, to find fault with bad arguments used in a good cause. There is danger of seeming to defend or to sympathise with the wrong when you try to show the weakness of some of the weapons which good men have wielded against it. It has been imagined that the course of recent events has inclined the people of this country to look on slavery with less abhorrence than before: that our admiration of the struggles of slaveholders trying to assert their national independence against opponents with immense material advantages, or our dislike of the arrogance of those opponents, and our fear that their too great strength may be dangerous to ourselves; our discovery that in very many cases slaves have been faithful to their masters under strong temptation to escape or revolt, and therefore may be presumed to be not dissatisfied with their treatment; it has been imagined, I say, that these causes may have inclined us to abate our aversion to the whole system, and to give a more favourable hearing to what can be said in defence of it. English travellers have reported that the negro race are naturally so indolent that they require a taskmaster to teach them submission to the great law of labour; and they have asserted that the negroes in America enjoy more material prosperity, have attained a higher civilisation and a greater knowledge of Christianity, than if they had continued in their own land, and therefore that they are gainers by the change.

Notwithstanding all this, I quite disbelieve that the aversion of the English people to slavery has been mitigated, and when I go over in my mind the arguments which we formerly used against slavery in order to find whether what we then said had any weight in it, or whether we are to own that we talked idly and foolishly about what we did not understand, it seems to me that time has made no change in them, and that what we thought conclusive before is conclusive still. God certainly often causes the wicked actions of men to result in beneficial consequences; and yet this does not justify us in sinning against our light in the confidence that He will turn all to greater good. If we admit that the negroes who are carried away from Africa gain by the change, who can venture to say that their gain compensates for the injury done to Africa by the slave trade in the resulting insecurity, mutual hostility, and destruction of lawful commerce? Besides that, the alleged gain itself is questionable; for a calculation that another man is the gainer by being deprived of liberty is not trustworthy if you who make the calculation have a strong interest in taking away his freedom and in keeping him so degraded that he will not wish for freedom nor know how to use it. I have, therefore, not a word to say in defence of slavery; but if it be asserted on the other hand that no man has, under any circumstances, a right to interfere with the freedom of another, I cannot assent to a principle stated so broadly. For all law is an interference with the liberty of the individual, and it is hard to fix limits to the extent to which that interference may proceed. In States supposed to be the freest, when the good of the community is believed to require it, law will deprive the individual of freedom of speech, will take from him the money he has earned, and will apply it to purposes of which he disapproves; will deprive him of freedom and send him against his will to fight as a soldier in a cause which he condemns. Law may indeed become so oppressive as to justify the subject in refusing his obedience; but the Bible is no book of casuistry, and we need no more expect it to lay down rules when subjects are justified in rebelling than when children ought to disobey their parents. It teaches in strong language the duty of reverence to law, seeing that human law is to be regarded as God's ordinance. In places where law sanctions slavery, as was the case where the Apostle wrote, it might conceivably be the duty of a Christian to keep slaves ; for if those of whom he found himself possessed had, as often happens, been so debased by slavery as to be unable to use freedom, sudden restoration to freedom might be very injurious, and their master might do better by keeping them for a time in subjection, and training them for freedom. If the master were really a Christian in heart as well as in profession,—one who was determined to use his power for no selfish ends, and to do to his servants as he would they should do to him,—power intrusted to such a man could not be abused. I believe it will be found on consideration that the Bible is not to be censured but rather commended for abstaining from deciding what forms of government are the best, and what are the exact limits to the authority which one man is justified in exercising over another ; for that some such authority must be exercised is undeniable. And I believe it did right also in shielding with the sanction of religion the authority of human law, and in deciding that the abolition of slavery must take place not in opposition to law, but by means of law : not by inciting individuals to disobedience, but by instilling principles which when received forced those in power to love and respect their poorer brethren, and so purified law by degrees from all that is oppressive and tyrannical.

The polemical discussion into which we have been led has carried us away from the region of practice ; yet it will not have been without some practical fruit if it have fastened more firmly in your memories and hearts the great rule which I have chosen as my text ; for the lessons of the Gospel come with equal force to men in every rank in life. There can be no better rule to regulate our discharge of the duties which fall to our lot than that which the Apostle gave for the conduct of slaves : that we too should do our work, not with eye-service as men-pleasers, but striving to commend ourselves to the approval of Christ whose purchased servants we are, whose benefits demand of us that we should show our gratitude by doing His will, and whose all-seeing eye cannot be deceived. "Whatsoever ye do, do it heartily, as to the Lord, and not unto men."

XIV

THE INTERPRETATION OF SCRIPTURE

"The Son of man shall come in the glory of His Father, with His angels; and then He shall reward every man according to his works."—MATTHEW xvi. 27.

"For by grace are ye saved through faith; and that not of yourselves: it is the gift of God: not of works, lest any man should boast."—EPHESIANS ii. 8, 9.

IT has been often remarked that the advocates of opposite doctrinal systems find no difficulty in each supporting his views by Scripture texts; and, accordingly, at the time of the Reformation, a leading Roman Catholic divine irreverently compared the Bible to a nose of wax which any one can twist into what shape he chooses. At the time when this comparison was made, there was far more justice in it than now. For there was then current a system of mystical and allegorical interpretation, which indeed had been handed down under the authority of some fathers of great antiquity and of the highest reputation, but by which it was possible for an ingenious man to find any doctrine in any text.

The principles, indeed, from which this method of interpretation started were such as might readily be granted by Christians, namely, that God's method of revelation was progressive; that truths were clearly made known to men of a later age of which their predecessors had had but dim perceptions; and yet that all was a continuous plan, and so that even to early times obscure intimations had been given of truths afterwards to be distinctly revealed. In particular that the Jewish dispensation spoke in type and shadow of the salvation afterwards to be revealed through Christ. The New Testament writers had given their sanction to the discovery, in Mosaic ordinances or in sayings of the ancient prophets, of a deeper meaning than was understood in the ages when these prophecies were delivered,—deeper, perhaps, than was understood by the prophets who had delivered them. Christian interpreters of the Old Testament could not then avoid putting to themselves the question, Are we limited to find Christ only in those typical or prophetical passages where the sacred writers of the New Testament have authorised us to find Him, or may we not follow out for ourselves the principles of interpretation on which they appear to have acted?

There is a multitude of Old Testament passages in which Christian interpreters of all ages have not hesitated to find a Messianic reference, although without any express authority from the New Testament for doing so ; a multitude of Old Testament institutions or incidents in which they have seen Christ prefigured, and have not doubted that the undeniable correspondence between type and antitype had been foreseen and ordained by the common author of the two dispensations. It would therefore be felt to be an overstringent rule if we were to insist on New Testament authority before we admitted any Messianic reference in our interpretation of the Old Testament.

Yet when the bounds assigned by such a rule have been passed, it has been found hard to keep interpretation within the limits of sobriety. Take, for example, Justin Martyr, one of the earliest of Christian writers, a great number of whose interpretations passed into the common stock of patristical exegesis. His own conversion had been mainly effected by the argument from prophecy ; yet a modern reader would reject, as strained, his interpretation of several passages which seem to him clearly Messianic ; and in his controversy with a Jewish opponent we cannot pronounce him uniformly successful. Nearly the same may be said of another second century writer, Irenæus, a man by no means deficient either in sobriety or good sense, and from whose interpretations, therefore, we are obliged to dissent, mainly on account of a difference in principle as to how far it is permissible to disregard the context or the original drift of an Old Testament passage which seems capable of a Messianic application. It will suffice to give one example of an interpretation which a modern commentator would reject without ceremony, and yet which many ancient commentators thought worth borrowing. In the terrible description given in Deuteronomy xxviii. of the sufferings which would follow if the Jewish nation rejected the Divine commands, we read, " Thy life shall hang in doubt before thee ; and thou shalt fear day and night, and shalt have none assurance of thy life : in the morning thou shalt say, Would God it were even ! and at even thou shalt say, Would God it were morning !" Here, instead of the commonplace interpretation of the words, " Thy life shall hang in doubt before thee," which the context suggests to us, the words, " Thy life shall hang," were taken as a plain prediction that Christ, who is our life, should hang upon the tree.[1]

It will easily be understood, however, that

[1] Iren. *Haer.* iv. 10 ; v. 18.

there is a number of passages which a modern Christian advocate would not venture to produce in controversy with an opponent, and yet which commend themselves to his own judgment as distinctly prophetical, or, at least, where he cannot reject as wholly fanciful the deeper meaning read into the text by early expositors. In truth it is not always easy to judge of the goodness of arguments advanced to prove a conclusion which we know to be true. They may, in our opinion, come short of being a logical proof, and therefore we may think it prudent to refrain from using them in controversy with an opponent, and yet we cannot bring ourselves to reject them as worthless, and they may sensibly add to the strength of our own conviction. If, therefore, the method of interpretation of which I speak had never been applied except to the establishment of doctrines which we believe to be true, we should probably have been content to accept it as in the main sound, and perhaps have hesitated to condemn the most violent wresting of a passage from its context in order to establish a true doctrine; being willing to surmise that those were not wholly wrong who discovered mysterious depths in Scripture likely to escape the notice of a hasty or irreverent reader.

But, naturally, they who used the allegorical

method of interpretation, employed it to elicit the doctrines not which we believe to be true, but which they themselves believed to be true; some of them to prove doctrines which no Christian of the present day believes to be true. When the Gnostics of the second century were challenged to give proof of the wild dreams which they had incorporated with the Christian scheme, while some of them appealed to secret traditions which they claimed to have derived from the Apostles, and while they rejected all the parts of the New Testament which were inconvenient to their system, one school, that of Valentinus, accepted the same canon of Scripture as the Catholic Church, but applying to it the current methods of interpretation, had no difficulty in finding Scripture proof of all the peculiarities of their system. Large fragments remain of a commentary on St. John emanating from this school; and it would be hard to say that the exegesis which made a Valentinian of St. John was more forced, or that it differed essentially in character from that which orthodox writers had made use of with general approbation.

Similarly, in later times, Roman Catholic interpreters have not been content with repeating the proofs which early fathers had found, in unexpected texts, of doctrines which we all hold in common. It has been equally easy for them to establish by Scripture proof the most recent novelties of their system. The authority of the Pope has been found in the first chapter of Genesis; the immaculate conception of the Virgin Mary in the Song of Solomon. What, then, is to guide us in our adoption of Scripture proofs? On what grounds can it be maintained that the Catholic interpretation was right and the Gnostic indefensible?

A little study of the feats which interpreters of different schools have performed is enough to convince one that the Roman Catholic illustration which I quoted in the beginning by no means exaggerates the plasticity of Scripture when the allegorical method of interpretation is applied to it. The most opposite conclusions may be derived by processes of which to an uninstructed judge one seems as legitimate as another. I don't know how one who adopts thoroughly the allegorical method of interpretation can justify the preference of his own interpretations over his rival's except by saying " My interpretations are right, because they elicit from the Bible true doctrine ; yours are wrong, because the doctrine which you derive from it is false." The practical result, then, is that instead of going to the Bible to find there the doctrine we are to believe, we must otherwise ascertain what doctrine is true, and only bring the true doctrine to the Bible to find there confirmation of our belief.

The necessary outcome of the allegorical method is the supreme authority of the Church, which both teaches the true doctrine and guarantees the legitimacy of the process by which it is derived from Scripture; and thus the decree of the Council of Trent would be justified that no man relying on his own wisdom should, in things relating to faith or morals, wrest the sacred Scriptures to his own sense contrary to that sense which has been and is held by the holy mother Church, whose province it is to judge of the true sense and interpretation of the Holy Scriptures. Again, if this allegorical method of interpretation be adopted, Cardinal Newman was quite right in saying that a Roman Catholic could subscribe to the sixth Article of the Church of England, and agree that the Church was not at liberty to teach for necessity of faith any doctrine of which she was not able to give Scripture proof. Only he explains, by "proof" you are to understand not a process of strict inference which a mere logician could pursue if not aided by the guidance of the Church, which is able to discern in Scripture testimony to the doctrines which she knows to be true, and having pointed out that testimony to her children has a right to demand that they shall receive it as proof.

Long, however, before Newman had followed the mystical method of interpreting Scripture to what I believe to be its legitimate result, he had proclaimed its vital necessity to the preservation of doctrinal truth, and had denounced the Syriac exegetical school which rejected the allegorical method as the parent of Arianism, Nestorianism, and a multitude of other heresies.[1] The birthplace of the allegorical method was Alexandria, where it was a good deal older than Christianity. With the growth of philosophy the time came when cultivated minds revolted at the absurdities and immoralities told of their divinities in the Theogony of Hesiod or in the Greek Bible, Homer. Explanations were given anticipating theories of modern times which find in the old mythologies only symbolical representations of the forces of Nature. Zeus was the æther, Hera his sister-wife was the lower air, a kindred but subordinate substance; the different fruits to which the fertilising heat of æther gives origin were symbolised in the various amours of Zeus. Each scandalous tale of incest, parricide, adultery or murder was manipulated until it was reduced to the harmless assertion of some physical

[1] *Arians of the Fourth Century*, chap. i.

fact,—explanations, however, which presented an obvious mark for the sarcasm of Christian apologists, who wondered that truths of such little value should have been wrapped in such filthy and so impenetrable disguises ; there being little to reward the initiated who were made acquainted with the true meaning of the riddles, much to scandalise the vulgar who accepted the unedifying tales as literal truth.

This device, however, of allegorical explanation was a recognised method ready for the use of Jewish apologists when their Scriptures were scrutinised in the schools of Alexandria, and when different Old Testament narratives were objected to as contrary to morality or as giving unworthy representations of God. The literal truth of the assailed narrative was given up, and the story was treated as valuable only for the sake of the deeper meaning which it symbolised. In the still extant writings of Philo, the most celebrated master of Alexandrian Judaism, the spiritual lessons derivable from the Old Testament are so dwelt on that much of the hard fact is volatilised away. In this school were trained some of the ablest and most learned of the early Christian teachers, and it was only natural that they should apply to the Old Testament, methods which their Jewish teachers had recognised as legitimate, in order to derive from it truths which unconverted Jews had been too prejudiced or too dull to discover.

It was only in the third century that there sprung up in Syria a different school of Biblical exegesis, which instead of bringing from without a meaning to be read into Scripture, strove to elicit the writer's meaning by the same aids of criticism, philology, and history as are used in the case of secular authors. I need not now inquire whether this method was not pushed too far in the direction of rationalism, and whether by fixing exclusive attention on the human element in Scripture it did not leave out of sight the Divine inspiration of the whole, refusing, for instance, to acknowledge that a prophecy could have any sense save that known and intended by the first speaker or writer of the words. But even if it had been perfectly free from blame in this respect it could not but meet opposition on its first introduction. If the interpreters of the mystical school had proceeded too far in their discovery of deeper meanings, it must have been shocking and distasteful to them when the literal school of interpreters insisted on being content with some commonplace explanation of passages which they had looked on as alive with high spiritual mysteries.

I have already mentioned how Newman attributes to this school of interpretation the fertility in heresy which he counts to be the unhappy distinction of the Syrian Church. "In all ages of the Church," he says, "her teachers have shown a disinclination to confine themselves to the mere literal interpretation of Scripture. Her most subtle and powerful method of proof, whether in ancient or modern times, is the mystical sense, which is so frequently used in doctrinal controversy as on many occasions to supersede any other. In the early centuries we find this method of interpretation to be the very ground for receiving as revealed the doctrine of the Holy Trinity. Whether we betake ourselves to the Ante-Nicene writers or the Nicene, certain texts will meet us which do not obviously refer to that doctrine, yet are put forward as palmary proofs of it." "It may almost be laid down as historical fact that the mystical interpretation and orthodoxy will stand or fall together."[1]

I believe that both in the case of Newman and also in that of the great glory of the Alexandrian school, Origen, fondness for the allegorical method had its root in the sceptical character of the critics' intellect. Feeling strongly the force of objections, and perhaps attributing to them more than their due weight, troubled with doubts whether the

[1] *Essay on Development*, p. 323. *Arians*, 3d edition, p. 414.

proofs alleged by orthodox advocates would, if tried by strict logic, bear the stress laid on them, they sought some means which would make them independent of strict logical proof. Certainly in Newman's case evidence constantly presents itself that it was despair of the success of what he accounts orthodoxy in the open field which has driven him to construct fortresses which he imagines she can hold securely as her own.

The Syrian school of exegesis can boast of several eminent commentators, including all those whom a modern reader finds most profit in studying, and it certainly succeeded in preventing the literal sense of Scripture from ever being totally ignored; but through the greater part of the Middle Ages (taking that word in a very wide sense), the allegorical method predominated, the mystical sense of Scripture being that which was most valued. It is certainly the reverse in our modern times, at least in Protestant countries. The use of the allegorical method would now be tied down by cautions and safeguards. A proof by this method would only be accepted in the case of a doctrine which could establish itself independently; and there is a growing tendency, even among the most orthodox commentators, to act on the principle of interpreting the Bible on the same principles as any other book.

It might be expected, perhaps, that the effect of this change of method would be, where it took place, to bring about uniformity of interpretation and to cause the contradictions of Scripture to disappear. It was easy to have Scripture ranged against Scripture when the methods of interpretation were so lax that each theorist found no difficulty in discovering texts which countenanced his theory, and when an array of Scripture texts on one side could, with small trouble, be confronted with as powerful an array on the other, and there being little to choose between the fairness of the procedure of the respective parties. But when some uniformity of agreement is arrived at as to principles of interpretation, if it be no longer so easy to draw opposite inferences from the same text, there is much more likelihood of finding different texts which seem to speak in opposite ways.

When the human element in Scripture was completely ignored, and all was treated as the continuous work of one Divine Author, it necessarily followed that it was impossible to admit either the occurrence of error of any kind, scientific or historical, or of any contradiction between different parts. If at any time the appearance of such presented itself, the allegorical method was able to solve the difficulty. St.

Augustine freely uses it as a canon in his interpretations of Scripture that when there appears to be what a modern interpreter might count as a contradiction between two passages, this contradiction had been divinely set as a signal flag to show that neither passage was to be understood literally, and that we were to dig below the literal sense to discover the deeper spiritual meaning concealed beneath. For example, the inscription of one of the Psalms speaks of David changing his behaviour before Abimelech, whereas the Book of Samuel names Achish as the king in question. St. Augustine infers that we are taught not to rest satisfied with the literal sense, but must inquire what is meant by these Hebrew names, and what is therein taught of Christ, to whom the whole Psalm relates.[1]

When, however, the human element in the Bible is fully acknowledged, it is known to be not a book but a library,—in other words, a collection of writings the composition of which was spread over hundreds of years. If it was a merely human work, it would be inevitable that there should be many contradictions between the views of independent thinkers, writing in different ages and under different circumstances. But

[1] *Enarr.* in Psalm xxxiii.

even when it is fully acknowledged that "the prophecy came not in old time by the will of man; but holy men of old spake as they were moved by the Holy Ghost," there remains ample room for diversities of aspect in the presentation of religious truth. The wants of one age are not those of another. The truths which it is needful loudly to proclaim are not at all times the same. If in one generation a successful battle has been made to rescue some great principle from denial or neglect, the vindicated principle runs the risk of being handed down to the next generation as a formula or a watchword repeated by men who have not entered into its spirit, and who, while they have no need to have its theoretical truth insisted on to them, may much need to be taught its practical meaning. Then, too, may come the need of insisting on counterbalancing truths which in the heat of controversy had been lost sight of,—for men's minds are seldom able to grasp several points at the same time; and when there is urgent necessity to struggle for the defence of some great truth which has been assailed, the work must be postponed to some calmer time of defining the qualifications and limitations with which the assailed principle can be asserted. Once more: in the proclamation of truth, regard must be paid to what men at the time are capable of receiving. "I have many things to say to you," said our Lord, "but ye cannot bear them now." Read the religious history of the world as it is told in the Bible, and we find a history of training and continual progress, even a lower moral code being tolerated for a time on account of the hardness of heart of those who were to accept it, and higher truths gradually delivered as the recipients were able to embrace them. That there should be differences then in the aspects of religious truth as presented by different divinely-commissioned teachers to men of different ages and of different degrees of culture is not only a thing not to be wondered at, but we should have cause to wonder if the fact were otherwise; and the only question is, whether or not these differences amount to contradictions.

But before we charge a book with being self-contradictory, we are bound to know something of the character of the book we criticise. The propositions of a scientific treatise will bear to be separated from their context, and the work may be condemned if one proposition is at variance with another; but we cannot deal in the same way with a work which is hortatory and practical. No preacher, for instance, feels himself to be guilty of inconsistency if at one time he exhorts his people to work as if everything depended on themselves; at another, to pray as if everything depended upon God. Much has the Bible been often misread when systematising theologians have caught up statements from it and attempted to draw them out to what they imagined to be their logical consequences.

In theology, as well as in other sciences, Lord Bacon's remark holds true that speculators have underrated the complexity of nature, and have been disappointed to find that its facts will not always consent to range themselves under the trim divisions they have marked out for them. The fact on which so much modern speculation has turned, that the lines of demarcation between different species are not as rigid as the early theorists had supposed, is but one of a class. When theologians have attempted to make a scientific definition of inspiration, and to classify its degrees and the various kinds of immunity from error which it confers, or when they have attempted to give a scientific account of the action of the grace of God on men's free will, they would find, if their theories were analysed, that they were showing their ignorance of the principle that the boundaries of the various provinces of nature are not sharply defined, but shaded off by insensible gradations; not here a line of light, there of absolute darkness; but between both, a penumbra such that it would not be easy to tell where the darkness ceases and the light begins. Again, it is seldom remembered that if an object be of any considerable magnitude the whole of it cannot be seen from one point of view. Possibly the attempt to sum up in a single formula a complete presentation of truth might produce something as monstrously unlike the real truth as the five-legged Assyrian bulls, which aim at enabling observers from different points of view to see all that it is supposed they ought to see. But whether such a summing up in a single formula be possible or not, the Bible does not attempt it. It is essentially a practical book, and countervailing or mutually limiting truths are presented, not simultaneously, but each in turn as the needs of the hearers require.

It is not only in religion, but in all departments of philosophy wherever controversy still reigns that different solutions of the same problem are obtained when it is attacked from opposite sides; and it is exasperating to see the confidence with which able and clear-headed men will assert conclusions, the evidence for which appears to them so plain that the denial of them must imply stupidity or dishonesty, when, in truth, the clearness of their view only arises from its narrowness, and those whom they condemn as stupid see things which they do not.

You will have understood from the texts which I read at the beginning, that what I have said in explanation of the fact that Scripture support has been claimed on behalf of opposing doctrines was intended as preliminary to a discussion of the Christian doctrine of reward, there being some texts which speak of reward as entirely gratuitous, God's free gift; others which speak of it as exactly proportioned to work. Having two Sundays at my disposal, I have thought it best to confine myself to-day to what I had to say respecting the interpretation of Scripture, leaving the discussion of the doctrine of reward to next Sunday.

XV

REWARD ACCORDING TO WORK

"The Son of man shall come in the glory of His Father, with His angels; and then He shall reward every man according to his works."—MATTHEW xvi. 27.

"For by grace are ye saved through faith; and that not of yourselves: it is the gift of God: not of works, lest any man should boast."—EPHESIANS ii. 8, 9.

ON last Sunday I attempted to give some explanation of the fact that the advocates on both sides of a controverted doctrine are so often able each to bring forward Scripture texts in support of his views. At the close of my sermon I referred to the fact that when, for the complete statement of a case, propositions which mutually limit each other must be asserted, the method of the Bible, which is pre-eminently a practical book, is not to attempt to embrace both at once in a formal scientific statement, but to dwell on each in turn as the immediate needs required of those at the time addressed. I intimated that these general observations were intended to be followed up by a particular application of them to the discussion of the Christian doctrine of merit and reward. The two verses which I prefixed as my text, suggest one obvious seeming opposition between different sides of the teaching of Scripture on this subject; and when the matter is thought over, another difficulty, less obvious, but not less perplexing, suggests itself, namely, that whereas in any scheme of reward according to work it seems almost a necessity that the recipients should form a continuous series, one member differenced from another by scarcely perceptible gradations, the Bible, as well as the theology founded on it, seems to divide men into two great classes, an immeasurable gulf dividing the lowest on the one side from the highest on the other.

To commence, then, with the first difficulty. Neither of the two verses which I read as my text can be described as an isolated passage, or can be set aside as a chance utterance at variance with the general tone of the book from which it is taken. The first is a specimen of the language on the subject of reward which clearly predominates in Scripture, though one who uses the Bible chiefly for controversial purposes may possibly be more impressed with the latter; because it happens that St. Paul had to fight very much the same battle against Judaising opponents that Protestants have had to fight with Roman Catholics, and so has had occasion to dwell on and enforce energetically some of the same truths for which we have been ourselves most anxious to contend.

Indeed, no very elaborate proof is necessary to show that any rational man who speaks of merit and reward as justly claimed by man from his Creator must use those words in a far different sense from that in which a man may be spoken of as claiming merit or reward from his fellow. We are most entitled to claim merit from another when we have done something for him which we had not been bound to do. If by our pains and labour we have conferred a benefit on him, it is reasonable to expect that he should be willing to confer on us some benefit in return, and if he has stipulated to do so, we can claim that return as a right. But the whole analogy breaks down when we apply it to our fulfilment of the Almighty's commands. What can we do for Him more than we had been bound to do? What is He the better of anything that we do for Him? If we believe in eternal life, and in the unspeakable good things which eye hath not seen nor ear heard, nor have entered into the heart of man to conceive, but God has promised to them that love Him, how can we imagine that works of ours, if ever so perfect, could be adequate to entitle us to claim a reward so far beyond the equivalent of our well-doing? And what works of ours are perfect? Human works must be seen from a great distance before any one can think of attributing to them perfection. If we are tempted sometimes to attribute that quality to the good deeds of some whom we admire from afar, what shall we say of those good deeds which we know most intimately—our own? Good works! Many of us would have to limit our claim to the merit of good intentions. For of the good resolutions we form how few are carried out to perfection! Some forgotten almost as soon as formed; some carried out for a time, but found too irksome to be persevered in; some fair-weather resolutions, sufficient when put to no unusual strain, but unable to stand against the storm of strong temptation. If, notwithstanding the assaults of indolence and other temptations, some few resolutions have survived and borne fruit, how small is the result compared with what might have been had we been more faithful! We have been entrusted with ten talents, and have, perhaps, one paltry talent to show as our gain.

And in our rare victories, when we reflect how much lower motives have contributed to keep us steady, we find little room for boasting, even if against any good we can claim to have done there were not to be set off evil so preponderating that we can only say, "If thou, Lord, wilt be extreme to mark what is done amiss, O Lord, who may abide it?"

We dare not then bring God to a reckoning or put Him in our debt books. Thankfully may we accept the glad tidings that He is willing to give us more than we have earned, more than we have deserved, more than we could venture to desire. And it is easy to believe His promise that He will thus deal with His people hereafter, for it is so that He deals with us here. The life-history of every one of us begins with love and benefits received which we have done nothing to earn, which we never repay, not even with the poor recompense of adequate gratitude. It is as our heavenly Father that our blessed Lord has taught us to regard Him in whom we live and move and have our being. "Can a woman forget her sucking child," says the Lord by the mouth of His prophet, "that she should not have compassion on the son of her womb? yea, they may forget, yet will I not forget thee." Well, of this paternal relation, which, even if Scripture had not so employed it, would naturally occur to us as offering the best image of Divine love, the very characteristic is that it is a relation of inequality—all the giving on one side, the receiving on the other; for by God's wonderful provision the infant's helplessness is ready to be shielded by love which looks for no worthiness in its object, which imputes it when it is not possessed, which bears patiently with waywardness, is discouraged by no thanklessness. Happy they who learn to understand something of the love which they have for so many years accepted as a matter of course, before it is altogether too late to make requital. As little as we should dream of drawing up a debtor and creditor account with our parents, or of boasting how well we had earned the benefits we have received from them, so little can we dream of claiming merit from the Father who gives us all.

Yet, if it is the clear teaching of Scripture, confirmed by our own reason, that nothing which God gives us has been earned by our works or deservings, it is equally clear that God does and will reward men according to their works. Perhaps some fulness of quotation may be advisable lest any of you should have overlooked how this doctrine pervades Scripture from end to end, not excepting the Epistles of Paul, who has done so

much to bring into prominence the other side of
the truth. The title which Abraham gave to
God, the "Judge of all the earth," designates the
character under which the Almighty is, perhaps,
most frequently contemplated in the Old Testament. It was as a righteous Judge, making just
retribution, that God revealed Himself on Mount
Sinai, abundant in mercy to those who love Him
and keep His commandments, but sternly visiting
the iniquity of the disobedient on them and on
their children's children. Job paraphrases the ex-
clamation of Abraham when he says (xxxiv. 11),
"Surely God will not do wickedly, neither will
the Almighty pervert judgment. The work of a
man shall He render unto him, and cause every
man to find according to his ways." Similar
is the language of the Psalmist (lxii. 11), "Power
belongeth unto God. Also unto Thee, O Lord,
belongeth mercy: for Thou renderest to every
man according to his work." In the Book of
Proverbs, the wise man cautions his disciples
against deceiving themselves with the hope that
excuses, which might pass current with ill-
informed men, can avert the condemnation of
an all-seeing and just Judge. "If thou sayest,
Behold, we knew it not; doth not He that
pondereth the heart consider it? and He that
keepeth thy soul, doth not He know it? and

shall not He render to every man according to his works" (Proverbs xxiv. 12). Quite akin to this is the language of Jeremiah (xvii. 10), "I the Lord search the heart, I try the reins, even to give every man according to his ways, and according to the fruit of his doings."

I need not multiply these Old Testament quotations, but it was important that I should remind you of enough to enable you to have in your mind the whole strain of the language concerning God, the righteous Judge; for if you did not recognise the same language when it recurs in the New Testament, you would miss an important topic of evidence as to what the New Testament writers thought of Him whom many of them had personally known a man like themselves dwelling among them in all humility. As to the principles on which future judgment is to be administered there is no opposition between the Old Testament and the New. Hear what St. John says in the Apocalypse (xx. 12). "I saw the dead, small and great, stand before God: and the books were opened; and another book was opened, which is the book of life: and the dead were judged out of those things which were written in the books, according to their works. And the sea gave up the dead which were in it; and death and hell delivered up the dead which were in them: and they were judged every man according to their works." But who is to execute this judgment? Turn back to a previous chapter of the Book of Revelation (ii. 23), and this is the language which He who is described as the Son of God directs to be sent in His name to the Church of Thyatira. "I am He which searcheth the reins and hearts: and I will give unto every one of you according to your works." Recall the words I cited a moment ago from Jeremiah, "I the Lord search the heart, I try the reins, even to give every man according to his ways," and the coincidence is too perfect to leave room for doubt that in this Book of the Apocalypse, so full of reproductions of the language of the Old Testament prophets, St. John has taken the very words used in the Book of Jeremiah concerning the all-seeing Jehovah, the righteous Judge, and claimed the same attributes for his Master.

It has been said by Strauss concerning the author of the fourth Gospel that he has rendered His Master a very perilous service when, in his attempt to do Him honour, he has put into His own mouth words claiming for Himself a dignity which no sane man would presume to arrogate to himself. Can any words which that Gospel has attributed to the Saviour be more impossible for a mere man, if a sane man, to utter concerning himself than this claim, which the apocalyptic seer, using some of the most solemn words of Old Testament prophecy, has put into the mouth of the exalted Son of God, to possess the omniscience of the all-seeing Jehovah, and in virtue of that attribute to perform a work for which nothing less than omniscience would be adequate,—the making a just award to every man according to his works? Some critics have pronounced the doctrine of the Apocalypse to be so unlike that of the fourth Gospel that both cannot be works of the same author. On this point, certainly, there is no disagreement. You will remember the words which the fourth Evangelist records of Jesus, "The Father judgeth no man, but hath committed all judgment unto the Son: that all men should honour the Son, even as they honour the Father. . . . The hour is coming, and now is, when the dead shall hear the voice of the Son of God; and they that hear shall live. The Father hath given Him authority to execute judgment also because He is the Son of man. The hour is coming, in the which all that are in the graves shall hear his voice, and shall come forth; they that have done good, unto the resurrection of life; and they that have done evil, unto the resurrection of damnation."

Again, it has been said that our Lord's language about Himself is different as presented in the synoptic Gospels and in St. John's. There is no difference as to His language about His coming again in judgment. One of the passages I have read as my text is from St. Matthew: "The Son of man shall come in the glory of His Father, with His angels; and then shall He reward every man according to his works." In a later chapter of St. Matthew there is a fuller description how the Son of man shall come in His glory, and all His holy angels with Him, and all nations be gathered before Him for judgment. And all three synoptic evangelists agree that the condemnation passed on our Lord by the Jewish council was in consequence of His having spoken what they accounted the blasphemy of asserting that they should see Him hereafter sitting on the right hand of power and coming in the clouds of heaven,—words plainly appropriating to Himself the picture of the judgment given in the seventh chapter of Daniel.

It would be unreasonable then to doubt that it was in language spoken by our Lord Himself that the belief originated which was held in common by all the New Testament writers, which was expressed in the words of St. Paul, "We must all appear before the judgment-seat of

Christ," and in the later hymn which we daily use, "We believe that Thou shalt come to be our Judge." Quoting more fully those words of St. Paul, we find that he states the rule of Christ's judgment in complete accordance with the language of the rest of Scripture. "We must all appear before the judgment-seat of Christ; that every man may receive the things done in his body, according to that he hath done, whether it be good or bad." Or as he elsewhere describes the righteous judgment of God, "Who will render to every man according to his deeds: to them who, by patient continuance in well-doing, seek for glory, and honour, and immortality, eternal life; to them that do not obey the truth, but obey unrighteousness, indignation and wrath, tribulation and anguish, upon every soul of man that doeth evil: but glory, honour, and peace, to every man that worketh good."

Now it is not merely the Scripture doctrine that, in a general way, righteousness will be rewarded and wickedness punished; but the Bible gives us to understand that there will be a correspondence between the amount of right or wrong-doing, and the amount of reward or punishment. In our Lord's parable, the servant whose pound gained ten pounds is made ruler over ten cities, he whose pound gained five pounds only over five. A gradation of rewards in which the most trifling good action should not be unremunerated is plainly intimated in our Lord's words, "He that receiveth a prophet, in the name of a prophet, shall receive a prophet's reward; and he that receiveth a righteous man, in the name of a righteous man, shall receive a righteous man's reward. And whosoever shall give to drink to one of these little ones a cup of cold water only in the name of a disciple, shall in no wise lose his reward." And, in short, the whole tenor of New Testament teaching is summed up in the words written in the last chapter of our Canon: "I come quickly; and My reward is with Me, to give every man according as his work shall be."

I have already tried to show how the experience of our daily life falls in with the Scripture doctrine that God has promised to bestow on us hereafter blessings earned by no works or deserving of ours. It is still more easy to establish as a truth of experience the supplementary doctrine that man shall receive retribution according to his deeds. If Christianity were abolished, there are some Christian institutions which an enlightened philosophy might find it for its advantage to retain. That, for instance, is surely an admirable institution, well worthy of adoption by any school of philosophy, which ordains that there shall be in every parish one or more persons charged with looking after the highest interests of the people, and of instructing them in the truths which it most concerns them to know. If we can imagine Christianity abolished, and our Christian parochial ministry superseded by the appointment of high priests of science, whose duty it should be to make men familiar with the laws of the world they live in—laws which cannot be violated with impunity—such preachers might still find, in the volume we have so long venerated, texts for the sermons they would find it most necessary to preach. In particular there is no law of the world we live in which it would be more profitable for men to be thoroughly convinced of than that which St. Paul has stated in the words, "Be not deceived; God is not mocked: whatsoever a man soweth, that shall he also reap."

It is a pathetic sight to one who has had much experience of the world to behold how young persons will in thoughtless lightness of heart fling seeds in all directions, and seem to make sure that nothing can come of them. To the child who walks the fields and sees here a bank clothed with gay flowers, there a corner choked with briers or noisome weeds, it does not occur to ask how these things came to be there. It seems to him natural that things should be as they are, and he has no thought of inquiring why they are not otherwise. But it is not the less true that this or that plant is there because the seeds had previously been dropped there, and that it is in man's power to determine what plants shall grow there and what not. In life the connection between the seed and its produce is often ignored on account of the length of time that sometimes elapses between the period when the seed is dropped and that when the fruits show themselves. "Because sentence on an evil work is not executed speedily," said the Preacher of old, "therefore the hearts of men are fully set on them to do evil."

Then again, owing to the complexity of causes it is easy to overlook the operations of any single cause. Even in carefully cultivated fields, the owner of which has been desirous to exclude from them seeds of any kind but one, weeds will spring up, taking their origin he knows not how. So the seeds which a man casts himself are sown in no empty field, but in one where many another has been planted before him; and so the young shoots of that which he himself has cast may push themselves up, yet remain for a good while undetected among those which have had a different origin. But however slow or unobserved the growth of the fruit of noxious seeds may be, they cannot be scattered with impunity. And so, long before the person himself is aware of it, others can see his character altering for the worse: temptations, by being yielded to, gaining power over him; evil habits winding chains round him, which, gossamer threads at first, grow into links of iron; powers stunted by disuse; energies dissipated, leaving him in mature life bankrupt for all good. And again, by God's bountiful provision, it is not only the evil seeds which a man sows that he reaps, but every effort for good he makes is blessed with its appropriate reward,—reward not denied him even when on other grounds and in other ways he is subject to punishment.

If, then, there be any natural connection between this life and another—if the character formed in us by the discipline of this life is to remain with us hereafter, it must make an abiding difference to us whether, and how far, during our earthly sojourn the evil has been subdued, the good cherished in our souls, our characters moulded to likeness to Him to be like whom is both to be holy and happy. It is rational to believe that the same natural laws which in this life cause well-doing to be rewarded, ill-doing punished, will operate, and, it is reasonable to think, with increased force, in any continuation of our present life; and in such wise that according to the infinite variety of talents originally entrusted, according to the infinite varieties of use made of them, there will be corresponding varieties of happiness hereafter.

The doctrine then of reward according to work being both conformable to reason and repeatedly asserted in a continuous strain of passages from one end of the Bible to the other, could not but be included as a necessary part of their system even in those Protestant confessions which most vehemently reject the Romish doctrine of merit and reward. It is enough for me to quote the Helvetic Confession : " Moreover, we teach that God gives an ample reward to those who work good, according to the saying of the prophet, ' Refrain thy voice from weeping, for thy work shall be rewarded ;' and as our Lord also says in the Gospel, ' Rejoice, for great shall be your reward in heaven.' And again, ' Whosoever shall give to one of these little ones a cup of cold water only, verily I say unto you he shall not lose his reward.' We refer, however, this reward that the Lord gives, not to the merit of the man who receives, but to the goodness, liberality, and truth of God who promises and gives, who though He owes nothing to any one, yet has promised that He will reward His faithful worshippers, to whose gift, too, they owe it that they do faithfully worship Him. There is, besides, much unworthy of God and imperfect even in the works of saints, but because God receives into His grace those who work, for Christ's sake He pays them the promised reward."

The distinction here enunciated is so obvious that it does not much need to be drawn out at length. Children at a charity school may be promised rewards by their teachers for the lessons they learn. Such rewards spring solely from the bounty of the giver. The work by which they are earned in no way benefits him who gives the reward, but the reward is given only to stimulate the child to an exertion which will profit himself more than any one else. The education by which he earns the reward he owes also to the same bounty: yet the reward will be proportioned to work, and in virtue of a promise may be claimed as a right. So again in the parable: the servant whose pound gained ten pounds is made ruler over ten cities; he whose pound gained five pounds, over five. The reward is proportioned to work: yet the pounds which gain the reward are not the servants' own but the entrusted property of the master; the cities which are bestowed are gifts immeasurably out of proportion to the work which earns them, and are themselves part of an inheritance which their master has gained without help from them.

The doctrine of reward thus established, and as to which contending sects of Christians are substantially agreed, might at first sight seem to be an eminently practical one. To accept it is to believe in the momentous importance of every part of our course. According to it, everything done in the body tells: not a single temptation which, according as it is yielded to or baffled, does not affect for evil or for good our interests throughout eternity.

But is it actually the case that men are much influenced by these considerations? I think not. Men who really believe the Christian doctrine of a future life have often been filled with terrible anxiety how they may escape hell, and win heaven; but the consideration whether in heaven they shall enjoy a higher or lower degree of happiness, and in the case of believers in purgatory whether they shall receive a greater or less degree of punishment, has the very faintest influence with them.

This brings me to a part of my subject with which I had thought it possible to deal to-day, but which now must be postponed to another occasion.

XVI

THE TWO CLASSES

"When the Son of man shall come in His glory, and all the holy angels with Him, then shall He sit upon the throne of His glory: And before Him shall be gathered all nations; and He shall separate them one from another, as a shepherd divideth his sheep from the goats: And He shall set the sheep on His right hand, but the goats on the left."—MATTHEW xxv. 31-33.

SOME of you will remember that of the two sermons I preached here last term the first had for its subject the antinomies of Scripture; in other words, it dealt with the fact that there are passages of Scripture which, taken separately, present different aspects of truth, and on which accordingly opposite systems have been founded. The second sermon dealt with a particular case of the kind, namely, the Christian doctrine of reward, there being passages which speak of man's reward as altogether proportioned to his works, others which seem to deny the possibility of man's works earning for him any reward at all. Yet when we came to examine this particular case, the opposition between the different utterances of

Scripture was seen to be so superficial that you may reasonably have wondered why I thought it necessary to prefix so elaborate an introduction. The ordinary rule of life certainly is that a man is rewarded according to his works; that according as a man sows, so he reaps; and yet to receive love and benefits we have not earned is the experience with which the life of every one of us of necessity begins, and is one which, if we judge ourselves fairly, we must in all thankfulness acknowledge, is daily repeated. It is manifest likewise that it can hardly be said that there is even apparent opposition between the statements that rewards are proportioned to work, and yet may be such that the workman could not claim them as his earned due except so far as the promise of his bountiful benefactor gave him a right to make such a claim.

But there is a difficulty connected with the Scripture doctrine of future retribution which lies deeper down; one not concerned with points on which Protestants have differed from Roman Catholics, or one Protestant sect or party from another, but relating to a doctrine which all Christians may be said to hold in common: the doctrine namely, that hereafter mankind will be divided into two great classes, separated from each other by a sharp and ineffaceable line of distinction. The text speaks but of two classes, " He will put the sheep on His right hand and the goats on His left," and such is the doctrine of all Christian sects; for though in Roman Catholic theology a third region in the unseen world is recognised, its use is supposed to be only temporary. At the Judgment Day the time of purgation will have passed, and all who are not finally rejected will have passed into the abodes of bliss.

But the difficulty presents itself that if men are to be rewarded according to their works, no such simplicity of classification is possible. If we were to judge men according to their conduct, even supposing we knew with all-seeing accuracy the deeds and the temptations of each, we cannot conceive it possible but that we should find them differenced from each other by scarcely perceptible gradations. We can hardly imagine that we should be able to place anywhere a broad line of separation, on one side of which all should be saints, or the other all sinners. Why, we condemn even a work of fiction if its villains are all black, its virtuous characters all faultless. We set down such a work as belonging to the signboard-painting school of art. We regard its author as one who was no observer of nature and did not draw after real life; where the worst men often surprise us by some redeeming virtues, the best often disappoint us by unexpected frailties, and intermediate there are many whose good qualities are so mixed with faults that we should find it hard to pronounce which predominates. The doctrine of inequality of future retribution, corresponding to the infinite variety of conduct here, is in itself so reasonable, and has so much countenance from Scripture, that it has been generally admitted to form a part of theological systems which in other points are at wide variance with each other. Our Lord distinctly taught that there would be inequality of punishment,—some being beaten with few stripes, while others who had only been guilty of the same sin, but had sinned against light and knowledge, should be beaten with many stripes. And He spoke with equal distinctness of the inequality of rewards,— the servant who had gained ten pounds being more richly rewarded than he who had only gained five; each good action, even a cup of cold water given in His name, receiving its separate reward.

So no theologian has had any difficulty in recognising that there may be among the blessed infinite varieties of happiness, indeed infinite varieties of capacity for happiness; and in like manner infinite variety in the sufferings of the lost. In Roman Catholic theology hell has its outer fringes or Limbi, the inhabitants of which suffer no pain of sense, but are only grieved by the pain of loss. Nay, modern Roman Catholic theology, as represented by the speculations of private divines though not formally sanctioned by their Church, is merciful enough to exempt unbaptized infants from even the pain of loss, and is willing to believe their state to be one of the highest physical enjoyment, and only deserving to be called damnation in comparison of the infinitely greater happiness which they are compelled to forego. Dante, whose representations of the unseen world only gave vividness and form to the beliefs which were current in his time, and which he helped to fix, saw as he descended into hell circles ever narrowing, the torments of which, as he went lower, constantly increased in intensity; while in like manner in Paradise the blessedness increased according to the degree of nearness which was permitted of approach to the Throne of the Supreme.

Theologians, then, have willingly agreed to admit a gradation in the conditions both of the saved and of the lost, but they have been nearly as unanimous in holding that there is an entire breach of continuity in passing from the one state to the other. When Paley was presented with the difficulty that there would probably be little to choose between the merits of the lowest person admitted into heaven and the highest of those excluded from it, he boldly answered that, for all he knew, there might be as little to choose between their conditions. I do not know that this answer found much acceptance at the time, and I daresay most Christians at the present day would find it startling; for though it does not expressly contradict anything that has been revealed, it is at variance with the general impression which the Scriptures convey.

And yet we must acknowledge, when we think on the subject, that the doctrine of the entire breach of continuity between the two states has killed the practical effect of the doctrine of gradation which is certainly very clearly taught in Scripture. In the case of ninety-nine out of a hundred of those who believe in the doctrines of Christianity, the one question concerning their eternal state which they feel to be of vital interest is whether they are to be among the saved or the lost. In comparison of that, what place in either division a man occupies is felt to be of infinitely little moment. It is the prominence given to this breach of continuity as I have called it which puts the real difference between the revival preaching of the present day and the older methods of the Church. In the revival teaching the prominent feature is that there is a great line to be stepped over, on one side of which is happiness, on the other misery. The first practical question for any man, in comparison of which any other shrinks into insignificance, is to make sure that he has passed over that line himself. The next thing is to induce others to step over it and so share his own security. What advance he or they might make on the other side is a matter of immeasurably less importance, and in point of fact is found not much to occupy his mind.

In the older Church methods, on the contrary, it was assumed, whether with or without good reason, that those within the pale of the Christian Church had already passed over this line. God's infinite willingness to save those who came to Him through His Son was taken for granted, and the preacher's efforts were directed to exhorting his people to walk worthy of the vocation to which they had been called. It is quite true that these older methods in many cases assumed what was not true. It is true that there were and have been many within the Church's pale who had as much need as those without it to inquire "What must we do to be saved?" men who, in the Apostle's words, "profess that they know God ; but in works deny Him, being abominable, disobedient, and to every good work reprobate." Surely all must own that the preacher does a good work if he can succeed in rousing such souls from the lethargy of sin, and through God's blessing on his labour effect in them an entire change of heart and life. Looking at the matter, then, practically, we see that it was not only in the beginning of the Gospel or in missionary efforts that men had need to be exhorted to pass from death unto life, from the power of Satan unto God; but that the visible Church contains multitudes who have as much need of a complete change of heart and state as if they had been born heathen. And yet just now we saw that the practical effect of dwelling too persistently on the need of such a change may be, in the case of a great many, to kill the practical effects of the other great Christian doctrine of reward according to works, and so to stunt men's growth in grace. Many will say, or if they do not say, will feel, All I care to know is to which of the two great classes do I belong; am I among God's friends or His enemies? If among the former, I am safe, and more than that I do not care to be. Some even have pushed the doctrine of the two classes to a consequence which by a Christian mind must be regarded as *reductio ad absurdum*, namely, the uselessness of prayer. We cannot believe it has been said that the prayers of God's enemies will be accepted by

Him; for He has said that the prayer of the wicked is abomination in His sight. It is therefore useless for an unconverted man to pray. But if you belong to the class of those whom He loves He will, without your prayer, do for you abundantly above what you can ask or think.

Now, it is plain that we interpret Scripture wrongly if we do it so as to make one part of it contradict another, and it was on this account that I spent so much time in speaking of the apparent contradictions of Scripture. What I said then may be briefly summed up in this: The Bible is a practical book, and not a scientific treatise. For practical purposes it is necessary, according as men's needs differ, that different sides of truth should be presented in turns, and this the Bible fully does. When men take one class of utterances, and treating them as if they were propositions in a scientific treatise, proceed to push them to what are taken to be their logical consequences, if the result is that they have formed a system the practical effect of which is at variance with the practical effect of the plain teaching of other parts of Scripture, the result condemns the method. We may be sure that in such a case these interpreters of the Bible have read it wrong.

Now, with respect to the two doctrines of

which I have been speaking from which opposite practical conclusions have been drawn, it is certain that both have their place in Scripture teaching. When I last addressed you I laid before you some of the evidence with regard to the place in the Bible of the doctrine of retribution according to man's deeds, and I need not go over the evidence again. And I showed also how entirely that doctrine agrees with the best explanation our reason can give of the objects with which God has placed us in this world, namely, in order that it should be a school for disciplining us for fitness for His heavenly kingdom, where the character that our earthly training has wrought in us will bear its appropriate fruits of more or less abundant happiness.

It is now the turn to speak of the other doctrine of the division of mankind into two classes. That this is a Scripture doctrine I need not look beyond the passage which I have read as my text, though no doubt abundance of other Scripture proofs will rise to your minds if such were needed. But that such a way of dividing mankind has nothing in it opposed to men's notions of what is right and reasonable is evident from the fact that it not only conforms to the prevalent opinion of Christians, but is a feature of all heathen speculation about the unseen world. I might remind you of Plato's tale of Er the Pamphylian whose report of the unseen world told but of two openings, through one of which the righteous ascended to happiness, through the other the wicked descended to punishment. But it is needless to particularise, for at the basis of all the mythological stories of Tartarus and the Elysian fields lies the conception of this twofold division of the human race. When we think on the matter, and especially with a view to self-examination, much of the superficial variety of human characters disappears, and it is found to be the great question whether in the contest between the powers of good and evil we are on the side of God or of His enemies. Suppose, for example, we desire to know where in this continuously graduated chain of human character we have a right to place ourselves ; how little confidence could we place in a comparison of our sins with those of others ? Should we even have a right to say, Others have robbed, or murdered, or committed adultery ; we may be certain that we can place ourselves above these. Well, David, for example, committed both murder and adultery —are we certain that we are in God's sight better than he? He had the temptation of absolute power, presenting to him the prospect of being able to sin with complete impunity, and he

Y

yielded to that temptation. But what corresponding temptation have we overcome? We know that if we committed offences such as his, the punishment they would draw down on us would be so severe that such things for us do not come within the practical possibilities of conduct. A general who fights an unsuccessful battle no doubt incurs a disgrace which is escaped by one who sits at home at ease, but we are not bound to believe that his arm-chair critic would have conducted affairs better if they had been entrusted to his management. In short, then, it is plain that we cannot estimate the comparative guilt of different persons if we only know the sins they have committed, and do not know also the temptations and opportunities of each—what temptations they have resisted as well as what they have yielded to. A child may have stolen a few shillings; a shop-boy ten times as much; a grown-up criminal a hundred times as much again. It would be absurd to classify their guilt according to the amount they had stolen. Their opportunities were different, but there may not have been a particle of difference between the dishonesty of purpose in the several cases. Men's temptations differ. The sins which lead one captive offer little attraction to another; so that it might be an act of supreme virtue for the one to resist what the other abstains from without an effort. And men's opportunities differ—some are guarded and hedged in by social restraints of various kinds, so that whole classes of sins are made for them practically impossible. But what puts the real difference between characters is how the temptations are met which *are* strongly felt as temptations. Does the thought arise, " How shall I do this wickedness and sin against God ?" This it is which the Apostle James has expressed in the saying, " Whosoever shall keep the whole law, and yet offend in one point, he is guilty of all. For He that said, Do not commit adultery, said also, Do not kill. Now, if thou commit no adultery, yet if thou kill, thou art become a transgressor of the law."

The Stoics exposed themselves to easy ridicule by stating in a paradoxical way their doctrine of the parity of offences, yet there is a deep truth at the bottom of their doctrine. The great question for any man, as stated from a Stoic point of view, is, Does he recognise the supreme authority of law, and make it his one aim to rule his conduct thereby? A Christian would add, Does he love the Law-giver, and is it his heart's desire to please Him ? But contempt for law may be shown in small things as well as in great. The posts assigned us in the battle against evil are different; but what worse can any man do than betray the post assigned to himself. "He that is faithful in that which is least, is faithful also in much: and he that is unjust in the least, is unjust also in much." Experience tells any who will observe that there is a much closer alliance between sins of different kinds than might at first have been imagined. Cherish wilfully one known sin, though you may flatter yourself it is a little one, and that sin is not likely to be your only one. When water has once found its way through an embankment it goes on enlarging the little aperture through which it began to flow, until what was once a little trickle swells to a great inundation. If in any case your faithless heart consent to the removal, in any part, of the barrier which the love of God and of His law ought to raise against sin, you will find your weakened will unable to withstand successfully other claimants for a like indulgence. I said a few minutes ago that there are some sins which to each of us do not count among practical possibilities. It is astonishing how any course of indulged sin enlarges the range of these practical possibilities; how this or that against which once conscience would have raised so loud a remonstrance that we should not have dreamed of disregarding her voice, is gradually met with fainter and fainter outcry, until at last it seems to us a light matter whether or not we are guilty of it.

I return, then, to what I said in the first sermon as to the supposed self-contradictions of Scripture. The key to the difficulties they present is to remember that the Bible is a practical book. Nothing is easier than to perplex oneself with speculative difficulties, but it is our own fault if any such obscure the path of duty. If there are any passages which we fancy present mutual contradictions, we may be sure that each contains a lesson which it is needful for us to learn; and we shall be sure to go wrong if pushing one of them to what we imagine to be its logical consequences, we make these our rule of action, neglecting the truth conveyed by the other.

It may be true that some have fixed their thoughts too exclusively on the importance of the transition from a state of indifference or enmity to God, to one in which we are His pledged servants and soldiers. They may have led disciples to feel as if, this transition once made, all was over that was of importance; as if the great point was enlisting as a soldier and not fighting the battle. And many may thereby have been led into dangerous mistakes:

in former days, thinking that because they had been baptized into Christ's Church they must be safe; in later days, because they had, as they believe, experienced conversion.

And yet, however that truth may have been distorted, it is no less true that it is a choice each of you has to make in which of two great classes you will be found; whether in the conflict with sin you will be on the side of the Lord or on that of His enemies. It does not follow that you are not fighting on His side because you may suffer occasional defeats. It is one thing to be worsted in a battle, another to make a shameful surrender or desert to the enemy's side. If temptations have overcome you, do not acquiesce in your defeat, let not your will consent to subjection to any form of known sin. But draw near for help to Him who is stronger than all your foes: seek strength from Him, and let the thought of Christ, our Example, who loved us and gave Himself for us, be ever with you as your shield against temptation. This is the battle you are bound to fight. Are you willing to do so? "Choose you this day whom you will serve." God give each of you grace to answer, "As for me I will serve the Lord."

XVII

WORKING TOGETHER WITH GOD

"We, then, as workers together with Him, beseech you also that ye receive not the grace of God in vain."—2 CORINTHIANS vi. 1.

IN this text we have one of the links that bind together the two Epistles to the Corinthians, and evidence their common authorship. The thought expressed here that the Christian minister is a joint-worker with God had been used by St. Paul in his First Epistle (iii. 9) in order to still the rivalries of those who did not look above the human agents to whom their conversion had been due. "We are joint-labourers," he said, "with God; it is God's husbandry, God's building you are." And the thought seems to have been habitual with Paul, for his disciple, St. Luke, on three several occasions reports that the language Paul used in relating his missionary successes was, "What things God had done with them;" "What wonders God had wrought among the Gentiles by them;" "What things God had wrought among the Gentiles by his ministry." For you will perceive that in the original conception of this familiar word "minister," the person spoken of was intended to be described not so much as a servant of the Church as a servant doing God's work.

Ever since the first preaching of Christianity, many a worker in the cause of benevolence or of religion has been sustained by the thought that he was doing God's work, labouring in God's service. And surely no worker could be animated by a more inspiriting idea; one presenting the thought that the work engaged in was the highest and best, and also that it was one which could not fail to succeed since a higher power was working with him. Yet the idea of labouring for God has not been confined to those who do work which we can acknowledge as divine. Our Lord warned His disciples that the time was coming when whosoever killed them should think that he was doing God service; and we know in the history of the Christian Church how the fires of the Inquisition were lit and the most cruel atrocities perpetrated by men who sincerely believed that they were thus doing God's work, and that the purging of the land in this way from heresy was the most acceptable service they could render Him. Attila, we are told, looked on himself as an instrument in God's hands, and called himself the scourge of God. Yet with respect to this last example it is necessary to remark, that it is a very different thing when a man takes up a work to gratify his own passions or promote his own interests, and then by an afterthought pleases himself with the reflection that his own enemies are God's enemies too, and that the injuries he has inflicted on them may be looked on as tokens of the Divine wrath: this is very different, I say, from a man's choosing an object and labouring at it solely from the belief that the cause at which he works is the cause of God.

It is necessary to point out how the phrase of the text and the corresponding passage in the First Epistle differ from the numerous passages in the Bible where men are spoken of as instruments in the hand of God. In everything that takes place the readers of the Bible are taught to see the hand of God. Inanimate nature obeys His commands; fire and hail, snow and vapours, wind and storm, fulfil His word. Even the wicked, though they mean it not, work out His designs; He maketh the wrath of man to praise Him. When the Assyrian king boasted of the cities he had overthrown, the prophet was commissioned to tell him that he had been but an instrument unconsciously employed by a higher power. "Hast thou not heard long ago, how I have done it; and of ancient times, that I have formed it? Now have I brought it to pass, that thou shouldst be to lay waste defenced cities into ruinous heaps. Therefore their inhabitants were of small power." Thus it is evident that we may speak of working for God or doing God's work in a sense in which nobody can help doing God's work; and clearly Paul meant something more than this when he described himself as co-operating in the Divine work.

It is curious how the conception of the universe, which is suggested by the most exalted Theism, runs up to meet simply Atheistic doctrine on the common ground of Pantheism. The devout man delights to see God's hand everywhere. Nothing takes place without His will. All things are overruled and directed by His sovereign all-disposing hand. How, then, is this view to be distinguished from that which looks on God and Nature as different names for the same thing? In fact it is only in the form of Pantheism that it is now possible for Atheism to exist. No one who has bestowed the most superficial study on the facts of the universe now dreams that blind chance can give a sufficient account of them. We find everywhere the same fixed laws—everywhere one uniform plan. This unity is compatible with much diversity. The same protoplasm may assume infinitely varied forms of life; yet in widely different forms we can discern the same ground ideas worked out in different ways. Each form is that which its time demands, and which is most in harmony with its surroundings. It might seem then a mere difference of language according as we use the names Nature or God, whether we describe all things as the work of God, or all things as different manifestations of the same ever-present, ever-bountiful Nature. But what, then, can be meant by working for God? or what by obeying the laws of nature? The laws of nature will make themselves obeyed whether we like it or not. What more need any man do—what more can any man do—than develop himself freely? Whatever he does will be the result of the nature with which he was endowed, and of the circumstances in which he has been placed. The results of his actions will work themselves out according to inevitable laws, so that no matter what he does he will fulfil the laws of nature; no matter what he does he will work out the will of God.

The difficulty is the same in another form as the old one that was presented by the ethical rule, to live according to nature; for there was need to explain why the vicious man does not live according to his nature, as much as the virtuous man according to his. In fact it is on the ethical side that lies the weakness of Pantheism, or indeed of any theory of the universe, which is founded on a mere study of the physical facts of external nature, and does not interpret all by a study of the nature of man. If science does nothing but register a succession of phenomena, why is one to be preferred to another? Why should we say that one term in the series is good, another bad? The tyranny of the oppressor, the patient suffering of the meek, the heroism of the patriot, the baseness of the coward and traitor, the self-indulgence of the profligate, the chastity of the virgin, are all alike manifestations of the changeful face of universal nature; one as much as another: one not more to be blamed or commended than another. To rise from Nature to God we need the revelations of conscience. It is conscience which tells us that all the parts of man's nature do not stand on a footing of equality: conscience, which claims a right to be obeyed, which threatens, which punishes if obedience be refused: conscience, which discriminates between the phenomena of the world outside us, which tells of a better and a worse, and proclaims it to be our duty to aid the progress from the worse to the better. True, we are told that conscience is an artificial growth; and we are presented with a history of its genesis, and are told that constituted as men are, and living in society as they do, those ideas of right and wrong must inevitably have sprung up. But what is such a history to us? Writers on Evolution may tell us the history of the development of the organ of vision,—how from a mere nerve speck, sensitive to light, has been evolved the wonderful organ which reveals to us the distant world,—but such a history is quite irrelevant to the question of the truth of the revelations of vision. Tell us, as you please, the history how men came to have eyes, and still it will remain that seeing is believing. And so no matter how conscience grew, we have it, and it is idle to dispute the truth of its revelations.

When the revelations of conscience are once recognised as authentic it becomes impossible to accept the totality of the universe as God. For conscience not only makes known that all the parts of man's nature do not stand on a footing of equality, by asserting her own supremacy over the other parts; she declares that all our actions are not alike; she condemns some and approves others. And so likewise with regard to the actions of other men: there are some which we stigmatise as mean, base, degrading; others which we honour as noble, generous, right. It then becomes impossible for us to treat all the phenomena that exhibit themselves as alike manifestations of the Deity; we cannot own as manifestations of God that which the nature He has given us teaches us to condemn and hate. Thus we cannot but arrive at the conclusion that the power that works through universal nature is something distinct from nature—something higher and better than nature—something from our conception of which we must exclude everything unworthy of the highest excellence.

Further, in the working of nature, our own intelligence enables us to discern a character. Leaving for a moment moral distinctions out of sight, we cannot even rank all the phenomena of merely physical nature as on the same level. Things that have what we call life we must look on as of higher nature than merely inanimate objects; and the meanest insect is, in our eyes, more wonderful than the huge rock on which it crawls. Higher again we set creatures of more complex organisation; when intelligence and reason manifest themselves we recognise something higher still; and we feel it to be no usurpation in man, but something to which his higher nature entitles him, that he claims dominion over the beasts of the field. Thus it is impossible for us to acquiesce in a Pantheistic view, the logical result of which is, that one manifestation of the Godhead has a right to claim equality with any other. We cannot help making a scale of higher and lower; and then observation tells us of a striving of nature to ascend in that scale. This is, in short, the doctrine of Evolution, now become so popular, that the ordinary course of things is the advance from lower to higher organisations; that every form of superior excellence that shows itself is selected and encouraged, and that inferior forms get crushed out in the struggle for existence. And in the moral world the general tendency of things is equally plain. That tendency is not indifferent to virtue or vice; but, as has been said, the force that rules through nature is a power that makes for righteousness. The moral laws, if violated, avenge themselves. In particular cases, through a favourable conjuncture of circumstances, the infliction of penalties may be postponed, or even averted, but every sin sows a seed of suffering which, in the ordinary course of things, will not fail in due time to bear its natural fruit. Thus in the moral world, as well as in the physical, nature exhibits a continual effort to ascend from the lower to the higher type. Shall we call this a process of unconscious nature, or not rather the work of God, who has constituted nature?

In this work God invites us to be co-operators. There are in the human body some actions necessary to our life which God has not left to be dependent on our care and thought; they are performed without volition of ours, and even without our consciousness. There are other things necessary to the perfection of our life which must be obtained by voluntary, and, it may be, not without skilful effort. But even the unconscious acts of the body may be aided and perfected by wisely directed will. There is, for example, one action which we begin to perform the moment we come into the world, and which we have been practising every minute of our lives ever since: I mean the action of breathing; and yet the well-trained singer would tell you how little people in general understand the art of filling their lungs with air, and what education is necessary in order to be able to make the deep inspirations his art has need of. Thus, then, there are, as I have said, processes of unconscious nature which God employs as His instruments in the elevation of our race—processes which do their work whether we choose it or not, and against which we cannot set ourselves, except to our destruction. But for the rapid success of His work, it is God's plan that what purely natural laws are effecting silently and slowly, should be taken up and urged on by the wills of His intelligent creatures, and made the subject of their conscious efforts. He has made known His will so plainly, both in nature and through revelation, that you can feel no perplexity what God's work is. The only question for you is, Will you accept the honour of being workers together with God, or will you be so mad as to try to arrest its progress?

The phrase, "workers together with God," may, perhaps, sound in your ears as a conventional phrase of pulpit rhetoric; but there is no difficulty in giving it a practical meaning, and turning it into a rule of conduct. If the work of God, which exhibits itself in nature, is the continuous elevation of His creatures in the scale of being, you must take your part in that work; and, to begin with, the creature with whose elevation you are most intimately concerned—elevation which has been committed to you as your special trust and duty—is yourself. It sounds worldly and selfish advice that I should tell you your first duty is to raise yourself; yet if you understand what true elevation is, it is sound advice; and if you take the most unselfish view possible of life, and regard it as given you merely that you might work for others and work for God, still the improvement of the instruments by which you are to work is the first condition of success in carrying out that end. The fact is, that God has so amply provided in the natural course of things for the development of your faculties, that you are in danger of thinking it superfluous to add any voluntary efforts for the same purpose. The majority of those whom I address are at an age when you are conscious of such vigorous growth of bodily and mental powers, that you can hardly conceive that any liberty you can take will permanently injure your health of body, that any experience can add ripeness to the decisions of your intellect. Further, in order to know how far the development of any creature is likely to proceed, we must know not only what are the powers inherent in its nature, but also how far these powers are aided or repressed by circumstances. In your case, not only is your age that when advance is likely to be most rapid and most easily marked, but the circumstances in which you are placed are highly favourable to mental and moral improvement. It might seem, then, as if you could safely let things take their course, and trust that you would make advance enough, even though you bestowed no thought on it. But in this case, too, real advance is only made when voluntary effort aids the unconscious strivings of nature. The popularity of the word "culture" indicates how thoughtful men at the present day have come to feel the necessity of training and discipline if we are to attain the highest excellence. We can all agree in insisting on culture, provided only that the culture is not regarded as an end in itself, aimed at in order that we might have a self-complacent satisfaction at our own elevation, but as a means for enabling us to do God's work in the world : and provided also that the culture is not limited to one part of our nature,—not merely that our taste should be refined, but that in intellect, will, affections, we should be formed into an instrument fit for the Master's use.

About bodily culture it is not necessary for me to say much, for the days are past when it was imagined that philosophy or religion taught that ill-treatment of the body was the way to exalt your spiritual health. The doctrine that a healthy body and a healthy mind go together is now so well understood that it is chiefly in romances, and not in actual university life, that one now often meets pale students who, in the pursuit of knowledge, have sacrificed their physical strength. In fact universities, whither young men are supposed to come for intellectual training, are now regarded by many who resort to them as if they were principally schools for bodily culture; and if there is danger of the balance of their powers not being duly preserved, the danger is lest that part should be neglected which you are supposed to come here specially to cultivate. It must be owned that in the excitement of competition, both for intellectual and for bodily pre-eminence, young men are sometimes tempted in their eagerness for temporary success to make exertions that are permanently injurious to them. Yet if there be a few whom it is right to caution against extravagantly expending on an immediate object the fund of powers which was intended to last them for their whole life, there are many more who commit the same sin, for sin it is, after a more ignoble fashion. The Apostle warned his youthful disciple to "abstain from fleshly lusts, which war against the soul;" and, he might have added, against the body also: for, as he elsewhere tells us, by these especially a man sins against his own body. And he who has to pay the penalty of this misdoing cannot console himself that he has spent his strength in contending for any worthy prize. Nay, he must make to himself the reproach, "What fruit have you in those things whereof you are now ashamed?" For believe me, that though sentence against an evil work be not executed speedily, the penalty is not remitted when the exaction of it is postponed. A man cannot with impunity stain the fair texture of his life, and it is often too late when he discovers that the stains are indelible. An ancient writer[1] gives this explanation of the need of death and a resurrection, that in the course of life our bodies receive so many stains, so many warps, that at length He who at first made the fair structure and pronounced it good, now sees nothing to be done but cast the materials into the melting-pot, and make the work anew. And this illustration often occurs to me when I mark how each sin writes its history on the constitution, making further sin more likely, breaking down the barrier of principle, storing the imagination with polluting images, and paralysing the will so as to incapacitate it for resistance. Lives have begun with prospects as fair as yours, which, through successive slips, one leading to another, have now become so stained through and through, that one asks, Is it within the compass of the Divine Omnipotence to make these pure again?

You have been called on, brethren, as your

---

[1] Methodius, *On the Resurrection*.

reasonable service, to present your bodies as a living sacrifice, holy and acceptable to God. But the Jewish law did not permit what natural piety forbids—the offering a blemished sacrifice to God. "If you offer the blind in sacrifice," said the prophet, "is it not evil? If you offer the lame and sick, is it not evil?" Will you not strive that that which you offer shall be pure and without blemish? Some have formed the generous idea of giving the present to reckless enjoyment, and at some distant time dedicating themselves to God. But that which they have got to offer is then no longer the same; and what have they done but deliberately prepared an unclean sacrifice to the King of kings? denying it to Him while it is unblemished, and hoping to appease Him by a sacrifice of the blind, the sick, and the lame.

Time will not permit me to say much more about your work on yourselves, though there are some other things I should have wished to speak of. In particular, I do not wish to leave quite unmentioned the importance of your cultivating and strengthening the power of the will to resist the demands of impulse, on your possession of which really depends whether you are a freeman or a slave. There is nothing it so much concerns your manhood to possess, nothing so easily lost.

A process is constantly going on through which habitual actions become automatic, and what it required much thoughtful attention for us to learn to do can now be performed without effort and almost without our consciousness. In this way a few decisions of the will make future action of the will needless : and so great part of our lives slips out of our control. Every form of vicious self-indulgence not only weakens power of resistance to the particular temptation yielded to, but produces a general paralysis of the will, and deprives the sinner of the power to set aside any impediment, and throw himself with all his energy on any desired task. And conversely, I believe that there is important moral discipline to be got from your intellectual training here, when you force yourselves to take up work that is not particularly attractive to you, and to put away wandering thoughts while you are engaged on it, and disregard impulses to turn to something less distasteful to you. By thus training your will to victory you may save yourself from sinking into that pitiable state of slavery to sin. It has been said to myself, " I know it is wrong ; I know it is injurious to me, but I can't help myself." I say, you must help yourself; it concerns your very life to help yourself. If soldiers set to defend a dangerous pass were told that they ought to lay down their arms because resistance was hopeless, they would know that that advice came from an enemy or a traitor. And believe me it is the enemy of your souls who tries to persuade you that his power over you has become so great that meek submission to him is your wisest policy. No; greater is He that is on your side than he that is against you; and if you let not yourself be discouraged by defeat, but go on to fight bravely your Master's battles, He will in the end give you the victory.

I have left myself little time to say anything of what people usually think of when working for God is spoken of—I mean working for others I do not very much regret this limitation because I believe that if your work on yourselves be rightly done, your work for others wil take care of itself. If, indeed, I had exhorted you in the worldly sense to raise yourself, you might feel tempted to gain elevation of that kind by the depression of others; but when once you have learned that the only true elevation consists in likeness to Christ, then every instinct of your nature urges you to bring others with you to every point you have gained. It is not natural to keep knowledge to oneself: one likes to communicate it: one looks about for sympathy: one wishes to speak to others of things that interest us: one does not willingly see one's neighbour stumble if we can help him up. And besides these ordinary natural motives, there is the Christian motive of love to that Saviour to whom we ourselves owe everything, and who asks us in return to love those whom He gave His life to save, and to help them on their way. I therefore care the less to dwell on this topic, because I believe that, at least at this time of your lives, the best work you do for others is that which you do unconsciously. I said already that the evolution of any creature depends partly on the original powers with which his nature has been endowed, and partly on the circumstances in which he has been placed. Well, *you* are the circumstances in which those who come to this University are placed; you make the atmosphere which they are to breathe. It is not the teachers, but the learners, who form the atmosphere of the place; you form the public opinion which for a time will rule their life. What prudent parent, thinking of sending a son here, would not inquire of what sort will be the companions with whom he is likely to mix? "In sending him away from the restraints and discipline of home, am I sending him to a place of temptation, or to a place where anything good he has learned will be strengthened and confirmed?"

It may be thought that I am not a fair judge, for the students with whom I come most in contact are those whose intended profession pledges them to aim at the highest standard. But I hope I am not judging too favourably in saying that the moral atmosphere here is, on the whole, a healthy one: uncongenial to anything mean, or base, or impure. But in the course of my fifty years of college life I have known exceptions. I have known men abuse the influence which their age, and sometimes their intellectual ability, gave them over younger students, by teaching them the ways of vice, and take delight in enlightening their simplicity and breaking down their home-bred scrupulosity. If you are at any loss to know how you are to do God's work, you can be at no loss to know how a man does the devil's work; you could not for a moment fancy you were doing God's work if you were trying to familiarise a lad's ears with profanity or impurity, or pressing him to join in revellings or excess. Just imagine any one saying, "As workers together with God, we beseech you to come with us to visit the harlots' houses."

If, therefore, you do not understand how to do good to your companions (and I daresay you do not, for really to do good to others is one of the hardest things in the world, and often one does most good when one thinks least about it), at least you can understand not to do them harm. One way of doing them harm you have been lately cautioned against,[1] namely, that of repelling them by exhibiting a gloomy, long-faced type of religion. The caution is very probably more necessary in Scotland than it is here; but even here it can be no harm to say, Be careful how you represent as sins things which God has not forbidden. In regulating your own conduct you will do well to avoid not only things actually sinful, but things which you find by experience to be injurious to your spiritual health. But if you lay too heavy burdens on others, there is danger lest they should cast off, not only these, but much more. It is often in breaking through restrictions that ought never to have been imposed that a young person learns the worst lesson he can be taught—that of disregarding the authority of his conscience; for an ill-informed conscience is likely not to be respected.

And now one word that shall embrace all the rest that I have said. When our Lord was asked, "What shall we do, that we might work the works of God?" He answered: "This is the work of God, that ye believe on Him whom He hath

[1] By Professor Drummond in an address delivered to the students of Trinity College.

sent." I will not attempt now to draw out all that is included in that familiar phrase, Believing in the Lord Jesus Christ: what duties it reveals, what motives it inspires. But to you, who know who He was and what He has done for you, and to whom the privilege is offered of being partners in His work, I will say, in the Apostle's words—"See that you receive not the grace of God in vain."

XVIII

THE FORGIVENESS OF SINS

"And such were some of you: but ye are washed, but ye are sanctified, but ye are justified in the name of the Lord Jesus, and by the Spirit of our God."—I CORINTHIANS vi. II.

THE earliest opponents of Christianity gave themselves little trouble to inform themselves about the tenets of the religion which they persecuted, and consequently a good deal of the first apologies written in defence of our religion has but a historic interest for us, being taken up with a refutation of idle calumnies which nobody now imagines to have ever had any foundation in truth. But when the head of the Roman empire became a professor of the new creed, it was no longer possible to treat its claims as unworthy of examination. Educated heathen made themselves acquainted with Christian literature, and a new generation of philosophic opponents of our faith drew from their study of our sacred books objections which have not lost their vitality in our own days.

Among other passages of the New Testament against which objections were brought, that which I have read as the text was fastened on by a heathen who lived at the end of the fourth century.[1] "Such were some of you," he cries. "Let us hear what 'such' means: 'Fornicators, idolaters, effeminate, abusers of themselves with mankind, thieves, covetous, drunkards, revilers, extortioners.' Yet having thus stained themselves with pollutions innumerable and abominable, by merely being baptized and calling on the name of Christ they are freed from all their guilt as easily as a snake casts its slough. Who, then, would not venture on all wickedness, mentionable or unmentionable, if he knew that he had but to believe and be baptized, and could then get pardon for the most abominable deeds from Him who shall judge the quick and the dead. This is downright encouragement to sin; this overturns all discipline and all law; this teaches the impious man to feel no terror, if by merely being baptized he can clear away a mass of ten thousand iniquities."

The same text had been also laid hold of by the Emperor Julian.[2] He enumerates in like manner the sins from which Paul's disciples had

---

[1] Macarius Magnes, *Apocritica*, iv. 19.
[2] Cyr. Alex., *Cont. Jul.* vii.

been washed, and scoffs at the idea that the baptismal water, which is unable to wash away leprosy, which cannot cleanse away gout or dysentery, which cannot take away even warts or whitlows or the very smallest disease of the body, should be supposed capable of penetrating to the soul and washing away adulteries, extortions, and all its other sins. The immorality of the Christian doctrine of the forgiveness of sins became a stock topic with heathen writers, who threw their objection into its most popular form in the myth which they circulated concerning the conversion of Constantine. The Emperor, their story went, being tormented with remorse for his many crimes, in particular for the murder of his wife and his son, consulted a philosopher of the school of Plotinus, by what lustral purifications he could be cleansed from his guilt. But this philosopher had the honesty to tell him that no purifications could avail to cleanse moral defilement such as his. The Emperor was grieved at his repulse, but afterwards fell in with some Christian bishops (Hosius of Corduba is said to have been principally intended) who told him that their baptism could obliterate the deepest stains of sin, and so Constantine eagerly sought at the hands of this new superstition a pardon which his older religious guides had been too pure and too true to promise.[1]

Thinking, as we have good reason to do, of heathen morality, we naturally feel some little amused surprise at the courage of the heathen advocates who challenged comparison of their doctrines with those of the Christians in respect of their moral tendencies. But the fact that it was as late as the fourth century before this line was taken may rather entitle us to set down among the benefits conferred by Christianity its indirect influence in elevating the moral conceptions even of those who did not embrace the religion. For the earlier objections to the new religion were not on account of the laxity of its morality, but on account of its puritanical over-strictness. "They think it strange," says St. Peter, "that ye run not with them to the same excess of riot." Tertullian, writing a couple of centuries before the heathen authors whom I have already cited, quotes as unwilling testimony to the purity of Christian morality, the lamentations which the unconverted used to raise over their former companions in riot who had been "spoiled" by Christianity. "What a jolly boon companion that young man was, and now he is good for nothing: he has become a Christian."

[1] Zosimus, ii. 29; Soz. *H. E.* i. 5.

"What a gay woman that was, how agreeably wanton, and now one dare not utter the least indecency in her presence."[1] Undoubtedly public opinion, at least among the educated classes, made a great advance in purity during the interval between the second century and the fourth, and the silent influence of Christianity is well entitled to the credit of the change, even though it may be true that there were at the latter period many nominal Christians whose lives would not bear comparison with those of the best of the unconverted.

This objection against the morality of the Christian doctrine of the forgiveness of sins is one that has not lost its vitality in our own day, and I am not concerned to deny that there have been Christian preachers who have given too much colour to the objection by the unguarded way in which they have preached the doctrine. I have no quarrel with those moralists who draw attention to an aspect of truth which is lost sight of by those who fancy that sin may be at any time repented of, and all be as well with them as if they had never sinned. "Sin," one of those moralists has told us,[2] "contains its own retributive penalty as surely and as naturally as the acorn contains the oak." Punishment has been

[1] Tert. *Apol.* 3. [2] Greg, *Creed of Christendom*, p. 265.

ordained to follow guilt by God, not as a Judge, but as the Creator and Legislator of the universe. God will not give us protection from the natural effects of our actions; He will not miraculously interpose between the cause and its consequences. "Whatever a man soweth, that shall he also reap." Even the omnipotence of God cannot uncommit a deed, cannot make that undone which has been done. Every act must bear its allotted fruit according to the everlasting laws, must remain for ever ineffaceably inscribed on the tablets of universal nature. We may bitterly repent that we have sinned, yet the consequences of our sin will remain. Our repentance will not undo injuries which our sins have done to our health, our fortune, our reputation, injury to our own moral character, which, in consequence of our sins, is now more frequently assailed by temptation and finds resistance more difficult, and what is perhaps most painful of all, injury done to others who, through our example and influence, have become sharers in our sins and do not share our repentance. If the truths of which I speak are not dwelt on in too one-sided a way the Christian teacher has no inclination to dispute them. The doctrine that "whatsoever a man soweth that shall he also reap," is as plainly taught in Scripture as it is in the universal experience of life.

One of the most recent attacks on our religion[1] undertakes to show that the influence of Christianity on morality has been either none at all or has been injurious. A portion of the author's proofs, though they take up great part of his book, may be lightly passed over. He draws pictures of the wickedness that prevailed in ages when the truth of the Christian religion was not seriously disputed, and favourably contrasts the morality of our own age when speculative doubt prevails to a much greater extent. But as there is no pretence that those of whose wickedness he tells deserved in any true sense to be called Christians; or that their misdeeds were wrought in consequence of their having embraced the Christian faith, and not rather in spite of their theoretic acknowledgment of it,—we need not now spend time in discussing them. Suppose a physician had acquired a high reputation for his success in treating, let us say, gout, what impeachment of his skill would it be if it could be shown that there were patients who had consulted him and had received no benefit, the fact being that they had used none of his remedies, thinking it too irksome to alter their manner of living as he recommended. Or again, if there were others who had never thought of putting themselves under his

[1] *The Service of Man*, p. 234, by J. C. Morison.

care until the disease had proceeded so far that they were at death's door.

Again, if the objector is obliged to own the influence exercised by Christianity in inducing men to make sacrifices for the good of their fellow-creatures, he represents the good effected by these sacrifices as infinitesimal compared with the benefits gained by the progress of science. He owns, for instance, the beauty of such a life as that of Sister Dora, but he asks,[1] What is the benefit conferred on the world by a whole tribe of hospital nurses bravely tending smallpox patients in their loathsome disease, compared with that conferred by Jenner in the discovery of vaccination? I need not inquire whether there is any propriety in attempting to estimate the relative worth of moral heroism and of intellectual sagacity, because it is plainly absurd to set Christianity on one side and science on the other, as if science were essentially unchristian, and were to be regarded as the exclusive property of Agnostics. Our Creator has encouraged us to study the laws of the world in which He has placed us, and has bestowed great rewards on the study when successful. But those laws, when once become known, are not the exclusive property of any one. And

[1] *The Service of Man*, p. 234.

surely the use that any one is likely to make of newly-discovered laws may be judged of by the use he has been willing to make of the laws he had previously known. Those whose zeal for the welfare of their fellows had been such as to induce them to disregard all personal risk in their efforts for the cure of disease would surely be also the foremost in using any methods for the prevention of disease that science might make known to them. I shall not then spend any time in discussing whether Christianity is to be blamed because men who do not act on its doctrines are not the better of them. The only important objection to our faith is whether there are any of the Christian doctrines which have an unfavourable moral tendency on those who truly accept them; and in particular whether, as has been asserted, this is the case with the doctrine of the forgiveness of sins.

Before proceeding farther it is necessary to point out that the doctrine assailed by the heathen objectors whom I quoted in the beginning is not exactly the same as that against which modern assaults are directed. The words of the text were translated in the Authorised Version with the disregard of the Greek tenses then habitual, which had no scruple in rendering aorists as if they were perfects or presents. But in the

Revised Version the text runs, " Such were some of you : but ye *were* washed, ye *were* sanctified, ye *were* justified," and it is plainly seen that the Apostle is not describing the state into which his disciples had come, but is referring to that former definite time when, in joining the Christian society, they broke with their old past, and in baptism put away their former sins. It was clearly the doctrine of baptismal forgiveness that was scoffed at in the story invented about Constantine, and as there is no doubt of the special pre-eminence attached to baptismal forgiveness in the early Church, it is certain that this was the doctrine assailed in the heathen objections which I have quoted. Now it will prevent us from wandering off to the discussion of irrelevant issues, if we clearly see that this doctrine of a special forgiveness of old sins on joining the Christian society, and of a pre-eminence of that forgiveness over any other, has no necessary connection with any superstitious idea about the rite of baptism, and that it might equally have been held, no matter what the initiatory ceremony used in the admission of new members into the Church, or even if they had been admitted without any material ceremony at all. The essential point was that the joining of the Christian society was a complete break with the old past and the beginning of an entirely new life. Although there was no necessary connection, there was undoubtedly a peculiar fitness in the rite of baptism, which not only represented in appropriate type the washing away of sin; but also in the form in which the rite was then administered denoted a death unto sin and a new birth unto righteousness. St. Paul frequently points out that the disciple, in going down into the water, was made like his Lord in His death and burial, while his coming up from it was like his Lord's resurrection, the beginning of a new life. To quote one out of many texts, in one which we read on Easter Sunday as containing a lesson specially appropriate to that day, St. Paul writes: "Therefore we are buried with Him by baptism into death; that like as Christ was raised up from the dead by the glory of the Father, even so we also should walk in newness of life."[1]

We have only to think of the circumstances of those to whom St. Paul wrote, and we see what lively truth there was in the image, when he spoke of their baptism as a death and a resurrection. Once they had lived in another world, mixing with heathen, taking their fill of heathen pleasures—lasciviousness, excess of wine, revellings, and abominable idolatries. Then the voice of

[1] Romans vi. 4.

God had sounded in their ears calling on them to come out of that world in which they lived. And though they feared to disobey, it must have seemed to them like death to make the change. They had to break every earthly tie, it may be to abandon their earthly possessions, perhaps to give up as unlawful the occupations by which they had earned their bread, to yield the place of honour and reputation they had enjoyed, to part with their dearest friends, to give up for Christ's sake, father, mother, brothers, sisters. From those who had loved them once they would be separated more completely than by death; for we do not cease to love those whom death tears from us; but their former friends, persuaded as was the common belief among the heathen, that they were joining a secret society for the practice of loathsome abominations would count them utterly disgraced, would cast off their society and hate the very mention of their name. You can imagine what the suspense and hesitation of an almost persuaded convert would be before he could decide on taking the step which would cut him off from all that he had loved and valued before; how he would shrink from the waters of baptism as we do from the waters of that dark river which separates us from a brighter land. But when at length his doubts were over, and he had resolved for Christ's sake to endure the loss of all things, then as he dipped his head beneath the water he felt that there he buried the dead past; he solemnly renounced the tyrants who formerly had held him in slavery,—the devil, the flesh, the world with its vain pomps and pleasures; his former sins he was resolved and solemnly promised to know no more, and he was told that God should know them no more; for His promise was, "Their sins and their iniquities will I remember no more."

And from that death he rose again to a new life,—a life with other society, other friends, other works, other duties; and he had a new principle of life, for the strength in which he was to overcome the fleshly lusts which till then had held him captive was not that of his earthly nature, but the Holy Spirit which through Christ was given unto him. Such was the doctrine of forgiveness which the Christian preachers announced to those whom they exhorted to arise and wash away their sins; and who can say that it gave encouragement to immorality? For the whole essence of the doctrine is that the pardoned sinner is supposed to have completely broken with his past, and to have hated and forsaken his former sins. Imagine that to be true, and can we say that forgiveness would then be improper? What punishment should we inflict if the apportionment of it were left to our own discretion? If punishment be intended for the reformation of the offender, that reformation by hypothesis has been already effected. Those sins of his, at which we feel indignation, he abhors as heartily as we do ourselves: if reparation of mischief he has done be due, he is ready cheerfully to make it. In actual life we cannot easily distinguish between true and feigned repentance, and, therefore, human laws cannot safely accept profession of sorrow as atonement for crime; but if we had the power of reading the heart, and thoroughly knew reformation to be genuine and hatred of former sins sincere, our wrath would certainly be disarmed, and forgiveness would be easy and natural. We need not then discuss the question of forgiveness; if there be a means of making the sinner holy, we must own the discovery of such means to be a blessing to the world; if the means be applied and found effectual, we shall consent that former sins shall be no longer remembered. The only question is whether or not such means exist. Is it possible consistently with the laws of human nature for a man thus to break with his past and wrench himself away from his former pleasures and pursuits?

Well, whether we think it possible or not without a miracle, it is historically certain that the thing was done. The text is one of several passages in the Apostolic Epistles, where confession is made of the low moral state of the Christian disciples in their heathen days: but in every one of these passages that previous state is contrasted with the utterly changed mode of life which had succeeded their conversion. They were distinctly told that unless such a change had taken place they had no share in the Christian promises. They must not "deceive themselves." If they remained under the thraldom of any of those vices for which "the wrath of God cometh on the children of disobedience," "they had no inheritance in the kingdom of Christ and of God." The early apologists were eager that their religion should be tested by its effects on the morals of those who embraced it. Thus Justin Martyr writes: "We who formerly delighted in fornication now embrace chastity alone; we who once used magical arts now dedicate ourselves to the good and unbegotten God; we who formerly aimed above all things at the acquirement of money and possessions, now bring what we have into the common fund, and share with every one who is in need; we who hated one another, and fought with one another, and would hold no intercourse with men of a different tribe, now all live together; and we pray for our enemies, and endeavour to persuade those who hate us unjustly to live according to the precepts of Christ, that they may share our good hope of blessing from God the ruler of all."[1] Tertullian appeals to the criminal registries. Not one Christian would be found in the prisons unless it was for the offence of *being* a Christian. It would be irrational to doubt the fact to which all the Christian advocates appeal so confidently, namely, the wonderful reformation of life which the new religion effected.

Nor is this fact inconsistent with anything we know of the principles of human nature. True, characters ordinarily go on in the same groove. Such as the man begins so he proceeds, the habits which he has formed only gaining firmer hold on him. But there do occur such things as sudden wrenches from the past. It would be easy to name individuals, St. Paul, St. Augustine, Colonel Gardiner, whose later life was utterly unlike their earlier, and where we cannot doubt the complete thoroughness of the change. Who has not known of profligates who, when some circumstance has opened their eyes to the ruin to which their courses were leading them, have entirely changed

---

[1] *Apol.* 14.

their life? and though in some cases the change has not been permanent, in many more it has been. But there is no such powerful agent of change as what a great preacher has called the expulsive influence of a new affection. Who does not know the power of a virtuous human love to alter the bent of a young man's desires, to make him lose his taste for grosser pleasures which had attraction for him before, to inspire him with ambition to make himself worthy of her whom he hopes to win? On those who embraced Christianity new and powerful motives were at work. There was terror at the threatenings of a future life, which was so vividly present to their minds that it seemed nothing to them to endure any torments persecutors could inflict if so they gained eternal happiness: there was love for the Master whom they pledged themselves to serve, who had given all for them; there was zeal for the interests and reputation of the society of which they became members,—one of the strongest of motives, for it is hard to say what a man will not sacrifice rather than be unfaithful to a society of which he is a member.

To make all these motives effectual it was absolutely necessary that despair should be banished. The publicans and sinners whom their respectable fellow countrymen had rejected as irreformable were welcomed by Christian preachers, and no matter how their past lives had been stained, were assured that they might wash their robes and make them white in the blood of the Lamb. They accepted the invitation, and the profligate became chaste, the drunkard became sober, the thief became honest. However men may theorise as to what the effect ought to have been of this free offer of forgiveness, there can be no doubt that the actual result was a reformation which could have been effected by no other means.

The heathen objections, then, to the doctrine of the text, of which I spoke in the beginning, would now be abandoned as worthless, and indeed it seems to cost our present opponents little to abandon the cause of their predecessors. Why, even the objections of the last century are now owned to have been worthless.[1] Bishop Butler, for instance, is quoted as complaining that it has come to be taken for granted by many persons that Christianity is not so much as a subject of inquiry, but that it is at length now discovered to be fictitious, and that this is an agreed point among all people of discernment; and it is owned that for a fictitious system Christianity still shows considerable vitality, and that the hopes of the sceptic of those days have turned out to be

[1] *The Service of Man*, p. 243.

shallow and groundless. But it is said the world has become wiser since Bishop Butler's days: the trivial conceptions of the deists of those days would be scorned now; and no one with a reputation to lose would speak of Christianity with such levity as theirs. The opponents of our religion are not in the least discouraged by the failure of former assaults on it, and they imagine that modern science has enabled them to attack it with better weapons.

Let us come, then, to the modern assaults on the doctrine of forgiveness of sins, and it will be found that they are assaults not upon Christianity, but on perversions of Christianity. In fact we have already seen that if he who embraced Christianity was promised forgiveness of sin, he also had to pledge himself to renounce and forsake sin. No forgiveness was promised on any other terms. If any Christian preachers have made such promises, they have done so without any authority from their religion. But let us trace the history.

The convert who on his admission to the Church professed his faith in one baptism for the remission of sins, did expect to receive then complete absolution for his former transgressions; but it was soon felt that this one forgiveness could not suffice. The acceptance of Christ's law brought with it a keener sense of sin, and the Christian felt the need of what he was taught on his Master's authority to do, namely to make "Forgive us our trespasses" a daily petition. But not only had provision to be made for the forgiveness of those comparatively secret sins from which even the best are not free. Cases would arise where a professed Christian brought scandal on the community by gross and open sin, and the question would arise whether his case had now become hopeless. There is nothing surprising in the fact that many were disposed to take a severe view of such cases: and you will easily perceive that when they asserted the uniqueness of baptismal forgiveness, nothing really turned on the particular form of the initiatory rite, and that a distinction was inevitable between sins committed before conversion, and transgressions against light and knowledge committed wilfully by men who had obtained the knowledge of the truth,— trangressions which implied that the privileges bestowed on them had been received in vain. We ourselves are willing to cast a veil on wrong-doing, for which the guilty person can claim the excuse that his conscience had not been awakened to a right sense of his duty. The orator of a temperance society does not lose his influence by confessing that in former days he himself had been a drunkard. And in revivalist pulpits, converted colliers or converted pugilists have been heard freely dilating on the enormity of their early life, with the object of encouraging their hearers to know that the worst of them need not despair of finding the same remedy which the preacher has found to be effectual.

But all this is because the former sinner is believed to have bid a complete farewell to his past. If the temperance orator were one night to come reeling drunk on the platform, his audience next evening would pay no very respectful attention to his addresses. And in like manner a preacher would entirely lose his influence if it were found that the vices which he had confessed as youthful transgressions had again entangled him in their snares. Now, every Christian convert undertook to be a preacher of righteousness to a corrupt world. As at the present day sins which might be condoned in the case of an ordinary person are felt to be peculiarly disgraceful in a preacher of the Gospel, so then the sins of *every* Christian showed like stains on a white garment, inasmuch as they professed higher aims than those which satisfied the vulgar. Every gross sin of a member of the Christian community was a disgrace to the whole body and an injury to its prospects of success. If at the present day some pious banker has embezzled his customers' money, or some popular preacher made love to his neighbour's wife, men who make no profession of religion will often be heard to assume that this is a fair specimen of the people who are called good, and that if the truth were known the rest are no better. Still more easily would this impression prevail against the early Christians, concerning whom gross calumnies were popularly current in heathen circles. When one of these was detected in open vice, it was easily believed that this incautious sinner showed how well founded were the suspicions entertained of the whole community. You will see then how natural were the feelings of resentment among Christians against those who had brought shame on the whole body, and their reluctance to give a second trial to men who had been already proved and found unworthy. What was to be done in such cases was one of the earliest of Christian controversies. Try them no more was the verdict of the more strict. Nay, cried others more merciful, give them one trial more, and only one. Let them have a single plank after shipwreck.

But the insisting on the uniqueness of baptismal forgiveness brought a new evil. Men came to think of baptism as a mechanical process for washing out sin, and were naturally unwilling rashly to use up a remedy that could only be applied once. Though their intellects were fully convinced of the truth of Christ's religion, and the danger of separation from Him, they preferred to remain outside the Church, taking their fill of heathen pleasures, assured that some day they would be able to blot out all their sinful past. It is to this epoch belong those heathen objections to the morality of the Christian doctrine of forgiveness which I have quoted ; objections which had not been heard of in the earlier ages of our faith.

Further, with the diffusion of Christianity, and the addition to the outward communion of the Church of many whose adhesion to it was only nominal, the line of distinction between the Church and the world once so clearly marked has been wellnigh obliterated, until in our own day a man, no matter how evil his life, runs no risk of being disowned and separated from the body of the others who call themselves Christians. It can well be conceived then that with this changed state of things some of the exhortations uttered by the preachers of early times may have now become inapplicable. Let us then examine how far this is really so, and whether we are to give up as indefensible the modern Christian preaching which has been objected to as immoral.

I take as an example what has been quoted

from Mr. Spurgeon: "My dear hearer, whatever thy past life may have been, if thou wilt trust Christ, thou shalt be saved from all thy sin in a moment, the whole of thy past life shall be blotted out. There shall not remain in God's book so much as a single charge against thy soul, for Christ who died for thee shall take thy guilt away, and leave thee without a blot before the face of God. Ah, my friend, let me assure you that there is hope for the vilest through the precious blood of Jesus. No man can have gone too far for the long arm of Christ to reach him. Christ delights to save the biggest sinner. Oh ye despairing sinners, there is no room for despair on this side of hell."

I do not pretend to be familiar with Mr. Spurgeon's writings, but I feel quite safe in saying that it would be easy to quote other passages from his sermons, which would show that the message delivered in the words I have quoted is not the whole of the message he is accustomed to deliver to his congregation. But the main point is whether the message here quoted is true, and, if not, what ought he to have delivered. We inquire from the critic, and we find that in place of the preacher's saying "O ye despairing sinners, there is no room for despair on this side of hell," what he ought to have said was, "O ye despairing sinners, you are quite right to despair, there is no hope for you."

Mr. Morison deprecates attempts to reform the abandoned, and thinks that nothing better can be done for them than to suppress them, or at least lock them up, so that they may not propagate their kind.[1] But what is a man to say who is not a closet speculator, but a practical preacher called on to address men for whom this remedy of locking-up must be owned to be too strong a measure, but who yet are groaning at being tied and bound by the chain of sin? Must he preach to them a Gospel of despair? If it be the truth that there is no hope for them, one who should tell them that there was could not be accused of immoral preaching. Their condition being by hypothesis irremediable, it is not made worse by one who allows them to indulge in the agreeable illusion of anticipated reform. But thanks be to God the message is not untrue. There are other truths which no doubt ought not to be thrown into the background. It is true that he who allows himself to slide down the downward slope of sin must find the retracing his steps a matter of constantly-increasing difficulty, difficulty which may at length become so great as to be scarcely distinguished from impossibility. It is true that those motives which others have found effectual to bring about a change of life tend to lose their efficacy as you

[1] See p. 294.

familiarise your minds with them and allow them to pass through your thoughts without any practical result. We cannot put you in the position of those who first heard the wonderful tidings of Christ's death and resurrection, to whom the truths then made known were a revelation transferring them from darkness to light. The same effect cannot be expected from repeating a message which has often been listened to and heard with contempt. And it is true also that the Gospel provides no mechanical method of forgiveness which will enable a man to live in sin until its pleasures can be enjoyed no longer; and then suddenly so make his peace with Him whom he has offended as to escape all evil consequences. No, those pervert the Gospel who represent it as a means for saving a man from the consequences of sin in any other way than releasing him from the dominion of sin.

Let all this be freely granted; let it be owned that God does not change our hearts in violation of the laws of our nature, but, on the contrary, in full conformity with those laws. Yet if you ask whether such a release from the dominion of sin is possible, we must answer Yes: if you ask whether any limit can be put to the time when it can be obtained we must answer No. It is no matter of theory; experience proves that many a sinner has found it, and has proved by subsequent holiness of life that his change of heart was a reality. The old familiar message which had often sounded in his ears has one day by God's grace struck his heart, and there awoke feelings which contained the seeds of a new life. We do not disparage the skill of the Great Physician if we dwell on the danger of those who refuse to follow His counsels, or who postpone compliance with them until their disease has become inveterate. But to whatever length it has proceeded, we must still say "Come to Him," and do not despair unless you have made trial of His skill and tried it in vain.

If the message "Do not despair" may be safely addressed to any, it may surely be addressed to those of the age of the majority of the congregation whom I now address. Listen to the Secularist preachers when they tell you of your danger. Have you already found occasion to complain of the small efficacy of good resolutions, and mourned how evil habits, which you had determined to forsake, still retain their hold on you. If the power of these habits be already so strong, what will it be when years have thickened their chains and confirmed their hold over you? Plainly the struggle for freedom must be made now, or there is danger that it may be made too late. Listen to them also when they tell you that it is useless to mourn over your faults and form resolutions against them if you do not take pains to trace these faults to their sources, and if you do not examine also whether there are not habits of yours which must be changed before your resolutions can possibly become effectual.

But do not listen to the Secularist preachers if they tell you that you are now to despair of your lives, and give up your contest before you have well entered on it. There might, indeed, be grounds for despair if no stronger motives could be brought to bear on you than those to which they appeal. But that which man cannot effect is not too great for the power of Christ.

"The grace of God hath appeared, bringing salvation to all men, instructing us, to the intent that, denying ungodliness and worldly lusts, we should live soberly and righteously and godly in this present world; looking for the blessed hope and appearing of the glory of our great God and Saviour Jesus Christ; who gave Himself for us, that He might redeem us from all iniquity, and purify unto Himself a people for His own possession, zealous of good works."

www.ingramcontent.com/pod-product-compliance
Lightning Source LLC
Chambersburg PA
CBHW030356230426
43664CB00007BB/611